ALSO BY HENRY MAKOW

A Long Way to Go for a Date (2000)

Cruel Hoax: Feminism and the New World Order (2007)

Illuminati: The Cult that Hijacked the World (2008)

Iluminati 2: Deceit and Seduction (2010)

SATANIC POSSESSION

HENRY MAKOW Ph.D.

SILAS GREEN

ILLUMINATI 3

Satanic Possession

Mailing address:
Silas Green
P.O. Box 26041
676 Portage Ave.
Winnipeg MB Canada
R3G 0M0
Contact: hmakow@gmail.com
www.henrymakow.com
www.cruelhoax.ca

ISBN – 978-0-9918211-2-9
Printed in the USA

You felt it your entire life. That there's something wrong

with the world. You don't know what it is, but it's there.

Like a splinter in your mind—driving you mad. It is this feeling

that has brought you to me.

—Morpheus, *The Matrix*

The part played by the liberals, utopian dreamers, will be finally played

out when our government is acknowledged.... Who will ever suspect then

that all these people were stage-managed by us according to a political plan

which no one has so much as guessed at in the course of many centuries?

—(Protocols of Zion, 13:4-6)

Woe unto them that call evil good, and good evil;

that put darkness for light, and light for darkness;

that put bitter for sweet, and sweet for bitter!

—Isaiah 5:20

Table of Contents

Book Six — *The Illuminati at Work and Play*

Book Seven — *Last But Not Least*

Overture

It's like the script for a '50s science fiction movie. Humanity is taken over by a satanic cult. Everyone who wants to advance must obey this cult wittingly or unwittingly. Our political leaders are sexually blackmailed to ensure loyalty.

Although this cult's phallic monuments and pyramids are everywhere, no one dares to mention its name or challenge its dominance.

We suffer from cognitive dissonance. We are under constant psychic attack by the mass media, which it never acknowledges. Society is a blind and deaf giant being led by demons.

Murphy's law is true. If it can go wrong, it will. For humanity, it has. Western society has been subverted by this cult.

A tiny clique of Cabalist bankers, the Illuminati, have supplanted God (i.e. the natural and moral laws of the universe) in the specious name of "humanism," "reason," "progress."

Henceforth, they will invert true and false, good and evil, and legislate that homosexuality, promiscuity, pedophilia, bestiality and incest are healthy and natural.

COMATOSE

The ship of civilization is sinking beneath the waves while the passengers sleep.

The Illuminati bankers are destroying the institutions of Christian civilization—religion (God), race, nation and family—in order to induct humanity into their satanic cult.

They instigated and financed wars to destroy the nations and hyped the authors that spread alienation and disillusionment. They hold humanity prisoner by their mind control. It's no coincidence the mass media is controlled by a handful of corporations with occult symbols in their logos.

The subversion of humanity is the true, suppressed history of the modern world. This is the only real conflict: Illuminati versus humanity. The others have been staged as diversions.

We don't want to believe it. It's like learning about a terminal cancer.

The mass media keep telling us our democratic and cultural institutions are sound. We'd prefer to believe that.

CONSPIRACY

The conspiracy is real and much worse than we think.

Powerful people have lived and breathed this plot for centuries. They have erected a vicious police state behind the facade of democratic government. The threat of terror is a pretext to further expand their control.

If they really cared about freedom, they'd empower us. They'd teach civic values, patriotism and history. They'd foster strong male-female relationships, marriage and families.

Instead they sabotage us. Educational and cultural standards are lowered. Their "entertainment" spews occultism, violence, porn and frightening apocalyptic visions.

Humanity suffers from arrested development. We are in a trance. Sequels and remakes. Nothing new or true. We are missing our rendezvous with our Creator.

The first job of government is to ensure that it isn't taken over by a satanic cult. Our governments have failed. They have no legitimacy.

WHAT TO DO?

A conspiracy requires secrecy and darkness to thrive. We can resist simply by shining the light on it.

We must expose its participants and their foul deeds, starting with 9-11 and including Newtown and Boston. Our leaders and mass media are liars and traitors, complicit in mass murder and coverup.

The Illuminati needs legitimacy to function. We can take that away.

Edward Snowden's revelation of NSA snooping has disturbed many people. We need to help the sleeping masses see the common enemy. But we must wait until they stir. We do not teach unless we are asked.

We must resist peacefully. Anything else plays into their hand. But we should be armed and prepared to defend ourselves. In my view, gun ownership is the main reason Americans are still relatively free.

We're dealing with Satanists. Given their track record, things are going to deteriorate unless they decide the cost is too great.

They are extinguishing civilization. Let it not be said, we slept and didn't even notice.

Turning the World Upside Down

Ye are of your father the devil... He was a murderer from the beginning, ... for he is a liar, and the father of it. Christ to the Pharisees. —*John 8:44*

It is not a matter of what is true that counts, but a matter of what is perceived to be true. —Henry Kissinger

Born in 1949, I have witnessed a steady decline in culture over my lifetime.

When I was young, a woman consecrated her virginity to husband and family.

Now, with the help of an app called *Tinder*, she "hooks up" with strangers in the vicinity.

Later, she participates in a "slut walk" to convince us that promiscuity is "empowering," as she has been taught.

When I was young, sex and bodily functions were not mentioned in public; now obscene references and potty talk are considered "edgy."

Entertainers who simulated sex on a public stage were banished; now, "twerking" is embraced and encouraged.

Homosexuality was a developmental disorder that aroused a visceral disgust. Now, it's a "sexual preference" that everyone should try or risk being called "homophobic."

The results of this veiled attack on heterosexuals are clear:

Since 1960, the US birthrate has declined by one-half. The divorce rate is up by 50%. In 2011, 36% of US births were to single women.

These and other baneful developments are not random or natural. They are the product of a careful program of social engineering by the Illuminati, a satanic secret society that controls the Western world using Freemasonry.

What passes as spontaneous "social change" is in fact an organized process of satanic possession.

This development is not an isolated or recent phenomenon. Western society is based on a rebellion against God and the natural and moral order.

The so-called "Enlightenment" refers to Lucifer as the "light giver." It represents the Illuminati's determination to reject Reality—the Creator's Design—and construct an artificial reality more conducive to their interests and perversions.

This is what the Cabalist bankers mean by "remaking the world" or "changing the world."

There is no way to sugarcoat this. Satanist (Cabalist) Jews and Freemasons are waging a covert war against God and man and are close to achieving victory. Many Jews and Freemasons have been a subversive force throughout history—the real reason for anti Semitism.

Of course, the majority of Jews (and Christians) aren't aware of this process of satanic possession. We have all succumbed to it.

Passing as "secularism" and "humanism," Satanism is the secret religion of the West.

In his book, *Behind the Lodge Door* (1994), Paul Fisher writes:

"Masons have succeeded in having their religion dominate American society. It is evident that International Freemasonry historically has been a revolutionary worldwide movement organized to advance Cabalistic Gnosticism, to undermine and if possible to destroy Christianity; to infuse Masonic philosophy into key government structures; and to subvert any government which does not comport with Masonic principles." (p.16)

PLAYING GOD

The Illuminati are the Establishment. They run the governments, militaries, intelligence agencies, think tanks, the media and corporate cartels. Government policy is *their policy.* Media spin is *their spin.*

The extent of Illuminati control was illustrated by the uniformity of Western condemnation of Russia's annexation of Crimea in March 2014. This blanket condemnation by media and politicians from *both* the Right and the Left came in spite of the illegal US overthrow the Ukraine government, and the endorsement of the annexation by 95% of the Crimean people.

The West is completely under satanic domination. Corporations, politicians, media, academics have all sold out. Everywhere, a castrated choir sings the same high pitched note. Everyone applauds the dismantling of independent governments like Iraq, Libya or Syria. Everyone castigates "racism" and praises "diversity" except when it applies to Israel.

The mainspring of Illuminati power is the Masonic Jewish central banking cartel that controls government credit worldwide. They create money out of nothing (based on our credit) and therefore think they are God.

The Cabala commands them to "remake the world" or euphemistically "heal the world." This is not positive change. It is satanic possession.

The Cabala says God is formless and unknowable. This is Satanism. The essence of any true religion is that God is knowable. How else do we obey his voice in our soul/conscience? The Cabalist says God is unknowable because he is the physical manifestation of God. He thinks he expresses God's will. He "remakes the world" in his own perverse image.

"PERCEPTION" (MAKE BELIEVE) IS REALITY

In the *Protocols of Zion,* the author says, "our watchwords are force and make believe."

The Illuminati control the levers of "make believe"—the mass media and education. They create a toxic false reality which we enter looking for meaning and direction, only to be entangled in a web like insects.

This is why so many Jews are consummate liars (excluding myself and a notable few like Myron Fagan, Benjamin Freedman, Israel Shahak, Henry Klein, Israel Shamir, Judith Reisman and Gilad Atzmon.)

This is why Jews are prominent in the "entertainment" industry—imagining reality. Most Jews have not heard of the Cabala but it seems to be in the cultural drinking water.

They create our reality in the same way as they create Hollywood movies. Notice the similarities between 9-11 and a disaster movie like *Towering Inferno.* Remember the image of people running away as the iconic towers crumbled into a cloud of dust behind them?

To build their satanic dispensation, they first have to destroy the old. They believe in "redemption through sin." The Messiah will return only when the world has descended into mayhem.

They managed the world wars and economic crises with the same directorial acumen. The world in which we live is very much their invention.

In contrast, imagine a society where the constant message from state, church, school and media is that our behaviour on earth determines if our souls achieve eternal life.

Can you see how different the world would be?

WE ARE ALL JEWS NOW

The bitter truth is that Judaism is a satanic cult masquerading as a religion. Most Jews and Christian Zionists are dupes.

Members of a satanic cult are never told the real agenda. Jews are manipulated with false information and specious platitudes. They believe anti Semitism is "an irrational sickness." Like most people, they want to conform and be accepted. Often this is a practical necessity.

Now, by extension, most of humanity is in this position. i.e. unwitting inductees into a satanic cult: Cabalist Judaism disguised as secularism. We are all Jews now.

"The Jews set themselves free in proportion as the Christians become Jews," Karl Marx wrote. "Thus, they contributed considerably to making money the means, the measure and the end of all human activity." (Cited by Leon de Poncins, *The Vatican and the Jews*, p. 76)

Judaism keeps two sets of books. Ordinary Jews and the general public see the Old Testament. (Even there, God is tribal and not universal, not really God but an egregore.)

Only the initiates see the true pernicious ideology: the Cabala and the Talmud which brazenly contradict the Old Testament. The Cabalists (i.e. Illuminati) are dedicated to inverting everything that is healthy, true and good. The Talmud envisages Jews as a master race and views non-Jews as subhuman and satanic.

"Jehovah created the non-Jew in human form so that the Jew would not be served by beasts. The non-Jew is consequently an animal in human form, and condemned to serve the Jew, day and night."—Midrasch Talpioth, page 225, L

"You are human beings but the nations of the world are not human beings, but beasts." Baba Mecia 114, 6

The human tragedy is the result of this Cabalist legacy of hate. And the New World Order is motivated by this desire to exploit and enslave mankind. However I emphasize the vast majority of Jews and Freemasons don't know about the Talmud and Cabala and would oppose this agenda if they believed it actually existed.

"REMAKING THE WORLD"

Even while they starved millions of Ukrainians to death in 1932-33, the Bolshevik Jewish leadership were infused with self righteous zeal.

"This pitiless fraternity lived in a sleepless frenzy of excitement and activity... Regarding themselves like God on the first day, *they were creating a new world* in a red-hot frenzy..." (Montefiore, *Young Stalin: The Court of the Red Tsar,* p.45.)

Illuminati banker Otto Kahn said the Jewish leadership will be God: "Our mission consists in promulgating the new law and in creating a God ... by identifying it with the nation of Israel, which has become its own Messiah." (Comte de St. Aulaire, *Geneva Versus Peace,* p. 78)

There it is in black and white: Jews, or specifically, the Cabalist Jewish leadership, replaces God using "the nation of Israel" as Trojan Horse.

Denying or supplanting God is the hallmark of Satanism. "Remaking the world" means turning it upside down. This is the real meaning of "revolution." Lucifer replaces God at the pinnacle.

As I have said, God is a state of consciousness in which spiritual ideals like truth, justice, goodness, love and beauty are self evident.

God is Reality. Our purpose on earth is to make Him ours.

God is a Spirit: and they that worship him must worship him in spirit and in truth. John 4:24

Satanists invert Reality. Evil becomes good, falsehood becomes truth, sick becomes healthy; ugly becomes beautiful, unnatural becomes natural and vice versa.

In this inverted reality, the attacker is the victim and the victim is the attacker.

As Ivor Benson noted, "anti-Gentilism becomes 'anti Semitism'; self-exclusion from the host population becomes hurtful discrimination and rejection; and aggressive finance-capitalism takes the form of Socialist and Communist "anti-capitalism"; the practitioners of genocide are represented as the greatest victims of genocide; etc., etc., and most audacious of all, a nation of atheists claims the land of Palestine 'in fulfillment of God's promise.'" (*Russia 1917-1918: A Key to the Riddle of An Age of Conflict*)

In the US, patriots like Charles Lindbergh, Henry Ford, Elizabeth Dilling or Louis Mc-Fadden are smeared as "bigots" and "anti Semites," while traitors (name any President except JFK) are honoured. Isn't this a measure of satanic possession?

"Remaking the world" requires that humanity loses touch with reality.

They make it up. For example, Saddam Hussein's "weapons of mass destruction." They have staged "terror attacks" like Oklahoma City, 9-11, Sandy Hook and the Boston Marathon. On 9-11, the Twin Towers fell at free-fall speed into their footprint and turned to dust. Clearly a demolition using some exotic explosive. A jetliner supposedly disappeared into the Pentagon. No wreckage. Don't believe your eyes; believe what we tell you.

The political elite and media are lying on an egregious scale.

Karl Rove repeated this Cabalist formula: "We're an empire now, and when we act, we create our own reality. And while you're studying that reality—judiciously, as you will—we'll act again, creating other new realities, which you can study too, and that's how things will sort out. We're history's actors...and you, all of you, will be left to just study what we do." (*New York Times Magazine*, Oct 17, 2004.)

These sanctimonious satanist liars just make it up and everyone sings *Hallelujah!*

If Russia is pushed too far, this disconnect from reality could easily degenerate into a nuclear confrontation. Moreover this "new Cold War" could give the Illuminati the excuse they need to fill their FEMA camps with "truthers," "homophobes," "anti Semites," "Christian extremists" and "right wing patriots."

SATANISM

Satanism is defined by its credo *Do as thou wilt.* Essentially this is giving free reign to our animal desires implying they represent our true nature. The Satanists "liberate" our base instincts by denying our connection to God (the soul) which normally serves as a check. Thus Satanists deliberately stymie man's spiritual evolution.

Throughout history, Cabalist Jews and Freemasons have subverted Christian nations by promoting pornography, promiscuity, mass migration, multiculturalism, miscegenation and homosexuality under the labels of Communism, Feminism, Liberalism, Socialism and "Gay rights."

We have been trained like Pavlov's dogs to reject anything that smacks of "anti Semitism." But anti Semitism is a red herring. There are more non-Jewish Freemasons who are just as culpable as any Jew, while most Jews don't have a clue.

The illuminati strategy is to divert public resentment onto these Jewish "useful idiots" and characterize all opposition as anti Semitism, i.e. "racism." They actually fund anti Semites so Jews will take the fall and toe the line. (See my website, *The Zionist Protection Racket,* and *The Dreyfus Affair was a Rothschild PsyOp* and *Zionists Double Crossed Iraqi Jews.*)

On the other hand, people who allow their government or organizations to do evil in their name without taking exception bear responsibility. The Trojan Horse was not an innocent bystander at the Fall of Troy.

FREEMASONRY

Freemasonry is Cabalism for Gentiles. The goyim get part of the Jewish banker credit scam in return for serving as their proxies.

Dr. Isaac Wise wrote: "Freemasonry is a Jewish Institution whose history, degrees, charges, passwords and explanations are Jewish from beginning to end."

Cabalism is a satanic sex cult dedicated to penis worship. Its symbols (obelisks like the Washington Monument) dot our cities.

In his book, *Morals and Dogma, 1871,* Albert Pike wrote that lower-level Masons are kept in the dark about Freemasonry's devil worship and embrace of homosexuality.

An initiate "commemorates in sacramental observance this mysterious passion; and while partaking of the raw flesh of the victim, seems to be invigorated by a fresh draught from the fountain of universal life....Hence the significance of the phallus." (p.393)

In 1919, the Masonic Archives in Budapest were seized. Christians read that at an 1897 B'nai Brith conclave, the Grand Master said:

"We must spread the spirit of revolt among the workers. It is they whom we shall send to the barricades, seeing that their desires are never satisfied, for we have need of their discontent to ruin Christian civilization and hasten anarchy. It is necessary that the moment arrive when the Christians shall come themselves and implore the Jews to take control." (Cecile Tormay, *An Outlaw's Diary,* 1924)

Father Maximilian Kolbe (1894-1941) who Pope John Paul II canonized in 1982, wrote, "We can safely identify a criminal mafia called 'Freemasonry.' The hand maneuvering all this toward a clear and specific goal is international Zionism."

"Freemasonry is the greatest enemy of the church. In fact, with tentacles reaching everywhere, it is able to affect everything and everyone... [Its ranks include] governors, ministers, businessmen, personalities of the highest rank, so it can rule the roost everywhere and always...The cinema, theatre, literature, art [are] largely directed by the invisible hand of Freemasonry."

(See *Freemasonry is a Jewish Proxy,* on my website.)

EXAMPLES OF SATANIC POSSESSION

If we wish to escape the ravages of modern life, we must understand that society is satanically possessed.

I am not speaking from a Christian or Biblical perspective. I come from a secular background. The difference is that I recognize that God is the magnificent moral and natural order governing the universe. Our obligation and reward lies in fulfilling His Will.

The prevalent Illuminist rebellion against God ultimately cannot be won.

The following are ten examples of our satanic possession:

1. *"God" is a dirty word, unmentionable in public discourse.* Prayer has also been banished from public places.

2. *Romance and sex have a disproportionate and unhealthy place in our culture.* Romantic love has become a religion. True religion is about self perfection. Instead we worship the imaginary virtues of someone we desperately want sex with. Almost every popular song affirms our devotion and dependence on this person who takes the place of God. In this bogus religion, orgasm is the Holy Sacrament.

   All love is really love of God. We love perfection (God.) That's divine love. We put up with people and nurture them. That's human love. The two shouldn't be confused.

   Romantic "relationships" are hyped as essential to happiness and personal development. They are not.

   "An erotomania is abroad through our civilization," Francis Parker Yockey wrote in 1948. It is "the identification of 'happiness' with sexual love, holding it up as the great value, before which all honor, duty, patriotism, consecration of Life to a higher aim, must give way." (*Imperium, 297*)

   Society is besotted with the attractive fertile female. The vagina is the Holy Grail. Since women are the gatekeepers, they are idealized and mystified.

   Women were designed to follow men, not vice versa. As Tolstoy said, "When religious feeling is waning in a society, it means woman's power is waxing."

3. *Sex has been divorced from love, marriage and procreation.* Sex for its own sake degrades all relationships to the level of *hot or not.* This is characteristic of homosexuals.

   Occult possession takes the form of sexual obsession. The Illuminati peddle porn and anonymous sex to dehumanize us. TV and movie actors are chosen for their sex appeal. We are constantly sexually titillated. Popular culture is replicating soft core porn. Society is hooked and craves it. The *Fifty Shades of Grey* trilogy has sold 100 million copies.

4. *The Illuminati are waging an insidious psychological war on heterosexuality, marriage and family.* Men want power. Women want love. Heterosexuality is based on the exchange of female worldly power for male power expressed as love. Thus female

empowerment neuters both sexes. Feminism's hidden agenda is for women to have careers *instead* of family. Only Satanists would undermine the love of man and woman, and mother and child. They should answer for this.

"Gay rights" masks a vicious attack on heterosexual identity and values. The aim is to replace heterosexual norms with homosexual ones. They have redefined marriage to suit less than one quarter of 1% of the population, i.e. gays who want to marry. Courtship has been replaced by "hooking up." Transgender confusion is encouraged. The media does a happy dance every time two gay Marines kiss.

5. *Incessant wars are contrived by the Illuminati* to increase their wealth and power, and to kill natural leaders, demoralize society and destroy nation states. Ironically, the Illuminati use wars to justify their "world government."

6. *Naturalism.* Erasing the line between spirit and matter by pretending spirit doesn't exist. Characterizing people strictly in animal terms by a reductive focus on bodily functions.

7. *The mass media including TV, newspapers, movies and music are the main instruments of public deception and occult indoctrination.* The dumbing down of the public through sports, entertainment and a defective education system. The promotion of collective over individualist values. The eradication of Christian heritage and the suppression of art and historical truth. Political correctness. Gratuitous violence. Occult ritual is our entertainment. Stars must be Satanists to succeed. Johnny Depp, Lady Gaga, Madonna and Miley Cyrus are examples.

    Human development has been arrested at the adolescent level. National governments are like high school student councils. The media—the high school newspaper. We have an ersatz democracy. There is no real opposition.

8. *The pervasive idea that Truth is relative and cannot be known is satanic.*

    God is absolute Truth. Knowing and obeying God is the essence of religion.

    Scientists who affirm an universal intelligence in nature are marginalized. Science that doesn't conform to "political correctness," i.e. satanic coercion, is suppressed.

    Modern culture eschews what is universal and true. Instead, it celebrates what is personal, subjective and usually sick.

9. *The mainstreaming of gambling (i.e. stock speculation) under the guise of "investing."* When not watching porn, millions are fixated on stock market fluctuations. Every middle class housewife and her dog has a "stock portfolio." Lust, whether sex or greed, is part of our satanic possession.

10. *Multiculturalism,* mass migration and "diversity" are underhanded Illuminati attacks on the cultural and racial heritage and cohesion of the West. Just as individuals have their own skin, people with common racial and cultural background should have their own countries. In the West, only Jews have this right.

In over 75 articles, I expand on many of these themes with the help of some valued contributors. One is James Perloff, whose book *The Shadows of Power* (1988) was the first conspiracy book I read. I am honored he's now a collaborator.

Since these articles originally were stand alone, there is some repetition. I beg your indulgence.

The template for the New World Order is a satanic cult, Cabalist Judaism a.k.a Communism. Although a charismatic world leader (the antichrist?) has not yet emerged, the satanic cult is devoted to increasing human depravity, exploitation and dictatorial control, body and soul. We already have gone a long way down this road.

Regarding the antichrist, a friend paints a post-nuclear war scenario. "Humanity everywhere will be in such a state of panic and despair, begging for a Savior, and this figure will arrive with solutions that really work. People will be so astonished and grateful that they'll declare that he must be God... and he will not refute that."

Finally, you and I were born during the last acts of this drama. I am not optimistic about the outcome. They control all the levers of power. Most people are brainwashed by the mass media. Society is not just complicit; it embraces its own subjugation. This is satanic possession. The best we can do is avoid contamination, possibly join like-minded people to bear witness, and steer our own course to higher ground.

Book One

The Cabala: Satanic Possession

What is Satanic Possession?

All nations will be swallowed up in the pursuit of gain, and in the race for it will not take note of their common foe. —Protocols of Zion 4

In 1976, for a payment, an Illuminati insider, Harold Wallace Rosenthal, lifted the veil on the "Jewish conspiracy" in an interview with a conservative editor, Walter White Jr.

Rosenthal worked for Senator Jacob Javits of New York. The interview is online (*The Hidden Tyranny*) and is summarized in my book *Illuminati (Protocols of Zion Updated.)*

Recently, my jaw dropped when I reread the following paragraphs which captured the essence of our satanic possession:

Rosenthal: "Your people never realize that we offer them only worthless baubles that cannot bring fulfillment. They procure one and consume it and are not filled. We present another. We have an infinite number of outward distractions, to the extent that life cannot again turn inward to find its definite fulfillment. You have become addicted to our medicine through which we have become your absolute masters...

We have converted the people to our philosophy of getting and acquiring so that they will never be satisfied. A dissatisfied people are pawns in our game of world conquest. Thus, they are always seeking and never able to find satisfaction. *The very moment they seek happiness outside themselves, they become our willing servants.*"

Rosenthal has hit the nail on the head. People are motivated by a desire to "feel good."

If we feel good because we serve and obey God, we don't need to buy or embrace anything else. We cannot be controlled.

Take God away and we will fill the vacuum with everything they sell, from money to sex, from learning to art, from bogus religions to material goods. By removing God from our lives, they artificially idealize everything else, and thereby control us.

"You can take away a man's gods, but only to give him others in return." Carl Jung, *The Undiscovered Self* (1958)

The essence of Communism is the denial of God. Communism is a system of complete control. Communism is the New World Order.

LOOKING OUTSIDE OURSELVES

These days people—especially the young—are more externalized than ever. They need others to validate them. If nobody reacts to their Facebook post, they feel slighted. Everyone wants to be a celebrity.

Our problem boils down to mistaken identity. We think we are the voice in our head. This voice constantly clamors for other people to make us feel good.

In fact, this is the mind speaking. We are the soul or "awareness" or "consciousness" —the entity that *hears* our thoughts.

The thought, "I'd like to have sex with that person," is not you. It is the mind, which is programmed by society and our animal instincts.

You are not an animal. You are the soul, which is your connection to God.

Human evolution, both personal and collective, depends on turning our energy away from the world, and looking inward to discover our true identity.

SLIDE PROJECTOR

Think of a slide projector. "You" are the beam of light. This light is Bliss: Truth, Goodness, Beauty, Love, i.e. our soul connection to God.

Your thoughts are the slides.

The slides usually depict things we think will fill the spiritual vacuum.

These days, we are bombarded by so many images, our heads are spinning. We're going out of our minds! In fact we are trapped inside them.

Our souls are kings but our minds are beggars. Each day we wake up and arrange our beggar bowls.

One is for recognition or love, another for money, a third for sex, power etc. We manipulate and twist the world in order to fill our bowls. Some people give something in return.

If, at the end of the day, our bowls are filled, it was a good day and "we" are happy. If they are empty, it was a bad day and "we" are frustrated.

People who fill their bowls on a regular basis are considered "successful." People who don't are "failures."

Either way, "we" are beggars. Even if we are rich, we feel poor.

BEING OUR REAL SELVES

The reason we are so nervous, miserable and false is because "we" are not our real selves. We are beggars.

In order to discover ourselves, the slide has to be transparent or better still, contain positive messages. The light has to shine through. Our minds have to be blank or reflect back bliss.

Illuminati 3: Satanic Possession

We have to renounce outside sources of "happiness." If we don't want to feel like a beggar, we must stop acting like one.

Instead, we must obey higher impulses that comes from the soul. I don't pretend to consistently follow this prescription, but when I am ready, I know the way.

The purpose of meditation is to reaffirm our true identity in terms of consciousness or light. Cambridge Platonist poet Henry More (1614-1687) wrote:

"When the inordinate desire after knowledge of things was allayed in me, and I aspired after nothing but purity and simplicity of mind, there shone in me daily a greater assurance than ever I could have expected, even of those things which before I had the greatest desire to know."

Amassing details about the Illuminati or world corruption isn't going to save us. We can foil the Satanists by having a moment-to-moment relationship with God. They hate that. Nothing would infuriate them more than a massive, worldwide religious revival. This is the only thing that will stop the NWO.

"My soul is a candle that burned away the veil; only the glorious duties of light I now have." St. John of the Cross

CONCLUSION

Gradually, our identity shifts from the thought-slides to the light, and we distance our self from our animal behavior.

This is the purpose of life. Self-perfection. Becoming the light. Shining the light. I expect Jesus literally shone. He referred to himself and his disciples as the "light of the world."

The light is the path of human development. Worldly desire is the path of death and destruction.

Some people reject this concept as "New Age." A living religion does not rely on scripture. It requires a constant living relationship to God within.

Religion is not what we believe. It is *what we do*. Our religion is our day.

As for sin. Forget what you have been told.

Sin is seeking happiness outside your soul-God relationship.

This is real meaning of "The Fall"—satanic possession—seeking happiness from anything but God.

Being a beggar.

NOTE:

These ideas are universal. An excellent teacher is Eckhart Tolle.

Check out his talks on YouTube.

The Devil and the Jews

Treason doth never prosper. What's the reason?
For if it prosper, none dare call it "treason."
—John Harrington (1561-1612)

There is no Wikipedia entry for *The Devil and the Jews* (Yale University Press, 1943) or its author Rabbi Joshua Trachtenberg (1904-1959.) There are no reviews on the Internet.

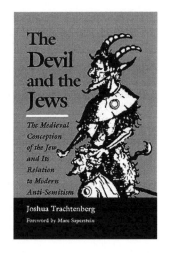

Our Illuminati Jewish masters have consigned this knowledge to the memory hole. Why?

When Europe was a Christian theocracy, say from 1050 -1650, Judaism was regarded as a satanic cult, and Jews were considered agents of the devil.

We're familiar with the Jewish persecution complex. During this period, Christians had a parallel fear. They believed that Jews both hated them and conspired to destroy Christendom. They believed the long-awaited Jewish "Messiah" was in fact the Antichrist.

"Their association with this awful figure...assumed really frightening proportions toward the end of the Middle Ages when Antichrist's Jewish parentage became definitely established and the Jews were expected to form the spearhead of his legions. They were not quite so weak...judging from their numbers and social position. For a terrible mysterious Jewish horde hidden somewhere in the East awaited the signal to pour out upon Christendom and annihilate it. The rumors of the birth of the Antichrist ...after the thirteenth century, kept Europe on edge awaiting the bloody outbreak of the "red Jews" .... (40)

Jews were accused of colluding with Mongol invaders on the Eastern frontiers. They were just as likely to desecrate a church, murder Christian infants in secret, spread poisons with the wind, or practise infamous sexual perversities.

"The catalogue of alleged Jewish crimes is long and varied indeed, and wholly unreasonable," writes Trachtenberg, "unless we accept the self-evident fact that, in medieval eyes, that as Satan's agents, nothing was beyond the depraved and evil nature of the Jews." (43)

While Trachtenberg and most uninformed Jews find this comical, many Christians believe this threat is more urgent today than ever. They point to the false flag terror, the creation of the American police state, and the general degradation of morals.

THE SALIENT FACT

Illuminati (Cabala) Jews and their Masonic henchmen don't want Jews or others to understand the hidden subversive and occult character of the collective Jewish enterprise.

They don't want Jews to understand that anti Semitism throughout the ages was not irrational. This realization would empower Gentiles, and allow "the lesser brethren" to escape their role as dupes, scapegoats, human shields and sacrifices for their demented leadership.

Cabala Jews believe that they define God's Will. In other words, God comes into the world through them. Otherwise, He is "formless and unknowable."

"As long as there remains among the Gentiles any moral conception of the social order, and until all faith, patriotism and dignity are uprooted, our reign over the world shall not come," Illuminati Jewish leaders said in 1936. (See online, *Catholics Unveiled Masonic Jewish Plot in 1936*.)

Cabalist Jews have been outsiders by choice because they cannot accept a world that is not an extension of their vanity. The alienated modern anti hero is based on the Cabalist's Luciferian rebellion.

JEWISH ACTIVITIES

Trachtenberg provides a litany of Jewish activities in the Middle Ages which suggests many age old "stereotypes" have deep roots.

"The Jews sell at cut prices as many dreams as you wish," he quotes the Roman poet Juvenal.

Throughout the ages Jews specialized in usury, magic, sorcery, fortune telling, astrology, potions and drugs, poisons, alchemy, amulets, incantations and curses, aphrodisiacs and cosmetics.

Pope Pius V explained his expulsion of the Jews from the Papal States in 569 thus:

"They seduce a great many imprudent and weak persons with their satanic illusions, their fortune-telling, their charms and magic tricks and witcheries, and make them believe that the future can be foretold, that stolen goods and hidden treasures can be recovered, and much else can be revealed." (77)

And of course, they were always the "doctors of unbelief" inciting heresies. "Everywhere, the church and the people discerned the diabolical hand of the Jews turning simple Christians aside from the true faith." (176)

CONCLUSION

Illuminati Jews have waged a covert war against man and God for millennia. This conspiracy is the real history of the world, the real cause of war and depression. Society has been subverted, and is constantly deceived.

Even Jews like Trachtenberg, writing in 1943, can't believe it.

"People will believe whatever they want," he says referring to "anti Semites" but this credulity also applies to him.

Ordinary Jews can't believe it because they are not Satanists. But many Cabalist Jews are. They have the money, comprise the secret leadership, and manipulate the rest.

Trachtenberg was a Reform Rabbi for 30 years. His portrait gazes down on his personal library housed at Temple Emeth in Teneck NJ.

He is one of many decent Jews like myself who have been used as a Trojan Horse for the Illuminati under the aegis of Communism, Socialism, Liberalism, Feminism, Zionism, Neo-conservatism and "gay rights."

We are all Jews now, Godless, deceived, and degraded. But at least we know where we stand, and can act accordingly.

NOTE: RELIGION OR SATANIC CULT?

Publisher's description of Trachtenberg's first book, *Jewish Magic & Superstition* (1939)

"Jewish Magic and Superstition is a masterful and utterly fascinating exploration of religious forms that have all but disappeared yet persist in the imagination. The volume begins with legends of Jewish sorcery and proceeds to discuss beliefs about the evil eye, spirits of the dead, powers of good, the famous legend of the golem, procedures for casting spells, the use of gems and amulets, how to battle spirits, the ritual of circumcision, herbal folk remedies, fortune telling, astrology, and the interpretation of dreams. First published more than sixty years ago, Trachtenberg's study remains the foundational scholarship on magical practices in the Jewish world and offers an understanding of folk beliefs and practices that expressed most eloquently the everyday religion of the Jewish people."

Leon de Poncins:
Why Judaism Hates Christianity

By Leon de Poncins

Translated by George F Held

Edited by henrymakow.com

On the morning of February 9, 1923, the following prophetic lines appeared in the Hebrew weekly *Jewish World:*

"The dispersion of the Jews has not made them a cosmopolitan people. In fact, [Jewry] is the only truly cosmopolitan people, and, as such, it must act—and in reality it does act—as a dissolver of any distinction of race and of nationality. The great ideal of Judaism is not that one day Jews will gather in a corner of the earth for separatist purposes, but that the entire world will be imbued with Jewish teaching, and then in an universal brotherhood of nations—in reality, a vaster Judaism—all the separate races and religions will disappear. They [...] go even further. With their literary and scientific activities, with their supremacy in all sectors of public activity, they are preparing to gradually melt thoughts and systems which are non-Jewish or which do not correspond to the Jewish models."

Vicomte Leon de Poncins (1897-1976) was a traditional Catholic French intellectual and author of 30 books that exposed the Masonic Jewish conspiracy.

This messianic dream can take many different forms, but the final goal remains unchanged: the triumph of Judaism, Jewish law, and the Jewish people. Under the universalist appearance, it is, indeed, a matter of Jewish imperialism which intends to govern and enslave the world.

Elie Faure, a Jew, writes: "The Jewish people, right from the time of Jesus Christ ... believed itself the people chosen as an instrument of a higher power. With respect to other nations, it still today believes itself the chosen people because [it is] representative of a supernatural force. [...] For it [the afterlife] does not exist. However often it has been spoken about, Israel has never believed in it. The pact of alliance [Covenant with God] is only a bilateral contract quite precise and positive. If the Jew obeys, he does so only in order to have dominion over the world. [...] "

CHRIST'S DIVINITY IS OBSTACLE TO JEWISH MESSIANISM

But to achieve this goal, it is necessary to abolish Christianity, which represents an insurmountable obstacle on the path to Jewish imperialism.

Until the coming of Jesus Christ, the position of Israel was simple and clear: according to the Prophets, by the grace of Yahweh, Israel was called upon to govern the world; if the people of the servants of Israel had complied with the divine requirements, the time would have come when Israel would had reigned over all the earth.

But here unexpectedly in Galilee was born a Prophet: A Prophet—Man and God—even He from the real race of David, and thence son of the Covenant. "Do not think that I have come to abolish the Law or the Prophets, I have come not to abolish them but to fulfill them" (Matt. 5:17)...

But...he interprets the promise in a completely new and different sense, so as to destroy the proud Hebrew edifice by spiritualizing and universalizing it. The realization of the promises was transferred from the material to the spiritual plane; surpassing the national level, it was no longer solely addressed to the Jews, until that moment the only beneficiaries, but was extended to the entire world.

... It was no more a matter of the supremacy of a race or a nation, or the triumph of a privileged nation: the chosen people were reduced to the rank of an ordinary people, one people among others.

The religious pride and nationalism of the Jews did not permit this leveling; it was contrary to the messianic promises, and put off ... the submission of all the kingdoms of the earth to Israel. The heads of the priests and the Pharisees could not tolerate such a blasphemy and such an attack on their privileges, and thus to get rid of that dangerous agitator, delivered him to the Romans and had him condemned to death...

Nevertheless, the Christian wave proceeded without respite, winning over the senior imperial power; then suddenly the world wavered and inclined in favor of the Church of Christ...

The Israelites have never accepted and will never accept this defeat. The rupture was total and definitive; the collision now became inevitable on both sides.

"If the Jew is right, Christianity is nothing but an illusion. If instead the Christian is right, the Jew is, under the best of hypotheses, an anachronism or at most the image of that which no longer has reason to exist. For the Jew, Christianity represents the renunciation of a monopoly, and the rejection of a "nationalist interpretation"—not to say racist—of his 'election.' [Christianity] is the opening up to the human brotherhood, and, at the same time, a big "amen" said to God, and to everything God decides...

And here we touch on the other reason (or excuse), which justifies the Jew's 'no' to Christ, who did not correspond to the idea that the Jew had made for himself of the Messiah and of salvation." ...

Cf. F. FEJTO, *Dieu et son Juif (God and his Jew)*, pp. 34, 190, 192.

Cabala "Destruction" Doctrine Behind War

The Cabalist Doctrine of Destruction is key to understanding world events.

According to the Cabala, which is the secret doctrine of Judaism and Freemasonry, **"Evil and catastrophe [are] endemic factors in the process of creation. Without evil there could be no good, without destruction, creation could not take place."** *(Cabala: An Introduction to Jewish Mysticism,* by Byron L. Sherwin, p. 72.)

Hiroshima

Cabalists believe the (Christian) Old Order must be ruthlessly destroyed before the (Satanic) New World Order can be built.

Hence, the Illuminati motto: *"Order Out of Chaos."* Hence, the Communist Manifesto advocates the destruction of nation, religion and family and the transfer of all private wealth to the Illuminati bankers, in the guise of the State.

The Doctrine of Destruction explains why war and revolution have been characterized by gratuitous genocide, terror and destruction.

It explains the banishment of God from public discourse and the widespread acceptance of obscenity, pornography and the occult. It explains the attack on gender and the promotion of homosexuality to heterosexuals.

It explains why humanity seems cursed by never-ending crises and catastrophes—economic, political and natural. They are engineered by the Illuminati to attack and destroy anything that smacks of the healthy divine order—spiritual, social or natural.

THE ILLUMINATI

The present day Illuminati grew out of the satanic "Sabbatean-Frankist" Jewish heresy in the 17th and 18th centuries. The bankers and half the Jews of Europe adopted this pestilence and spread it to the Gentile elites through Freemasonry.

Thus, Illuminati Jews characterize the "Jewish" role in terms of the destruction of civilization.

For example, in the book *"You Gentiles"* (1924) Maurice Samuel writes: "In everything, we are destroyers—even in the instruments of destruction to which we turn for relief... We Jews, we, the destroyers, will remain the destroyers for ever. Nothing that you will do will meet our needs and demands. We will forever destroy because we want a world of our own." (p. 155)

In 1928, Marcus Ravage, a Jewish Rothschild biographer wrote an essay entitled, *"The Real Case Against the Jews."*

"You have not begun to appreciate the real depth of our guilt. We are intruders. We are disturbers. We are subverters. We have taken your natural world, your ideals, your destiny, and played havoc with them. We have been at the bottom not merely of the latest great war but of nearly all your wars, not only of the Russian but of every other major revolution in your history. We have brought discord and confusion and frustration into your personal and public life. We are still doing it. No one can tell how long we shall go on doing it." (*The Century Magazine*, Jan 1928, 346-350.)

Most Jews (and liberals/leftists in general) are unaware of this Cabalistic plot. They have been duped by spurious appeals to ideals of "social justice" and "equality."

WHY THE CABALA IS SATANIC

Religio means "to go within" i.e. "to know and obey" God. In any true religion, God comprises absolute spiritual ideals—love, truth, justice, goodness, beauty, harmony—pure and unalloyed. God is nothing if not Moral—i.e. Good.

Evil is the *absence of God*, just as darkness is the absence of light.

The Cabala is satanic because it says God is unknowable and has no form.

"To the Cabalists, God is an infinite Sea of Being (*En Sof*) without any limits; hence without any qualities, without desire or will of any kind. He is totally incomprehensible." Jacob Agus, *The Meaning of Jewish History* (1963) p. 286

In fact, God is perfection, the form necessary for human evolution. *Be ye therefore perfect as your father in heaven is perfect.* (Mathew 5:48)

True religion assumes God is present in the human soul. Obeying this voice, (conscience) is what makes us human.

Anyone who denies the existence of God is a Satanist, not an atheist.

The Cabala is satanic because it says *evil is part of God*: "God has two sides; [both] are essentially one thing; what we experience as evil is as Divine as what we experience as good."

Hence the expression gaining currency today: "It's all good."

The Cabalist exegesis continues:

"Many texts in the Cabala, including the Zohar, say that the task is not to destroy evil but to return it to its source—to "include the left within the right," in the Zoharic metaphor, "to uplift the fallen sparks" in the Lurianic one. In Chabad Hasidism, it is stated that evil exists as part of the Divine revelation itself. Indeed, to think that evil really is separate from God is, itself, the essence of evil, which is precisely the illusion of separation."

"Letting go of the reality of separate evil, and really accepting that the *sitra achra* [impurity, occult, evil] is a side of Divinity, is... indeed life-changing. Everything is a flavor of Divinity."

Cabalists also believe in "redemption through sin" i.e. deliberately flaunting the Old Law by doing evil (adultery, incest, pedophilia.) The destruction of civilization (i.e. chaos) will provoke the return of the Messiah (the antiChrist) who will rebuild the world according to Cabalist specifications, with the Illuminati bankers playing God.

This is all Satanism. God is inherently good. In a true religion, you do not obey God by doing evil, or pretending evil is part of God.

SATANICALLY POSSESSED

Call it paganism, secularism, luciferianism, humanism or the occult: It's all Cabala.

Modern Western civilization has no moral legitimacy (and no future) because it is based on a rebellion against God, who represents the path of our spiritual development.

Humanity has been hijacked by psychopaths intent on torching the "old order" and building a bizarre, solipsistic, violent, depraved dystopia in its place.

These psychopaths control our government's credit and the mass media. Thus, they are able to purchase our leaders and dupe society into embracing its own downfall.

The Cabala is a Hoax

By Richard Evans and Henry Makow

In 1946, George Brock Chisholm, first Director of the World Heath Organization, gave three lectures laying the foundation for sex education and sensitivity training in America's public school system.

Their goal was "severing children's beliefs and morality from the influence of their elders." The sensitivity training method he proposed was imported from Nazi Germany and the Soviet Union. Chisolm said they would "replace the conventional concept of right and wrong in accord with the Kabbalah." 1.

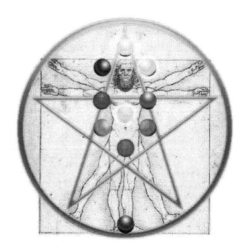

The Cabala is the unacknowledged religion of the West, a fact that will become evident over time. It is the belief system of Freemasonry and organized Jewry, the two forces that govern the world. It is the reason God and the Ten Commandments have been banished from public life, why Christianity has been gutted and replaced by moral relativity.

In its current form, the Cabala was created by Isaac Luria (1534-1572.) He derived it from the Zohar, a 13th century 23-volume work by a Spanish Jew, Moses de Leon.

According to Wikipedia, Moses "knew how to charm with brilliant and striking phrases without expressing any well-defined thought. He was a ready writer and wrote several mystical and cabalistic works in quick succession."

These books were arguments against assigning any moral attributes to God or "the endless one" (Ein Sof). He argued that distinction between good and evil place limits on the infinity of the Ein Sof. Further, Ein Sof is so transcendent that God's not in this universe and has no direct interactions in it, but can be known through ten emanations or qualities of energy called the "Ten Sefirot."

The Sefirot are the ten circles depicted in the 'Tree of Life' diagram pictured in the Zohar and Cabala. These mysterious medieval elements continue to intrigue credulous minds and made it a Middle Ages best seller.

THE ORIGIN OF THE HOAX

The Cabala is largely based on the Zohar. According to the *Jewish Encyclopedia*, this is its origin:

"There is a story told about how after the death of Moses de Leon, a rich man of Avila named Joseph offered the widow, who had been left without means, a large sum of money for the original from which her husband had made the copy; and she then confessed that her husband himself was the author of the work. She had asked him several times, she said, why he had chosen to credit his own teachings to another, and he had always answered that doctrines put into the mouth of the miracle-working Simeon ben Yohai would be a rich source of profit."

The specious notion of a Jewish secret mystery school complete with systems of divination and reality-altering magic created a sensation among Jews throughout Europe. However the scholarly Sephardic Jewish leaders in Moorish Spain dismissed the Zohar as a hoax full of heretical and dangerous ideas and banned it.

When the Catholics regained control of Spain from the Moors and expelled (or converted) the Jews in 1492, the dominance of Sephardi culture over Jewry waned.

Many intellectuals went into exile in Jerusalem, where Issac Luria was teaching the Zohar. The ban forbidding study of the Zohar was lifted in 1540 when the balance of power shifted to the Ashkenazi rabbis. Luria's Cabala opus was published after his death, and Cabala replaced Hakirah (*Mishne Torah*) as Judaism's mainstream theology.

The main reason for mainstreaming Cabala was to underpin belief in the arrival of the Messiah and with it, Jewish world dominion. Rumors spread like wildfire that the arrival of the Moshiac (Messiah) was at hand.

SATANISTS CHAMPION THE CABALA

In the midst of this wishful fervor, the infamous Cabalist Sabbatai Zevi (1626-1276) announced in Smyrna in 1666 that he was the Messiah. Over a million Jews worldwide became his followers called Sabbateans. Jacob Frank (1726-1779) took up the torch in the 18th century and the movement which spawned the Illuminati was called "Sabbatean-Frankist."

Sabbatai Zevi preached the satanic doctrine, *Praised be He who permits the forbidden.*

He reasoned that doing good keeps the universe too balanced and slows down the return of God. Therefore sin is virtue; and observance of the Torah morality was the sin. The essence of Satanism is to turn good and evil on their head.

Sabbatai Zevi's movement thrived until he promised to overthrow the Caliph of Istanbul. The Caliph gave him the choice of converting to Islam or execution. Sabbatai Zevi converted without hesitation, telling his followers to do the same.

Conversion to Islam was a bit over the top for many rabbis who excommunicated the Sabbateans. However, a core of followers converted with him.

Rabbi Martin Antelman believes an unknown number of Sabbatai's followers returned to the mainstream fold of Judaism but remained secret practitioners of the cult.

The Nobel Prize winning Yiddish storyteller Isaac Bashevis Singer recounted legends among pre-holocaust Jews in Poland of entire villages that succumbed to these satanic Cabalists. His novel *Satan in Goray* is devoted to this subject.

Sabbateanism went underground and a century later had a revival as the semi-secret cult of Jacob Frank (1726-1791.) When Adam Weishaupt's branch of the Illuminati was exposed, Amschel Mayer Rothschild set Frank and his cult up in Frankfurt as the new head of the Illuminati.

Frank followed Sabbatai Zevi's strategy of pretending to convert to a target religion in order to infiltrate and destroy it. Frank later returned to Poland with his followers and "converted" to Catholicism. His sponsor had been the King of Poland. But within a year his infamy was obvious and he was imprisoned.

CONCLUSION: SMOKE AND MIRRORS

The Cabala is a hoax, but one which governs our deluded and degenerate society.

For the Cabalist, good and evil are 'relative' so evil is an illusion. Instead of right and wrong, Cabala says every action is like the moon, with a light side and dark side. The Cabalists say that the adept must embrace his or her dark side to become, "a fully integrated human being."

Not everyone who studies Cabala becomes a Satanist. But, Cabala is a prerequisite for ALL Luciferian practitioners. Albert Pike, the 19th century "Pope of Freemasonry," said Masonry worships the devil.

"The Masonic Religion should be, by all of us initiates of the higher degrees, maintained in the Purity of the Luciferian doctrine. If Lucifer were not God, would Adonay and his priests calumniate him?

Yes, Lucifer is God, and unfortunately Adonay is also god. For the eternal law is that there is no light without shade, no beauty without ugliness, no white without black, for the absolute can only exist as two gods..."

(Morals and Dogma by Albert Pike, cited in Lady Queensborough, *Occult Theocracy* pp. 220-221.)

There is only one God. Lucifer is the spine-chilling vacuum that results from the absence of God. The Cabala is a hoax that allows its followers to reformulate reality to serve their selfish interests. This is why they teach that "truth is by its nature subjective."

-----

1. The three Washington DC speeches were organized by Alger Hiss.

"The psychiatry of enduring peace and social progress" Dr. Brock Chisolm. (The William Alanson White memorial lectures). Psychiatry Journal; 1st standard Edition edition, 1946 ASIN: B0007IV8WY

Cabala: How Sex Became our Religion

Sex, love and "relationships" have become the ersatz religion of modern society. Indeed the societal obsession with romantic love is a sublimation of the religious impulse.

The implied message—Sex is the Way to God—has been in our cultural drinking water since the 1960s and longer.

Movies portrayed sexual intercourse in mystical terms, perfect bodies coupling to the accompaniment of angels singing.

The Illuminati music industry pushed the theme that romantic love and sex take the place of God. Consider *Kathy's Song* (1965) by Paul Simon:

So you see I have come to doubt/ All that I once held as true/ I stand alone without beliefs/ The only truth I know is you.

Could they say it any more plainly? I know I was deeply influence by this propaganda.

This was followed by this scholarly exegesis: Man is "alienated" and alone in the universe. Life has no intrinsic meaning so we must make one up. Man overcomes his separation from God through sexual intercourse, which is mystical in nature. In other words, man becomes One with God by copulating.

Little did we know that the mystification of sex is pure Cabala. Cabala, the Illuminati "religion," is Satanism.

HOW SEX BECAME A MYSTICAL EXPERIENCE

In *Sigmund Freud & the Jewish Mystical Tradition*, (1958) Jewish psychology professor David Bakan writes:

"The soul, according to the Zohar, [i.e. Cabala] has an unquenchable yearning to be united with its source in God. This union is characteristically discussed in the metaphor of sex. Generally speaking, the union of male and female is taken as the ideal form of existence. Thus, human sexual relations become symbolic vehicles of Divine acts; and the Divine creativity is understood as of a deeply erotic character itself." (p.273)

According to the Cabala, God has a female side, called the Shekinah.

Just as man seeks unity with God through sex, so God supposedly seeks union with His female nature. In other words, man both imitates and helps God by having sexual intercourse.

The key to change the material world is magical manipulation in the supernatural realm which is the basic definition of sorcery. It is the rationale behind *Tikkun Olam*, the "healing" of the world of the Cabala.

When the Cabalist prays, it is so the gods can have their incestuous tryst in heaven so that things will go better on earth.

According to Israel Shahak, "the duty of pious Jews is to restore through their prayers ...the perfect divine unity, in the form of sexual union between the male and female deities..." [The prayer corresponds to the various stages of foreplay.] (*Jewish History, Jewish Religion: The Weight of 3000 Years*, p. 34)

All of this is nonsense. As we have seen, even Jewish sources dismiss the Cabala as a hoax. Nevertheless, this hoax, along with the Talmud, defines Judaism.

WHY SATANIC?

Here are two more reasons the Cabala is satanic.

First, by making the sex act a means for reaching God, the Cabalist sets up a false God. According to the Cabalist, sexual intercourse is tantamount to mystical union. Orgasm is revelation.

In fact, unity with God is reached by grace, worship, prayer, selfless service, meditation and spiritual discipline, not by copulating. But just as homosexuals use sexual excess to compensate for loss of healthy intimacy between a man and woman, heterosexuals use it to compensate for loss of God. Naturally, the Illuminati want us to imitate homosexuals.

Second, Bakan writes: "Never in the Jewish tradition was sexual asceticism a religious value." (272)

This alone disqualifies Judaism as a religion. All true religions require a renunciation of carnal desire.

Far from ascetic, the Talmud and Cabala are degenerate, opening the door to pederasty and incest. The Cabala also holds that man is bisexual, which explains Illuminati promotion of homosexuality and androgyny. Satanists will do anything to overturn the natural order and spit in God's eye.

Most Jews have hardly heard of the Talmud and Cabala, let alone read or understand them.

GODDESSES

Thus, the Cabala is the reason why pussy is the Holy Grail and young women are idealized as goddesses.

This pagan sex cult is peddled by the Illuminati-controlled media. Here are some recent headlines from the *Huffington Post*, which considers itself a serious news source:

Jan 28: "Oops Amanda Seyfried Slips Off Her Undies"
--------- " Did Jennifer Lawrence's Dress Rip at SAG Awards?"
Jan 31: "Chloe Kardasian—My Vagina Smells Like Roses"
Feb 1: "Jennifer Lawrence Describes her Breasts?"
Feb 3: "'Girls' Star's Dress Debuts Boob Windows"
Feb 3: "Fmr Miss France Flashes her Headlights" (breasts)

Are we adults? Apparently not. "Adult" now designates porn, violence and arrested development. This constant harping on sex and nudity is designed to normalize it, to give it importance and acceptance, and keep us fixated.

The elevation of young women to Goddess status is more than sexual. Hollywood portrays them as warriors and geniuses as well. In *Zero Dark Thirty,* a 98-pound Jessica Chastain gets credit for tracking down and killing Osama Bin Laden. Even lesbians thought the movie was "propaganda." But Illuminati filmmakers think portraying a falsehood as a truth is enough to make it so. As George Orwell observed, when everyone is deviant (sick), deviant becomes the new normal.

The female focus is also reflected in the obsession with "relationships," encouraging more woman-worship and co-dependency. "Relationships" are a female preoccupation. None of this means the Illuminati give a damn about women. They are promoting them to feminize and destabilize society, and because women are easier to manipulate and control.

NOTE: MORE ON THE ILLUMINATI SEX CULT

According to David Livingstone's book, *Surrendering Islam,* Cabalism is a sex cult tied to the cycle of the seasons. It is concerned with the incestuous mating of the god and goddess to ensure fertility.

The Cabala is based on ancient pagan mythologies which recount the story of an original god who created the universe, and an usurper god (Lucifer) who eventually defeats him and comes to rule the universe in his stead.

Lucifer is the offspring of the father-god and his wife, the goddess. But the son-god also marries his mother. The son-god was identified with the sun while the goddess was identified with the planet Venus, the first star seen at sunrise.

"Essentially, the god and the goddess were seen as two aspects of a single god." Livingstone writes. "As such, other names for Satan have included "Prince of Dawn" or "Son of the Dawn."

Lucifer, who exemplified evil, was known as a "dying God" because every winter he died and descended to the underworld where he ruled over the spirits of the dead.

Lucifer demands sacrifices. He must be appeased to direct his evil against one's enemies. The most significant sacrifice is the slaughter of a child. Livingstone explains:

"This [child sacrifice] became the basis of this cult as it was worshipped throughout the ancient world. Rituals of death and resurrection imitated that of the god [Lucifer.] Participants would imbibe intoxicants and dance to music in order to achieve a state of ecstasy, or Jinn [demon] possession, by which they believed they could achieve supernatural abilities like shape-shifting, clairvoyance and other magical powers. In this state, they would slaughter a child and eat its flesh and drink its blood so that the god could be reborn in them."

Illuminati defectors testify that these practices continue today. Livingstone says these rituals usually involve sexual orgies where a priest and priestess impersonate the god and goddess in a "sacred marriage." They become possessed and produce a "son of god" who would then rule as king.

This is the basis of a satanic sex cult that secretly dominates the world.

"It is this secret religion which is so often referred to as the occult. Its proponents have been advancing the satanic plan for a New World Order, and the elimination of Islam." (*Surrendering Islam* pp. 11-13)

Freud's Part in Our Satanic Possession

Sigmund Shlomo Freud's career illustrates how the Illuminati cast its satanic spell over humanity.

Sigmund Freud (1856-1939) was a Sabbatean who sold his perverted satanist beliefs to the world in the guise of science and medicine. The Illuminati-controlled media and education system hailed him as a great prophet.

Sigmund Freud

The Sabbateans indulged in every sexual perversion imaginable as a way of spitting in God's eye. This is what Satanists do to thumb their nose at God: incest, pedophilia, orgies, homosexuality, everything that is unnatural and unhealthy.

Freud and his B'nai Brith (Illuminati) backers convinced the world that sexual desire (libido) is the primary motivation of human life, and that sexual satisfaction is the universal panacea. He taught that repressing sexual urges is harmful and results in neuroses. Males experience castration anxiety and females suffer penis envy.

As an overture to incest and pedophilia, he taught that children have sexual feelings for their opposite-sexed parents and feel hostility to their same-sex parent. At the extreme, his "Oedipus Complex" states that a boy subconsciously wants to kill his father and rape his mother.

The philosopher Karl Popper said Freudian psychoanalysis is as devoid of scientific method as palm reading. Freud's Oedipus Complex "has absolutely no scientific basis."

According to Wikipedia, Freud "is considered one of the most prominent thinkers of the first half of the 20th century, in terms of originality and intellectual influence."

LEARNING FROM A SATANIST

After joining the Masonic Jewish B'nai Brith in 1897, Freud's stillborn career began a meteoric rise.

Psychology Professor David Bakan describes Freudian psychoanalysis as derivative of the Lurianic Cabala and the Zohar. Lurianic Cabala is a 2nd century Gnostic formulation which was picked up by Jewish heretic Sabbatai Zevi. [*Sigmund Freud and The Jewish Mystical Tradition*, (Beacon Press, Boston 1958)]

Freud discussed Cabala with a rabbi Chaim Bloch in 1920. The rabbi told Prof. Bakan that he saw books in Freud's study which identified him as a follower of Sabbatai Zevi, (the Sabbatean founder.)

In a speech to the B'nai Brith on his 70th birthday, Freud emphasized his Jewishness. He said he joined the Masonic Jewish lodge because of "many *dark* emotional forces" that made "Jews and Judaism irresistible." He was drawn to "the clear consciousness of our inner identity, the intimacy that comes from the same psychic structure." (Bakan, p.305)

Indeed, several members of the lodge provided the initiating cadre who founded the quackery of psychoanalysis.

According to E. Michael Jones, Freud's Psychoanalytical Association was structured as a secret society. (*Libido Dominandi*, p. 122) Presumably, it had the same secret goals as the B'nai Brith, to subvert, exploit and enslave mankind.

THE REAL FREUD

Freud's letters revealed he regarded his clients as suckers. He compared himself to a lion in a cartoon he saw. The lion is checking his watch at feeding time and asks, "where are my Negroes?" Freud said his patients were his "Negroes." (Jones p. 116)

Freud declined an invitation to travel saying, "a wealthy woman client might get well during my absence."

"My mood depends very much on my earnings. Money is laughing gas for me," he wrote. (116)

Called the "talking cure," psychoanalysis was a scam. As Michael Jones writes, for a fee, rich people received absolution for their guilty pleasures and permission to proceed.

Jones believes psychoanalysis was based on the Illuminati initiatory ritual and is a form of mind control.

"Both were based on having the patient or adept give in-depth, quasi-confessional "examinations of conscience" during which they told the Illuminist controller or psychotherapist details of their personal lives which could later be used against them. Both Illuminism and psychoanalysis ended up as covert forms of psychic control, whereby the controller learned of the adepts dominant passion and manipulated him accordingly." (p.127)

CONCLUSION

The bottom line is that psychiatrists are part of this satanic secret society. The true Illuminati goal is to make people sick and take their money. This would explain why psychiatrists are putting millions of people, including children, on drugs. See also online my: *The Soviet Art of Brainwashing.*

The secret society model may apply to the medical profession as a whole, as well as to other professions.

Freud was a precursor of Alfred Kinsey, the pervert who contracted a fatal disease from self abuse. Kinsey filled his famous Rockefeller-sponsored report with the behavior patterns of his fellow homosexuals. Thus, he convinced Americans that promiscuity and deviance were now the norm.

Similarly, Freud had an affair with his wife's sister, Minna Bernays, who got pregnant. His psychiatric theories about incest and sex were attempts to exonerate himself. Ironically, Adam Weishaupt, the Illuminati organizer, also got his sister-in-law pregnant.

Freud went through a period where he embraced the salutary properties of cocaine. When some friends became addicted, he supposedly gave it up. However Wikipedia reports: "Some critics have suggested that most of Freud's psychoanalytical theory was a byproduct of his cocaine use."

Sigmund Freud illustrates that modern culture was determined by Satanists in white coats.

How the Illuminati Hooked the Young on Porn

"We aspire to corrupt in order to rule." — Giuseppe Mazzini (1805-1872) Freemason leader.

Mankind has been colonized by a satanic cult, the Illuminati, Cabalist Jewish bankers & Freemasons who used their fraudulent monopoly over government credit (currency) to buy the world and hold mankind in debt-servitude.

So effective is their control over culture that humanity only now realizes it is the hostage of an emerging globalist police state.

American Pie

We also recognize that "sexual liberation" and pornography are political weapons designed to degrade and control us.

The Illuminati know that real men supported by loyal wives will defend their families and ensure that their children have a wholesome future.

Better to turn these men and women into sex addicts who betray their spouses for a cheap transitory thrill.

Porn is literally a weapon of war. In occupied Poland, the Nazis corrupted Polish society:

"The authorities turned a blind eye to the illicit distillation of alcohol. In Warsaw, gambling halls were opened which only Poles were allowed to attend. Prostitution was tolerated. The printing and distribution of pornography was encouraged." (*Poland Under Nazi Occupation* 1961, p.218.)

Casinos. Prostitution. Porn. Sound familiar?

Porn is a favorite weapon of colonizers. When Israel took over Palestinian TV stations in the West Bank, they broadcast porn. After the US invaded Iraq, porn flourished.

For most people, sex has become an addiction. Porn is the crack. In the 19th Century the British fought the Opium Wars because the Chinese wouldn't take their "medicine."

For the past 50-100 years this weapon has been used against us and increasingly porn is setting societal norms.

WEAPONIZED PORN

Just as "social change" is really "social engineering," Hollywood entertainment is really behavior modification and occult possession.

Risky Business (1983) is described as "a teen comedy-drama" when it was designed to hook a new generation on pornography. Tom Cruise plays Joel "Goodson" an innocent whose teenage fantasy comes true when a comely young prostitute (Rebecca de Mornay) moves in while his parents are away on vacation.

The film contains many steamy sex scenes and implicitly condones prostitution and sex for its own sake. No coincidence, it was made by David Geffin, a homosexual Jew and written and directed by Paul Brickman, a Jew whose "sexual preference" is unknown.

This film about corrupting innocence is bookmarked by the *American Pie* series (1999-2012) another Illuminati Jewish "teen comedy" which begins with four teenagers who vow to lose their virginity before graduation. The Google images for "Shannon Elizabeth"/ "American Pie" will confirm that this is porn plain and simple, aimed at adolescents.

In the sequel, *American Wedding*, (2003), the future bride performs fellatio on the groom under a table in a crowded restaurant.

At the wedding reception, the groom's unruly friend has sex with the groom's grandmother in a darkened closet thinking she is the bride's sluttish sister.

Granny is so pleased she blesses her grandson's marriage to a "shiksa." In the final scene, another friend performs cunnilingus on the unruly friend's mother in a bubble bath.

This crude psychological assault on our morals and decency is part of the Illuminati's hate-filled (Talmudic) strategy to destroy the institution of the family.

In this context, *Fast Times at Ridgemont High* (1982) and *Pretty Women* (1990) are significant for their nudity and for legitimizing abortion and prostitution.

All these movies played a major role in removing moral constraints and allowing obscenity, porn and Satanism to flourish in the mass media today.

How much easier to create a police state if people enslave themselves.

The Masonic System of Control

By Stephen Knight

(Stephen Knight 1951-1985, was murdered for his exposure of Freemasonry in his book, The Brotherhood, 1983. This is an abridgment of pp. 140-149.)

I received a phone call from a man who said he would very much like to meet me...

"Christopher" was tall, more than six feet, slim and aged about fifty. Everything about him spoke of affluence, except his plain National Health Service glasses. We went to his club, which he pledged me not to name as it could be used to identify him.

I wondered what a person might have to fear from Freemasons if circumstances made him, for instance, a threat to them in the business world; or if he discovered they were using Masonry for corrupt purposes; or ... if he would not heed warnings not to oppose them.

Stephen Knight

"It is not difficult to ruin a man," he said. "And I will tell you how it is done time and again. There are more than half a million brethren under the jurisdiction of Grand Lodge..."

It transpired that Christopher was one of a small and unpopular group within Masonry who some time in the early seventies had decided that ... they had to do something "to stop the rot" which the blinkered officers of Great Queen Street refused to admit was there...

Thumb on knuckle, Tony Blair and Ratzinger signal collusion

"PRIVATE INTELLIGENCE NETWORK"

Christopher explained that Masonry's nationwide organization of men from most walks of life provided one of the most efficient private intelligence networks imaginable.

Private information on anybody in the country could normally be accessed very rapidly through endless permutations of masonic contacts—police, magistrates, solicitors, bank managers, Post Office staff ("very useful in supplying copies of a man's mail"), doctors, government employee bosses of firms and nationalized industries etc., etc. dossier of personal data could be built up on anybody very quickly.

When the major facts of an individual's life were known, areas of vulnerability would become apparent. Perhaps he is in financial difficulties; perhaps he has some social vice—if married he might "retain a mistress" or have proclivity for visiting prostitutes; perhaps there is something in his past he wishes keep buried, some guilty secret, a criminal offense (easily obtainable through Freemason police of doubtful virtue), or other blemish on his character: all these and more could be discovered via the wide-ranging masons network of 600,000 contacts, a great many of whom were disposed to do favors for one another because that had been their prime motive for joining...

Sometimes this information gathering process—often involving a long chain of masonic contacts all over the country and possibly abroad—would be unnecessary. Enough would be known in advance about the adversary to initiate any desired action against him.

I asked how this "action" might be taken.

"Solicitors are very good at it," said Christopher. "Get your man involved in something illegal—it need not be serious—and you have him." Solicitors, I was told, are "past masters" at causing endless delays, generating useless paperwork, ignoring instructions, running up immense bills, misleading clients into taking decisions damaging to themselves.

Masonic police can harass, arrest on false charges, and plant evidence. "A businessman in a small community or person in public office arrested for dealing in child pornography, for indecent exposure, or for trafficking in drugs is at the end of the line," said Christopher. "He will never work again. Some people have committed suicide after experiences of that kind."

CREDIT IS CUT OFF

Masons can bring about the situation where credit companies and banks withdraw credit facilities from individual clients and tradesmen, said my informant. Bank can foreclose. People who rely on the telephone for their work can be cut off for long periods. Masonic employees of local authorities can arrange for a person's drains to be inspected and extensive damage to be reported, thus burdening the person with huge repair bills; workmen carrying out the job can "find"—In reality cause—further damage.

"Again with regard to legal matters, a fair hearing is hard to get when a man in ordinary circumstances is in financial difficulties. If he is trying to fight a group of unprincipled Freemasons skilled in using the "network" it will be impossible because Masonic Department of Health and Social Security and Law Society officials can delay applications for Legal Aid endlessly.

"Employers, if they are Freemasons or not, can be given private information about a man who has made himself an enemy of Masonry. At worst he will be dismissed (if the information is true) or consistently passed over for promotion"...

"Most people, fighters or not, are beaten in the end, though. It's ... you see, I ... you finish up not knowing who you can trust. You can get no help because your story sounds so paranoid that you are thought a crank, one of those nuts who think the whole world is a conspiracy against them. It is a strange phenomenon. By setting up a situation that most people will think of as fantasy, these people can poison every part of a person's life.

"If they give in, they go under. If they don't give in, it's only putting off the day because if they fight, so much unhappiness will be brought to the people around them that ... even their families turn against them out of desperation. When that happens and they are without friends wherever they look, they become easy meat. The newspapers will not touch them"...

"There is no defense against an evil which only the victims and the perpetrators know exists."

Anti-Jewish Manifesto (1882) Puts NWO in Perspective

But no man said anything about him [Jesus] openly for fear of the Jews. (John 7:13)

The last significant effort to defend Christian national values was the "First International Anti-Jewish Conference" held in Dresden in September 1882.

The conference which attracted 300 prominent businessmen, aristocrats, politicians, clergy, lawyers, physicians, farmers and intellectuals from Germany, Austria, Hungry and Russia, produced a Manifesto addressed to "the Governments and Peoples of Christian Nations Threatened by Judaism."

The document shows how 130 years ago Jewish hegemony was a fait accompli, and explains why the West's Christian heritage and racial cohesion are still under attack today.

Adolf Stoecker (1835 -1909) was a German Lutheran theologian who founded the Christian Social Party and helped organize the 1882 "Anti Jewish Conference.")

FINANCIAL AND CULTURAL INVASION

The Manifesto begins by saying Europe has been invaded by a foreign race more dangerous and insidious than Arabs, Tartars or Turks in the past because of "its means and objectives."

Jewish "emancipation" following the French Revolution ("Equality, Fraternity, Liberty") removed protections against "a race whose first and foremost thoughts and energies are everywhere aimed at putting other nations in the moral and material shackles of slaves..."

"According to the Jews' religious and national traditions, all of these peoples were created merely to serve them. The principle of equality was also applied to a race that does not wish to be equal with us, that considers itself a people privileged by God and [regards] the rest of mankind as lower beings, impure animals. The principle of fraternity was also applied to a race that does not even acknowledge non-Jews as neighbors and fellow human beings and according to whose Talmud non-Jews are enemies destined for eradication."

"Moreover, cheating, stealing from them, bleeding them dry, bringing ruin upon them, perjuring against them, dishonoring, and even killing them constitutes an activity pleasing to their God. Small wonder, therefore, if modern liberalism, identifying more and more with the ascendant Jews, has taken the shape of pseudo-liberalism. In the Jews' hands, it has turned into a convenient tool for realizing their plans for world domination and putting irons on the European peoples."

As a result of Jewish monopoly on government and finance, "the farmer, the big land-owner, the industrialist, the artisan, the merchant, etc. have all gotten caught up in material dependency upon Jews...they were forced to turn into their obedient servants, their train bearers. What's more, the Jews hire influential men who are active in public life to fill well-paid positions at banks, railways, insurance companies, etc. These individuals are thus virtually kept as Jewish vassals and are the most zealous and influential supporters of Jewish power in the legislatures and governments. "

As a result of Illuminati Jewish-instigated wars, "the governments of some indebted countries have become nothing more than Jewish institutions, Jewish collection agencies. This explains the complete inactivity of these governments with respect to the Jewish question and also their hostile behavior against their own populations in favor of Jewry."

THE MASS MEDIA

Due to media ownership, "until recently no newspaper in Central Europe would have dared to speak the truth vis-à-vis Jewry. Thus the Jews have become absolute masters, fabricators of public opinion. Any complaint raised against them, however justified it may be, is suppressed. Any article that addresses the subject of Jewish dominance to the slightest extent is done away with."

Political advancement "is dependent upon the favorable position of the Jewish press.... As a result, intellectual slavery and moral cowardice vis-à-vis Jewry is one of the most characteristic features of our age."

Ambitious Christians "become train bearers of Jewish power; they turn into traitors to their own nation and race and thus to their own blood relations. In many countries, the Jews have adulterated the system of [Freemason] lodges, stripped it of its essence, and degraded it into one of the most dangerous and effective instruments of Jewish power."

"Mainly by means of the press, Jewry increasingly undermines the Christian religion, which ... during Roman times,... saved the European Aryan race from moral bankruptcy, on the one hand, and semi-civilized barbarity, on the other, and also regenerated it. It did so by setting the civilization and culture of the European Aryan race on firm religious, moral, and social foundations."

"Christian religion is the most powerful reaction against Jewish tendencies to achieve world domination. It is an insurmountable protest against the elevation of the Semitic above the Aryan race, and so it is only natural that the Jewish clan is a sworn mortal enemy of both the founder of this religion and the Christian religion itself.

"Accordingly, Jewry can only firmly establish the superiority and rule of the Semitic race when it has managed to defeat the natural reaction opposing it and to destroy the institution of Christianity."

CONCLUSION

The 1882 Manifesto deftly describes the impotence of Christian leadership which is just as obvious today. There was no "Second International Anti Jewish Conference." The participants recognized they were fighting a lost cause. They did not propose measures because "this nation of parasites has become much too deeply engrained in the body of our societal and state life for this first congress to operate under the delusion that its potentially detailed propositions could be carried out today."

This was in spite of the fact that economist and philosopher Eugen Duhring had just laid out a detailed program in his book *On the Jews* (1881.) Ironically, it required the Illuminati Jewish-sponsored Nazis to enact many of Duhring's proposals, which were similar to racial policies in effect in Israel today.

The rise of the Nazis led to the genocide of about six million German anti Semites (i.e. Nazis) in WW2 and some 50 million other non-Jews. Given the 1882 Manifesto, do you think the Nazis could have achieved power without Illuminati Jewish sponsorship? As in chess, often you sacrifice a player (i.e. non-Zionist Jews) to win the game.

Generally, the tone of the Manifesto gets more petty and racist, tarring all Jews with the same brush, saying all Jews are cosmopolitans with no loyalty to country or attachment to land, incapable of honesty, hard work and scientific or creative originality, driving farmers to destitution with their usury.

While I agree with the Manifesto's description of Jewish leadership and its goals, many if not most Jews were very patriotic, hard working and wanted to assimilate. In the 1930's, 60% of all German Jewish marriages were interracial. The Illuminati had to create Hitler to get them to go to Israel.

Christian leaders should have encouraged assimilation. Instead the 1882 Conference concluded that the only solution was expulsion.

"Europe belongs to the Christian peoples and therefore should not be the testing ground for the hunger for power of any hostile, domineering, non-Christian national element. The history of past centuries amply proves that legal decrees restricting the Jewish race —no matter how strict they are—do not achieve the desired result."

Whatever we think of this Manifesto, it does provide a unique historical perspective on our world today. We are living in the twilight of Christian civilization which has suffered a series of colossal failures and defeats which have been disguised as just wars, depressions, gay rights, diversity, sexual liberation etc. But this perspective can strengthen our resolve to oppose the further degradation of society by the satanist Illuminati.

Satanic Signs Are Everywhere

Baphomet, the pagan devil, has a crescent moon on the top left and bottom right.

Illuminati motifs in logos signal their control to insiders.

The swoosh is a reference to the horizon, the rising sun, the Son of Dawn, Lucifer.

BAPHOMET
KNIGHTS TEMPLARS' GOD

The Dot in Circle symbolizes penis in vagina. This is a sex cult. VOA and CBS.

Obama logo uses rising sun and swoosh motifs

Chrome logo below also incorporates 666.

Below; 666 and Disney.

Logo of the City of Ottawa. 666 is on every street sign, and every city bus and police car.

Winnipeg logo includes swoosh and stylized 666.

Monster drink; 666 in Hebrew

Eye of Horus in Time Warner and APTN logos

Logos with a Pentagram;

Rising Sun Motifs; In the British Columbia logo, the golden arch, the sun, is like an eye at the top of the pyramid/mountain. On the far right is the emblem of the socialist party that runs Greece.

Rising sun, dot in circle;   Pyramid motifs; The kangaroo doubles as Eye of Horus

                         Swoosh and sunrise;   Two towers;

American Federation of State, County and Municipal Employees

Does the Devil Own all these Companies ???

A reader, DD, wrote: "Please notice that all corporate logos now have the crescent half moon sickle. For example Bud Light, AOL, Capital One, Minuteman Press, Weight Watchers, Comcast, Ryder Trucking, Newport cigarettes, Sandisk, Washington Wizards and plenty more—too many to be a coincidence. With all copyrights laws etc. why are they all using the crescent half-moon? Are they all owned by Freemasons?

Satan Worship:
The Coming One-World Religion

By James Perloff

The Illuminati set out to systematically destroy Christianity and belief in God. Do we need any more proof that we are ruled by a satanic cult?

The Bible and the Protocols both agree that the Illuminati's one-world government and religion are coming.

Illuminati Jewish program to discredit the Bible and Christianity includes claims that a tomb containing the bones of Jesus and Mary Magdalene was found.

Revelation 13:7 says the Antichrist will have "authority over every tribe, people, language and nation." *Protocol* 5:11 says the Illuminati plan to "absorb all the state forces of the world and to form a super-government."

Revelation 13:8 says that "inhabitants of the earth will worship the beast." *Protocol* 15:20 brags "they will acknowledge the autocracy of our ruler with a devotion bordering on 'apotheosis'" [glorification as a god]. He "will be the real pope of the universe, the patriarch of the international church." (17:4)

For Satan to rule Earth autocratically, he must not only consolidate governments and currencies, but belief systems. But how could he unite something so diverse as religions?

THE PLAN

The long-term strategy: (1) splinter a religion into sects on the "divide and conquer" principle; (2) assault the religion's foundations, creating doubts among believers; (3) finally, herd the remnants together with other religions, i.e., ecumenism.

Let's see how this played out in Christianity. *Protocol* 17:5 says of churches: "we shall fight against them by criticism calculated to produce schism." Over centuries, Christianity has been splintered into increasingly smaller sects. For example, the Jehovah's Witnesses were founded by a Freemason, Charles Taze Russell.

To plant doubts in believers, Darwin's theory of evolution was introduced as a "scientific" alternative to creation by God. *Protocol*s 2:3 flaunts "the successes we arranged for Darwinism."

Attacks on the Bible achieved what *Protocol* 17:2 terms "the complete wrecking of that Christian religion." The Rockefellers funded seminaries that questioned the Gospel, most notoriously the Union Theological Seminary. In the late 19th century, Union Theological professor Charles Briggs introduced "Higher Criticism," in America claiming the Bible was error-ridden.

In 1922, Harry Emerson Fosdick gave a landmark sermon which cast doubt on the Bible being God's Word, the Virgin Birth, the Second Coming, and Christ's death as atonement for sins. He declared those holding these beliefs "intolerant."

His sermon sparked outrage, and Fosdick was forced to resign. However, he was immediately hired as pastor of Riverside Church—attended and built by John D. Rockefeller, Jr. for $4 million. Rockefeller paid for 130,000 copies of Fosdick's sermon to be printed and distributed to ministers. Fosdick's brother Raymond was president of the Rockefeller Foundation.

The views expressed by theologians like Briggs and Fosdick were called "Modernism," which included denying Christ's divinity, miracles and resurrection. Modernism was not a quibbling over some gray area of theology; it was total repudiation of Christianity's major tenets. With Rockefeller funding, it permeated seminaries and churches.

Recently Modernism has gone further; the Jesus Seminar (financial backers unpublicized) declared over 80 percent of sayings attributed to Jesus weren't authentic. The Da Vinci Code—this century's best-selling novel, thought by John Coleman to be a Tavistock creation—claimed Jesus wasn't resurrected and married Mary Magdalene. Shortly after the film version's release, a Discovery Channel documentary claimed a tomb had been found containing the bones of Jesus and Mary Magdalene.

ECUMENISM AND SOCIAL GOSPEL REPLACING FAITH

Consolidation of churches required organizations. The Rockefellers funded the National Council of Churches. John Foster Dulles was chosen to spearhead the ecumenism drive. Dulles was a Rockefeller in-law, chairman of the Rockefeller Foundation trustees, a founding CFR member who helped draft the UN Charter (which never mentions God.)

In 1942, Dulles chaired a 30-denomination meeting which called for "a world government of delegated powers." Not content with unifying America's churches, Dulles helped to found the World Council of Churches in 1948.

Among today's ecumenical traps: the Tony Blair Faith Foundation. The former British prime minister—a consummate insider—said he wanted to "promote respect, friendship and understanding between the major religious faiths" since "globalization pushes us ever closer."

But even with structures for consolidation, the question remained: how to motivate churches to unite. Since denominations often disagree on theology, the strategy was to encourage collaboration where they did agree: values (e.g., helping the poor and sick.) This materialized in an action-based program, "the Social Gospel" (religion transformed into socialism.)

Walter Rauschenbusch, trained at Rockefeller-funded Rochester Theological Seminary, became "Father of the Social Gospel," declaring that "the only power that can make socialism succeed, if it is established, is religion."

Perhaps the most notorious "Social Gospel" pusher: Rockefeller-backed Reverend Harry F. Ward, who long taught at Union Theological. Union boss Samuel Gompers called Ward, the ACLU's first chairman, "the most ardent pro-Bolshevik cleric in this country."

Ward helped found the Methodist Federation for Social Action, which advised Christians to downplay the Gospel and fight for things like social justice, better labor conditions, and "world peace." i.e., the goals Marxists proclaimed.

Missionary work was targeted. In 1930, John D. Rockefeller, Jr. funded the "Laymen's Foreign Missions Inquiry," which recommended missionaries downplay Christian doctrines and ally with other religions in doing good works. Although most denominations were critical of the report, former missionary Pearl Buck praised it in the media. Subsequently her novel *The Good Earth* received the Nobel Prize.

Rick Warren, author of *The Purpose Driven Life* (over 30 million sold) is America's current Social Gospel point man. In 2008, backed by a $2 million Rupert Murdoch donation, Warren launched the Peace Coalition. *Time* magazine headlined it: "RICK WARREN GOES GLOBAL." Warren said the coalition's goal was "to mobilize 1 billion Christians worldwide."

Warren, who is a CFR member, gave the invocation at Obama's inauguration, and was dubbed "America's pastor" by CNN. He's anointed, but by who?

CATHOLICS

The Illuminati haven't forgotten Catholicism. *Protocol* 17:3: "When the time comes finally to destroy the papal court...we shall penetrate to its very bowels."

Like other churches, Catholics have recently seen major ecumenical developments such as: the signing of the Joint Declaration on the Doctrine of Justification by Lutheran and Catholic representatives (1999); dialogue with Eastern Orthodox churches, resulting in the Common Declaration of Pope Benedict XVI and Ecumenical Patriarch Bartholomew I (2006); an unprecedented Catholic-Muslim summit at the Vatican (2008); and visits of Pope Benedict XVI to Israel and to the Great Synagogue of Rome (2009).

And Catholicism has experienced its own "social action" movement—comparable to the tactics of Harry F. Ward and Rick Warren—as in the doctrine of liberation theology, which was prominent in Latin America beginning in the 1950s and 60s, where the Gospel took a back seat to fighting poverty and social injustice via Marxist precepts.

Protocols 17:2: "as to other religions we shall have still less difficulty in dealing with them, but it would be premature to speak of this now."

ONE WORLD RELIGION

The final mechanism for one-world religion might be Project Blue Beam. According to Serge Monast, satellite-projected holograms in the sky (the "image of the beast" predicted by the Bible), will be tailored to religious populations in Earth's different regions.

To induce worship, the Antichrist will not initially appear as a tyrant, but as a "savior." To save us from what? Probably from all the chaos the satanic Illuminati will have created: wars ignited by false flags, famines from artificial food shortages, plagues from viruses synthesized in laboratories, HAARP-generated storms and earthquakes, and perhaps even a fake "Blue Beam" alien attack, simulated by holograms of spaceships.

Having contrived these disasters, it will easy for him to stop them. By turning off HAARP, for example, he will appear to duplicate the feat of Jesus in quelling the storm on the Sea of Galilee. These high-tech counterfeit "miracles" will allow him to be accepted as God, as Christ returned.

But any "saving" will be short-lived. Once enthroned in Jerusalem (the end goal of Zionism), Satan will use his absolute dictatorship to unleash his greatest cruelties on the world. Worshiping the Antichrist will undoubtedly include human sacrifices—a practice consistently associated with Satan worship, from child sacrifices offered to the demonic Baal in the Old Testament, to today's mock human sacrifices carried out by America's elite at Bohemian Grove.

People of faith should stand united; not in a one-world religion but against the Illuminati.

Jesus warned: *Beware of false prophets, who come to you in sheep's clothing, but inwardly they are ravenous wolves.*

Protocol 11:4: The goyim are a flock of sheep, and we are their wolves. And you know what happens when the wolves get hold of the flock.

Book Two

Normalizing Sexual Perversion

The Meaning of Perversion

Since the world is controlled by a satanic cult, the meaning of the word "perversion" is naturally obscured.

Perversion is anything that deviates from what is natural and healthy. The word "perverse" is synonymous with "sick."

For the last 100 years or more, the Illuminati has sold sex for its own sake under the labels of "free love" and "sexual liberation."

Satanists invert sick and healthy. Perversion is sold as "liberation."

Next to survival, reproduction is our most powerful natural instinct. The purpose of sex is to ensure the survival of the species and the continuity of civilization. To turn it into an end in itself, for sensual pleasure, is a perversion.

Female sex appeal is mostly a function of fertility. After menopause, women are rarely sexually attractive to males. Male sexual attraction is largely based on natural reproductive programming.

In a healthy society, sexual intercourse would be confined to marriage or at least to long-term committed relationships. Thus, sexual energy would strengthen the marriage bond and provide a firm foundation for family. Women want to be desired exclusively rather than used and discarded like kleenex .

"Sexual liberation," on the other hand, weakens the institution of marriage by normalizing promiscuity. It dehumanizes us by promoting physical intimacy without human intimacy.

Young women have been told promiscuity is "empowering." In fact, marriage is empowering. Marriage ensures a woman is loved as a human being.

Women were always cherished for the love they gave their husbands and children. Now that Feminism has reprogrammed them to be self-seeking, young women have nothing to offer but their bodies. They have been transformed into sluts and would-be porn stars. This is perversion and satanic possession.

Society Blind to Psy War on Heterosexuals

Every day, heterosexuals are immersed in a toxic bath of lesbianism, homosexuality, obscenity, pedophilia and sexual promiscuity designed to transform them and society. Yet, they are blissfully unconscious of this attack.

In June 10, 2011, NYC police ticketed two women sitting on a park bench eating doughnuts.

They violated a regulation, (one of 15 listed on a sign,) prohibiting adults from entering the playground unless accompanied by a child.

This is supposed to deter pedophiles. Other US cities, including Miami Beach and San Francisco, have similar ordinances which have been extended to libraries and children's museums.

Last winter, seven NYC men were ticketed for playing chess in a playground. In Idaho, a man was arrested for taking pictures of a child, who turned out to be his grandson.

"It's pedophile panic," says NYC writer Lenore Skenazy. "Everyone is a pedophile until proven otherwise."

In a clever sleight-of-hand, they transfer the stigma of pedophilia to heterosexuals. Studies show that while homosexuals are only 2 per cent of the population, they account for 25-40% of child molestation. But the goal is for heterosexuality to be seen as a pathology (e.g. domestic abuse, etc.)

"I for one would want a couple of women sitting in a playground as an extra pair of eyes," Skenazy writes. "When you start treating everyone as evil, you can't have community." (*Playground Panic, Maclean's,* Sept 5, 2011)

Bingo. Instead of one big human family, we are a world of sexual predators. You must hand it to Satanists; they know how to create hell.

HETEROSEXUALITY ERASED

The Illuminati are trying to transform our human identity from father, mother, husband, wife, sister, brother, son and daughter to isolated and autonomous worker-consumer-drones.

If we want healthy families, society must encourage men and women to consecrate themselves to the task. Our children represent our organic growth, our tie with eternity.

Instead, heterosexuals are under constant psychological attack.

"Progressive" young women march for the right to behave like "sluts." Schools favor homosexuals for scholarships. Pop songs like Katy Perry's *I Kissed a Girl (and I liked it!)* get four million paid downloads. Mainstream TV story-lines feature gays and gay porn. Teachers encourage children to engage in sex and gay sex under the guise of "sex education." Little girls are sexualized. *Sesame Street* had to fight off demands that two puppets, Bert and Ernie, serve as positive role models for gay marriage.

This undermines marriage and family. Almost 50% of women who lost their virginity as teenagers were divorced within ten years. Forty three percent of the college-educated women born between 1965 and 1978 have no children.

Our society has been subverted by satanist (Cabalist) Jewish central bankers and their traitorous Masonic minions who want the state to handle procreation, (as envisaged in Aldous Huxley's *Brave New World*.) We are being re-engineered to serve them.

The reason we are blind to this vicious underhanded attack on our identity is that it is disguised as "homosexual rights;" and they portray opposition as "homophobia." In fact, they practise "heterophobia" which is not even in the dictionary. Orwellian.

A few Google searches illustrate how this vicious heterophobic assault flies under our radar.

If you google "heterophobia" (i.e. fear of heterosexuality) you'll get 115,000 entries, most unrelated to what is really happening.

Google "homophobia" (i.e. fear of homosexuality) and you'll get 9,270,000 entries, eighty times more references, mostly disparaging. Since gays are 1/50th of the population, the awareness disparity is roughly 4000 to one.

I first noticed this when looking for a Google image for heterophobia. There were 11,700, but hardly any were applicable. There were 979,000 images for homophobia, 836 times as many.

Homosexuality gets almost seven times as many hits as heterosexuality, despite being 1/50 the demographic segment.

We are mind controlled and manipulated and we haven't a clue it is happening.

DENIAL OF GENDER = DENIAL OF REALITY

Male and female gender spans nature from the human to the most rudimentary sea creatures. Gender differences are documented in science:

"There has seldom been a greater divide between what intelligent, enlightened opinion presumes—that men and women have the same brain—and what science knows: that they do not," neuropsychologist Dr. Anne Moir writes.

"Conclusive scientific research presents an irrefutable truth: The difference between men and women is not merely physical. It is neurological, too. Male and female human brains are wired differently, causing us to think, feel, react and respond in strikingly different ways." (http://www.brainsexmatters.com/index.php)

Women are different because they have babies. Children must be conceived in love and raised in a secure and wholesome environment. Men and women have complementary roles based on different skills and temperaments.

Heterosexuality and homosexuality are not compatible. If heterosexuals don't determine societal norms, the tiny homosexual minority will (empowered by the Illuminati.) As this happens, the majority will erode, become a minority and eventually disappear.

The 1852 Occult Plan to Worship Women & Disinherit Men

M. Comte aims at establishing ...a despotism of society over the individual, surpassing anything contemplated in the political ideal of the most rigid disciplinarian among the ancient philosophers —John Stuart Mill

In *Brave New World* (1931), Aldous Huxley envisioned test tube babies. But as early as 1852, Illuminati philosopher Auguste Comte had similar visions of reengineering society. He said social progress required that human reproduction "depend solely on the woman." Men should be shut out of the family.

August Comte

"If in human reproduction, the man contributes merely a stimulus, one that is but an incidental accompaniment of the real office of his generative system, then it is conceivable that we might substitute for this stimulus one or more which should be at women's free disposal..." he wrote.

The goal seems to be to eliminate sexual attraction altogether.

"Woman, even in her physical functions, may become independent of men...The highest species of production would no longer be at the mercy of a capricious and unruly instinct, the proper restraint of which has hitherto been the chief stumbling-block in the way of human discipline." (*System of Positive Polity,* 1851-1854, Vol. IV, P. 60, 61.)

In a chilling presentiment, he wrote, "A female friend, if well chosen, who could make herself a member of the family, would in most cases do better than the father himself." (Vol. IV, P. 195.)

The Illuminati believed they could control society by "liberating women" from marriage. Cults anticipated the "single mother."

"The change would complete the just emancipation of women, thus rendered independent of men, even physically, it would no longer be possible to contest the full ascendancy of the affective sex over children which were its offspring exclusively." (Vol. IV, P. 244)

Mankind would be members of one great family as "the offspring of a spouse-less mother." (Vol. IV, P. 359)

THE WORSHIP OF WOMAN

Comte said the first step in the "worship of humanity" (Humanism) was to make women goddesses.

"By substituting goddesses for gods, we sanction the legitimate preeminence of women.... In a word, the new doctrine will institute the worship of Woman, publicly and privately, in a far more perfect way than has ever before been possible. It is the first permanent step towards the worship of Humanity." (Vol. 4, 446; Vol. I, P. 205.)

While Comte himself supposedly was not a Freemason, according to one source, [Comte's philosophy] positivism "played a particularly strong role in French Freemasonry in the nineteenth century. Part of the reason for this partnership was positivism's own political undertones of resistance against authoritarian means of knowledge, most notably from the Church. "

CONCLUSION

With the "Enlightenment" the Illuminati embarked on a multi-generational project to wrest humanity from its natural and spiritual moorings, and re-engineer it into a large penal colony that serves their interests.

For religion, which seeks to obey the Creator's Design, the Illuminists substituted the religion of man, or Humanism.

Man becomes "his own God" as he makes the world a heaven. This is just a ruse to re-engineer him according to elite specifications. Comte is known as the "father of sociology"—an indication that the social sciences are really devoted to establishing a totalitarian society.

Any substitute for God is satanic. Auguste Comte is proof that modern social trends—the idealization of women, the destruction of marriage and family—are satanic in origin and have deep roots.

This article is based on research by Erica Carle in 2010. http://www.newswithviews.com/Erica/Carle172.htm

Smoking Gun! Predators Draft "Sex Education"

We shouldn't forget the case of former Ontario Deputy Minister of Education, Benjamin Levin. Released July 9, 2013 on $100,000 bail, Levin was charged with making and distributing child pornography. As Deputy Minister of Education, he drafted a "sex education" program to sexualize Ontario children.

This is more evidence that a Masonic (Cabalist Jewish) satanic sex cult controls society using liberal and "progressive" groups as fronts. He was a professor at the University of Toronto; his brother is Registrar there and another is Canadian ambassador to Cuba. Another brother was the Book Editor of the (Toronto) *Globe and Mail*.

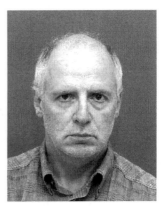

Ben Levin

BY *REALITY* (REAL WOMEN OF CANADA – SEPTEMBER, 2012)

From 2004 to 2009, Ben Levin served as Deputy Minister of Education of Ontario under the lesbian Minister of Education, Kathleen Wynne, who is currently (2014) the Liberal Premier of the Province.

During Levin's time as Deputy Minister, a new sex education curriculum, called the Equity and Inclusive Education Strategy (EIES), was developed. According to this curriculum, six-year-olds were to be taught "gender identity" in grade one, sex orientation in grade three, masturbation in grade six, and oral and anal sex by grade seven.

In a letter, dated April 6, 2009, Mr. Levin stated, "Today, the ministry released its new equity and inclusive education strategy paper, realizing the Promise of Diversity... This province-wide strategy has been a priority for our Minister of Education Kathleen Wynne and me."

This program was introduced in September, 2010. Horrified parents raised such a storm of protest that the then Premier, Dalton McGuinty, was forced to withdraw the program after two days. Undaunted by this rejection, Premier Wynne, who succeeded McGuinty, announced in January, 2013, that she planned to bring back this controversial sex education program.

In June, 2013, Mr. Levin published an article in the *Literary Review of Canada* which criticized the provincial requirement that all adults working with children be required to undergo criminal record checks. He claimed that this was a barrier to partnerships between the schools and the communities.

Mr. Levin was so highly thought of by now Premier Wynne that she appointed him a member of her transition team in January, 2013. He also sat proudly in a privileged front row spot next to Ms. Wynne, federal Liberal leader, Justin Trudeau, and former leader Bob Rae at Toronto's Gay Parade in June, 2013.

Mr. Levin has now been charged with two counts of distributing child pornography, one count each of making child pornography, counseling to commit an indictable offense, and agreeing to or arranging for an indictable offense against a child under 16 years of age.

Two further charges were also levied against him for possessing and accessing child pornography.

EARLY CHILDHOOD EDUCATION AND CHILD PREDATORS

It was not by mere chance that Mr. Levin, as Deputy Minister of Education, was promoting early sex education program for children. By sexualizing children before they are ready—psychologically, emotionally and physically—children may engage in sexual activity with predators believing it is normal, acceptable and expected of them.

This makes them both vulnerable and an easy prey. It was only the common sense and intuition of concerned parents in Ontario that stopped this sex curriculum from being implemented.

Who's the Bully? Manitoba Forces Homosexuality on Children

We must introduce into their education all those principles which have so brilliantly broken up their order. Protocols of the Elders of Zion (16)

In December 2012, Nancy Allan, Manitoba Minster of Re Education and Child Procurement, announced a coercive law to persecute students who object to homosexuality, ensuring that school children are groomed for homosexual pedophiles.

Nancy Allan

The "Anti Bullying Action Plan," which became law Oct. 9, 2013, will teach children how to report anyone who has reservations about homosexuality. This has been extended beyond the school to include all venues, including the Internet and social media. There will be political commissars trained to take complaints and hunt down and intimidate offenders. (Source: *CBC Information Radio Interview* with Allan)

All school boards will be forced to adopt a "Human Diversity" Mission Statement which emphasizes "inclusiveness" i.e. approval for the "homosexual lifestyle." It will insist that "gay-straight alliances" be established in all Manitoba schools. These clubs are meeting places where straight children can be inverted and have their first gay sexual experience. These trysting places have been established in 31 Manitoba schools so far.

The Illuminati always have a good reason and the real reason. They talk about making schools "safe" and "friendly" for gays. The real reason is to encourage gay sexual experimentation. Manitoba schools are no longer "safe" places for the 98% of the school population that is heterosexual. Our political leaders demonstrate a subversive hatred for heterosexual society and its institutions.

I live in Winnipeg. Manitoba's NDP government is a member of the Socialist International, a Communist (Illuminati Masonic) front. Their logo, fist and red rose are both Communist front symbols. The Illuminati have crossed the line. They have been caught red handed procuring children for pedophiles. They are gambling the public is too stupid and cowardly to recognize this and resist.

PSY OP

You know it's an Illuminati psy-op when local, state and federal governments, corporations, celebrities and the mass media all start singing from the same songbook.

The "psy-op" is "bullying." Supposedly it's an epidemic. The Obama administration "estimates that bullying affects 13 million students, or about a third of those attending school."

One-third of all children attending school? Have you ever heard such nonsense in your life?

Back in the 1950s I was bullied in the schoolyard at Fairfield school. I didn't go whinging on YouTube for government, public or celebrity assistance.

I hired a tough kid named Louis and he took care of the problem. It cost me some marbles.

Some kids ostracized me in later grades. So what? I shunned them. Personality conflicts and disagreements are a normal part of life. They do not require legislation unless there is a pernicious hidden agenda.

"Bullying" is not the real issue here. "Bullying" is a euphemism for something else, non-acceptance of homosexuality.

Gay kids are being portrayed as a persecuted minority. Anyone who refuses to experiment with homosexuality is being set up as a "bully" or "hater."

"Lady" Gag wants to make "bullying" a "hate crime." Did you know most homosexuals prefer heterosexuals? They don't like rejection.

Watch the report on ABC News, Dec. 6, 2011. It was about how satanist slut Lady Gag is going to the White House to discuss bullying. But it quickly emerges that bullying isn't the problem, resistance to homosexuality is.

Jonah Mowry's video is trotted out and Jonah is quoted as saying Gag inspired him because of her "born that way" campaign.

Earth to Jonah. Very few homosexuals are "born that way." Most become that way because of family dysfunction (abusive or no father, overbearing mother) or sexual abuse by an older member of the same sex.

[Kevin, a reader, used to live in San Francisco. He asked gay men questions like "Were you always attracted to men?" EVERY LAST GAY MALE HE SPOKE TO had been either abused by his father or (more likely) step-father or raped by a person in authority; all while young or teenaged children.]

This dysfunction is what the Illuminati perverts are trying to normalize. This is why they give shots against STD's to babies and children.

Don't have any illusions about the monsters who govern us. They are practicing Satanists. They don't care about gays, women, children, or anyone but themselves. But they will adopt a pious pose to advance their perverse agenda.

I believe homosexuality is a developmental disorder and gays should be treated like anyone else with a health problem, with compassion and support. I do not encourage or condone hurtful behavior.

Don't be fooled. "Bullying" is really about heterosexuals being coerced to have gay sex. The media and government perverts and traitors are bullying you.

Nancy Allan was dropped from Cabinet in Oct. 2013, a week after her heterophobic bill became law.

FIRST COMMENT BY JUDITH REISMAN PH.D. AUTHOR OF *SEXUAL SABO-TAGE*, (2010)

This is a wholly accurate account of the state mandated pedophile/pederast grooming increasingly found worldwide. Only a worldwide institution could produce the same global sexual "party line." The campaign to sexualize all infants and children for use and abuse emerges as an "Anti Bullying Action Plan" in Manitoba. The program induces child sexual experimentation—the same encouraged by Havana-trained sexologists in Brazil, and similar pedo-advocates in Great Britain, the USA and worldwide under the closet umbrella of International Planned Parenthood.

These programs are entry level for the child sexual traffic—a financial growth industry. Picture perverts sitting around a conference table for the last 20 years planning how to, "get the kids away from the controls of parents and religion and they are wholly vulnerable. Let's call it anti bullying, hate crimes. Once we get pedo-grooming—we get global control."

Ridiculous you say? Time is telling us it is not.

Judith Reisman, Ph.D.
Visiting Professor of Law
Liberty University School of Law

Nancy Allan's Guide to Gay Sex

Nancy Allan was the Minister of Education in Manitoba until October 2013. Manitoba schools rank among the lowest in Canada. The answer: Teach Manitoba children to eat shit (i.e. "rimming.")

Yes literally. She wants Manitoba school children to embrace homosexuality. Her Bill 18 forces schools to establish "gay-straight alliances" and criminalize resistance to homosexuality as "bullying."

At these meetings, I can imagine the lesson plan would include the following information about gay sex:

1. Anal sex is one of the principal homosexual pleasures. Anal intercourse is analogous to normal sex. You may disregard the fact that the anus was not intended to be a receptacle. Disregard the fact that when sodomy is performed, the peculiar forced inward expansion of the anal canal results in a tearing of the lining as well as bleeding anal fissures. This gives rise to a litany of diseases.

2. Anilingus, usually referred to as "rimming." This practice involves licking the rim of the anus, and often ingesting faecal matter—in other words, eating shit. If they don't actually eat shit, some homosexuals defecate on each other. This bizarre practice is known as scat. Urination into the mouth and over the bleeding body of the participant...is likewise a common practice. This is known as golden showers or water sports. Go for it, children!

3. Fisting or hand-balling involves inserting the hand or fist into the anus. While it is difficult to believe that a fist can be inserted into a human anus, it is possible. Don't worry that the damage from fisting can result in a sphincterectomy or colostomy. Some individuals can then have sodomy performed through the colostomy opening, causing further damage.

Try to imagine how you can sink to lower depths of depravity than this. As well as fists, you can also insert toys into the anus: dildos, vibrators etc. This leads to serious internal damage; in particular puncturing of the intestinal wall and seepage of faecal matter into the abdomen, which can result in death. But at least you will die in a politically correct way.

An American publication said of sex toys that, "Most are small, but physicians have removed such large items as a six-ounce Coca-Cola bottle, an entire pencil, and a

Henry Makow PhD   67 vibrator head." The record must be an after-shaving lotion bottle 14.2 cm in length, 21.5 cm circumference.

4. Another homosexuals practice is sado-masochism. About a third of homosexuals engage in sexual torture. The top six US male serial murderers were all gay. Thanks to the Manitoba Dept. of Education, you may end up seriously injuring or murdering someone, or being seriously injured or murdered.

5. As the thrills diminish, you will need to employ drugs to heighten your experience. Drug use is seven times higher among gays. Crystal meth and cocaine are the drugs of choice.

6. As a homosexual, you will enjoy an extraordinary degree of promiscuity. You may enjoy many dozen sex partners in a year, hundreds in a lifetime. "Marriages" are rarely exclusive.

Denis Altman, a veteran of this courageous endeavor to reshape human nature has written: "Large-scale luxurious pleasure palaces where everyone is potentially a sexual partner are a common sexual fantasy; only for gay men they are a commonplace reality...Men in bathhouses rarely talk much, and it is quite common for sex to take place without words, let alone names, being exchanged."

Altman pretends that this is a display of brotherhood: "The willingness to have sex immediately, promiscuously, and with people about whom one knows nothing and from whom one demands only physical contact can be seen as a sort of Whitmanesque democracy, a desire to know and trust other men in a type of brotherhood."

Apart from bathhouses, homosexuals often engage in totally anonymous sex in public toilets—a practice known as "cottaging"—and in public parks and elsewhere. The personal columns of homosexual publications are crammed full of advertisements for male whores—rent boys.

Bend over children! That's what the New World Order is about: Induction into a satanic sex cult. Anyone who objects is a "bully" and will be prosecuted accordingly.

Teachers Applaud as Prof Defends Pedophiles

Despite the fact that 3000 people signed a petition to bar James Kincaid from Canada, there were no protesters when this defender of pedophilia spoke to a conference, *Bodies at Play; Sexuality, Childhood and Classroom Life* at the University of Toronto Oct. 19, 2013. The talk was sponsored by the *Centre for Sexual Diversity Studies.* (Should be "sexual perversity.")

Although the 125,000 members of the Institute for Canadian Values and Canada Family Action petitioned the government, the only dissenter present was henrymakow.com reader Nathan Wiedmann, 32, a tradesman and father of three, who drove three hours through the night to be there.

Nathan expected to join other protesters. When none appeared, he decided to attend the lecture instead.

Normally, he would have to register in advance but they let him in anyway, despite heavy security outside. Thanks to the recording Nathan made of the 45-minute talk, I can report what transpired.

Kincaid, 76, who is a Professor Emeritus at the University of Southern California, did not come right out and advocate pedophilia in so many words. Rather he downplayed the negatives while in general terms, promoting the positives of seeing children erotically. His euphemism for erotic is "the surrealistic child."

Kincaid is a confident and charming speaker as you'd expect from a retired English professor. The audience treated him like a guru and social reformer, not like the ideological pederast he is.

They laughed at his little jokes and concluded with a round of applause. No questions were allowed but people were invited to approach him individually.

TRADEMARK MESSAGE

The first half of the talk featured the display of unintelligible "erudition" professors use to hypnotize their audiences. Then Kincaid came out with his trademark message. He implied that everyone is sexually attracted to children but only pedophiles are honest enough to admit it.

This is the strategy homosexual activists also use. Anyone who doesn't want their "lifestyle" to become the societal norm must be a closeted gay himself.

Kincaid said there was no need to protect children from predators. Conservatives created this bogeyman to uphold the outdated institution of family and "US identity." Society is hypocritical because it eroticizes children at the same time as it persecutes pedophiles.

I beg to differ, Prof. Kincaid. Illuminati social engineers, homosexuals and pedophiles sexualize children. Society objects because your values have not yet taken over.

The audience laughed in agreement when he said child predators are really FBI agents arranging a sting. He pictured two FBI agents making an assignation. "Nothing ever happens," he says."It's a thought crime."

Please. Nothing ever happens when a pedophile meets a child?

He said there were only 115 child abductions a year in the US, and hysteria over pedophilia diverts resources from more urgent child welfare issues like the 750,000 children who run away from home.

As if "child abductions" were any measure of pedophilia. These are probably custody cases, and there are probably many more. Child porn is a $20 billion a year industry online alone, and Kincaid thinks pedophilia can be measured in terms of 115 abductions.

He said 90% of sexual abuse took place in a "family context." Pedophiles are being scapegoated to shield the "faltering family unit."

This is what homosexual activists call "jamming," making outrageous, indefensible assertions as if they were facts. Here, he is blaming pedophilia on the protector of children, the traditional family.

He said we objected to Calvin Klein portraying children in underwear on billboards because we were attracted to them. He said people claimed that boys genital shapes were air-brushed out of Sears catalog underwear ads. He said this was not true and he would have brought the pictures to prove it but was afraid being stopped at the border. He chuckled and the audience laughed.

MESSAGE TO KINCAID

Healthy adults want to hug, nurture and protect children. We do not want to have sex with them. Only sick people do.

He implies that pre-puberty children are sexual. I don't think so, but whether they are or not, they are not ready for sex. They are not fair game for people who can't control their worst impulses.

Can't Kincaid remember what childhood is like? Children are weak, vulnerable and extremely dependent. They lack understanding. They are in an unformed state.

Can't pedophiles see the harm they do to children? Can't they see the horrific results? Why do they only think of themselves?

Kincaid ended with a Dionysian rhapsody about the wonder and beauty of children. It sounded like a sexual overture couched in spiritual terms: "oceanic bliss;" "ecstatic intoxication;" "find out what we have lost;" "the moment is all we have;" "experience is all that matters;" "everything else is death" etc. etc.

SATANISM

He ended by condemning education as an obstacle to these wonderful creatures, children, who should be teaching their teachers. The audience of 50 education students and profs politely applauded, and the host thanked Kincaid for a "wonderful talk." Clearly, they didn't understand the talk or have lost their moral bearings.

A cognitive dissonance happens and reality shifts under our feet when people who are socially accepted say abhorrent and irrational things, especially when they are couched in vague, elaborate language.

Kincaid probably got $5,000 plus expenses to fly to Toronto with his wife and stay at a fancy hotel. Is this how our tax dollars should be spent?

Courts Help Gays Pimp Their Sons

By Miriam Silver

My 11-year-old son reported that his father's gay lover was massaging him in bed with his underwear on, and that he no longer wanted to visit his father's house while this man was there as he gave him the creeps and hated him.

I tried to speak to his father, but he said he wanted his son to get used to another man touching him, that it was natural.

My attorney brought this to the judge's attention and was immediately shut down. Judge wrote an order stating I was a liar, and she wouldn't let me or my son testify again.

My son who was a big boy started to have physical fights with his father on his days of visitation as he didn't want to be around his boyfriend...

I was accused of "Parental Alienation," even though the man my son was complaining about wasn't his father, but his gay lover.

The judge told me he didn't have to follow any of the laws of the USA and that my son needed to get used to a homosexual lifestyle, and he then ordered no contact between me and my son.

My son begged me to help him, so we ran away. Bounty hunters were hired; private investigators followed my entire family; all our phones were tapped; my family's bank accounts were frozen, and my parent's mail was sent to the police before they could receive it.

Finally in Feb 11, 2002 I was placed on FBI "Ten Most Wanted" list with Osama bin Laden.

I voluntarily returned with my son after the judge was removed from my case for bias, but it was too late, as the new judge upheld the actions of the previous judge....

I went to jail for six-months, spent four years under house arrest and was denied contact with my son who kept asking for me.

My case is not unusual. As of this writing, 2.2 million moms have been denied primary physical custody of their children.

http://www.workingmother.com/special-reports/custody-lost

My son testified against me after his father actually put him into foster care to scare him. Nancy Grace did a small section on this trial, wondering why I was put on trial.

I am a libertarian and if you worry about Obama not following the law, surely this can't be a surprise by now.

Little by little our government has been trying its best to take control over our children. If you think losing your doctor or healthcare is bad, imagine losing your child. This is it folks—our government is already starting the practices of Nazi Germany and no one wants to see it.

My book is available at my website www.protectingmychild.org. I ask you not to ignore this story. How many more children must be devastated, harmed, sexually abused and killed before one person in the media is willing to do an investigative report?

I think our government has reached it's tipping point.

Miriam Silver is the pen name of a Florida mother.

Disgrace: Canada Protects Porn Queen Judge

When a society fails to recognize and exorcise evil, and instead rewards it, it is in deep trouble.

In an unprecedented act Nov. 21, 2013, a panel of judges charged with removing a family court judge whose naked pictures appeared on the Internet threw up their hands and quit because of lack of support from Freemasons in the federal Conservative government.

Associate Chief Justice of Manitoba, Lori Douglas

The mass media does not mention any of this. Instead it gave the long delay as the reason, as if starting over won't further retard the process. The inquiry had already cost $3 million.

Before becoming a family court judge in Winnipeg in 2005, Lori Douglas was required to disclose any information that would compromise her. She hid that she had posed for scores of disgusting porn and bondage pictures on the Internet. She hid that her husband Jack King had solicited a Black client, Alex Chapman, to participate in making more such obscene pictures.

When Chapman revealed this in 2010, Douglas was already Associate Chief Justice of Manitoba *in charge of family law.* She should have been forced to resign, plain and simple.

Instead, Winnipeg's Masonic elite rallied around her, arguing that her private life had no bearing on her job capacity. *Winnipeg Free(mason) Press* columnist Lyndor Reynolds opined, "there's no reason she can't continue as a judge. One has nothing to do with the other."

Perhaps if she were still in private practice. But chief family court judge is a public position. Do they expect decent citizens to allow a degenerate to determine their fate?

University of Manitoba Law Professor, and outspoken feminist, Karen Busby said: "Most people have sex pictures out there somewhere, then it's an impossible standard for anyone to meet to become a judge."

Have you ever heard anything so ridiculous?

The Masons claim Douglas didn't know what her husband did with the photos. Alex Chapman begs to differ. He had two exploratory lunch dates with her and she knew why.

Instead of resigning, Lori Douglas has been receiving full salary of $315,000 for performing "administrative duties." It's been three years already. How long are taxpayers going to tolerate this?

CANADIAN JUDICIAL COUNCIL

In 2011-2012, a Canadian Judicial Council Inquiry began hearings to determine if Douglas should be cashiered. The panel included the Chief Justices of Newfoundland and Prince Edward Island and was chaired by the Chief Justice of Alberta, Catherine Fraser.

In July 2012, the hearings were going badly for Douglas. After some particularly withering cross examination, Douglas' lawyer Sheila Block accused the Committee of being "biased" and called for the proceedings to be stayed. Her motion was rejected by the Committee.

Nevertheless, she was able to take her accusation of "bias" to the Federal Court. This is obviously an obstruction tactic. Instead of rejecting it, the Federal Court entertained the motion for twenty months, until March 2014 when it finally denied it.

By this time the Canadian Judicial Council Committee had quit in disgust. "This Committee does not agree that the Federal Court has the jurisdiction to judicially review the proceedings of an inquiry committee which is deemed to be a superior court under the Judges Act , RSC 1985, c. J-1."

In Section 9, the Committee cited many instances where Freemason Peter MacKay, the Attorney General of Canada failed to defend the Canadian Judicial Council in federal court proceedings.

These include: "The AGC did not oppose the stay of the Committee's hearings requested by the Judge which was consequently granted, unopposed; The AGC did not appeal any of the decisions of the Federal Court denying intervener status to the Committee or restricting intervener status for the Council and the new Independent Counsel, despite having consented to these applications."

The Committee concludes: "There is no voice in defense of the process and an inquiry committee's role in it. Thus, this fundamental part of the process is silenced and paralyzed."

CONCLUSION

The hearing was to continue with testimony from Justice Martin Freedman of the Manitoba Court of Appeal, who was involved in Douglas's application to be a judge.

The Lori Douglas Inquiry threatened to unveil Masonic control of the justice system. Obviously, this control extends right up to the offices of the Attorney General of Canada, Peter MacKay, and the Prime Minister, Stephen Harper.

Lori Douglas was appointed a judge because she had posed for porn, not in spite of it. Freemasons have to be blackmailable in order to be controlled.

While the media is focused on trivia, the ignominious failure of the justice system to purge an unfit judge was largely ignored.

I sent this article to MacKay and received a reply Dec. 2, 2013, to the effect that he will act when he gets the Judicial Council's recommendation. The Canadian Judicial Council announced the appointment of a new panel on March 13, 2014. I hope Lori Douglas' lawyer doesn't find them "biased" as well.

FIRST COMMENT FROM ALOYSIUS FOZDYKE

(Satanist, Member of the Alpha Lodge in Sydney Australia.)

"We have weakened societies by reforms which undermine authority, together with the destruction of national and communal identity and legal systems that are complex and pro-criminal."

Canadian Serial Killer Linked to Elite Satanists?

In February 2010, Canadians had their mental paradigm shattered when the Commander of the largest air force base, CFB Trenton, Col. Russell Williams, was arrested and charged with sexually assaulting and murdering two women.

"The accusations shook the armed forces and the Canadian public. Col. Williams had been hand-picked and 'pipelined' into the upper echelons of the air force. He trained new pilots, flew the prime minister's plane and last summer was awarded command of S-Wing Trenton, with 2300 men and women, the country's largest and busiest air force base." (*Globe and Mail,* April 17, 2010.)

On Oct 21, 2010, Williams was given two life sentences for murdering a subordinate, Cpl Marie-France Comeau in her home last October, and another woman Jessica Lloyd on Jan. 28. He confessed to breaking into the homes of other women, stripping them, beating them and photographing them naked. He also made some 80 panty raids on women's homes.

Serial killer Russell Williams, center, with former Canadian Defense Minister Peter MacKay, right, and Chief of Defence Staff General Walter Natyncyk. Williams wearing bra and panties below

He will still collect his $60,000-a-year pension while in prison.

He was arrested by the Ontario Provincial Police at a roadblock when an officer noticed his tire treads matched those found near Lloyd's home.

Canadians were dumbfounded. As the *Globe and Mail* put it: "How is it possible that someone so polished and groomed for leadership could stand accused of such crimes?"

Canadians will continue to be baffled until they realize that such events, including cases of missing persons and child molestation, are symptomatic of the presence of a satanic cult, the Illuminati, subverting "respectable" society. This is true of most countries.

PAUL BERNARDO

On February 12, the *Ottawa Sun* revealed that Russell Williams was a college pal of Paul Bernardo who murdered and dismembered three teenage girls and raped 19 others in Toronto in the late 1980s. They both studied economics at the Scarborough campus of the University of Toronto.

The police speculated that the two may have "competed" in terms of sex crimes. From prison, Bernardo suggested police go back 20 years and look at everything, because that's when his testosterone would have been at the highest.

What the Bernardo trial covered up and the newspaper ignored, is that Bernardo's murders were satanic in nature. They were so horrific that the trial proceedings were made secret. Bernardo and his wife Karla Homolka made snuff films for the entertainment of a network of prominent Illuminati Satanists. This is the real reason the trial was hit with a publication ban.

This information is contained in a rare encyclopedic work entitled *New World Order— Corruption in Canada* (1994) edited by Robert O'Driscoll and Elizabeth Elliott. The editors had many contacts inside the Illuminati. They were told these ritual murders are a source of spiritual power for Satanists.

"The serial killer's dissection of the body always parallels his attempt to vivisect the soul. In many cases, the limbs of the body are kept in close proximity for long periods of time even after they decompose; Dahmer in the US kept parts of the body in his fridge to be consumed at his will. Reports of these vivisections [and snuff films] go straight to the Illuminati or their political agents [and] to other cells of the Church [of Satan] as distant as far flung Japan." (p.25)

CONCLUSION

We will continue to have our paradigm shattered until we stop looking at the symptoms and address the cause: a vast satanic underground whose members are respected citizens by day and monsters at night.

If Russell Williams is any indication, its tentacles reach into the highest offices of the land.

Satanist Pedophiles Rule Great Britain

By David Richards

Pedophilia is common practice in the British establishment. This is difficult for the British public to believe. At our level, pedophilia is a crime heavily punished by the law and condemned by the mainstream media.

However, Illuminati members are above the law and partake in pedophile rings without fear of prosecution.

Jimmy Savile and a younger Tony Blair

The Illuminati operate pedophile rings for three main reasons:

1. Most members of the cult have a psychopathic and sadomasochistic make-up, and therefore have perverted sexual desires.

2. Pedophile rings operate as a system of blackmail, enforcing conformity to the NWO. All members of the establishment are vetted by security services. Hidden cameras are placed at child sex parties to gather incriminating material.

3. Perversion is the way Satanists worship. Just as a Christian might perform works of charity, the Satanist will prey on children.

FOUR EXAMPLES OF ELITE SATANISM

The following cases prove the existence of establishment pedophile rings in Britain.

1) Gordon Brown—English journalist Mike James claims former Prime Minister Brown is a well-known pedophile. James worked in the mainstream media and was first told of Brown's perversions by Norman Lamont (Chancellor of the Exchequer 1990-93) at a private party in 1986.

He later did his own research into the man, and wrote in 2010: "Gordon Brown, the current British prime minister, is a practicing pedophile whose activities are known not only to the British, American and Israeli intelligence services, but also by Rupert Murdoch and his senior editor at the *Sunday Times*."

The fact that intelligence services have dirt on Brown means he is controlled. Brown became Prime Minister because of his perversions, not in spite of them.

Mike James places Brown as a member of a ring of senior British pedophiles, including Lord Robertson and Lord Peter Mandelson. All of them are major members of Masonic lodges.

2) Thatcher Pedo Ring—It has been revealed that a pedophile ring operated within the Thatcher government (1979-90).

In the '80s, a teenage rent boy went to the police claiming he and other boys were sexually abused by top people.

The parties were held by millionaires and attended by British politicians, judges, senior civil servants and members of the European elite. Some of the VIPs were said to have flown in via RAF (Royal Air Force) Northolt on the outskirts of London.

This case has been revealed by a disgruntled former policeman who interviewed the rent boy. He says when he began to investigate the claims, his superior demanded he stop.

"It was a case of 'get rid of everything, never say a word to anyone'. It was made very clear to me that to continue asking questions would jeopardize my career."

3) Sir Jimmy Savile (1926-2011)—For over 40 years Savile presented TV shows aimed at young people.

In recent months he has been exposed as a violent pedophile who abused children over a period of four decades.

With each passing day, more people come forward to testify against the dead presenter. Police are currently processing the testimonies of hundreds of victims.

The details are astounding: he abused children who appeared on his television programs, organized pedophile parties with other entertainment stars, and molested sick children in hospitals. A former BBC radio DJ claims he was also a necrophiliac.

However, the most damning reports—and least commented on in the mainstream media—are those which reveal Savile took part in establishment pedophile rings.

In 2011, the *News of the World* newspaper reported that 'Savile is known for supplying a number of high profile MP's with children for them to sexually abuse.'

The article revealed Savile was a regular visitor to the notorious Haut de la Gaurenne care home in Jersey in the 70s, and was witnessed taking young boys onboard the yacht of former British Prime Minister Ted Heath.

Ex-Jersey deputy police Chief Lenny Harper explains how children were abused on the island:

"We know from court cases and statements made to my team [during a 2008 inquiry] that children in Jersey care homes were 'loaned out' to members of the yachting fraternity and other prominent citizens on the pretense of recreational trips but during which they were savagely abused and often raped. When these children complained, they were beaten and locked in cellars [at Haut de la Garenne.]"

Allegations circled around Savile for decades, but due to his establishment connections he was protected. In 1990, the Queen honoured Savile with a knighthood (Member of the Order of the British Empire.)

The revelations have only emerged now because Savile died in Oct. 2011 and can no longer be protected by libel laws.

SATANIC RING

On January 13, 2013, the *Daily Express*, a major British newspaper came right out and said, in a headline, "Jimmy Savile was part of satanic ring."

JIMMY SAVILE beat and raped a 12-year-old girl during a secret satanic ritual in a hospital.

The perverted star wore a hooded robe and mask as he abused the terrified victim in a candle-lit basement.

He also chanted "Hail Satan" in Latin as other paedophile devil worshippers joined in and assaulted the girl at Stoke Mandeville Hospital in Buckinghamshire. The attack, which happened in 1975, shines a sinister new light on the former DJ's 54-year reign of terror.

Savile, who died aged 84 in October 2011, is now Britain's worst sex offender after police revealed he preyed on at least 450 victims aged eight to 47.

The victim recalled being led into a room that was filled with candles on the lowest level of the hospital, somewhere that was not regularly used by staff. Several adults were there, including Jimmy Savile who, like the others, was wearing a robe and a mask.

She recognized him because of his distinctive voice and the fact that his blond hair was protruding from the side of the mask. He was not the leader but he was seen as important because of his fame.

She was molested, raped and beaten and heard words that sounded like 'Ave Satanas', a Latinized version of 'Hail Satan', being chanted. There was no mention of any other child being there and she cannot remember how long the attack lasted but she was left extremely frightened and shaken.

http://www.express.co.uk/news/uk/370439/Jimmy-Savile-was-part-of-satanic-ring

(David Richards, 25, is a Brit who teaches English in Mongolia.)

Sexual Revolution:
Bestiality & Pedophilia are Next

By Ron

As you correctly note, bestiality is next in the New World Order effort to enslave us. It's been tried before. A look at history shows that in the 1970s, the Illuminati pushed a mentally ill young Danish woman named Bodil Joensen into world-wide prominence by filming her pornographic performances with animals.

Briefly, bestiality porn looked like it was going to go mainstream before it was pushed back underground through the efforts of decent people. The tragic Ms. Joensen died in the early '80s, a broken prostitute, after the porn industry had finished exploiting her.

If at first you don't succeed, try again, and so the Illuminati are trying a different approach this go round. The Wikipedia entry on zoophilia discusses this subject in some detail, including the marketing of dildos in the shape of animal penises.

A woman Ph.D. originally from Israel named Hani Miletski is among those leading the charge to normalize bestiality today. Not surprisingly, she has strong connections to think tanks and government agencies that suggest Illuminati entanglements.

Her promotion of bestiality in her book *Understanding Bestiality and Zoophilia* takes the form that you might expect—the desire to have sex with animals is just another sexual orientation. That approach worked with homosexuality and it's now being used to promote and normalize incest, bestiality, and pedophilia.

THE INTERNET

Turning to the Internet, as you say, pornography is dictating norms. There is an "app" called Vine that is a video version of Twitter. Vine allows users to post six-second long videos, mirroring Twitter's 140 character tweets. If you search the word "naughty" on Vine you will see videos posted by everyday adult women and men, not porn stars. These women and men are exposing themselves, with tight close-ups of their genitals. Most masturbate for Vine. There are also websites picking up these videos for viewing on the Internet...

You also bring up the subject of flashing vaginas in public, and how it may become common. Before I left my career in academia, I had as early as 2003 seen panty-less, pruned private parts being flashed in class.

Narcissism, the addiction to thrills, and the influence of the porn industry played a part, in my opinion. There was a "celebrity" at the time named Paris Hilton who was flashing her shaved lady bits to the paparazzi, and I think this behavior also influenced a number of females on campus. Since then a wide variety of these untalented "celebrities" have engaged in similar exposure. It's no longer shocking for them to do it, so why should anyone be shocked when the girl next door does it?

Many celebrities are creations of the Illuminati, themselves enslaved by mind-control methods invented by the New World Order. They not only promote pornographic lifestyles, but also Satanism. From Madonna to Lady Gaga, and now to poor Miley Cyrus, these and other entertainers are cogs in a larger Illuminati machine that practices cultural engineering on a vast scale—all of it intended to enslave us to our carnal appetites.

PEDOPHILIA, NECROPHILIA & ANAL SEX

Pornography is introduced into the lives of children in some new and highly creative ways, and this should also be considered by parents concerned for their children's welfare. The *Bratz* dolls look like hookers or porn stars.

The new *Monster High* dolls look more like dead hookers or dead porn stars. I consider these toys to be an entrée to necrophilia porn, i.e. porn portraying sex with the dead. As children graduate from playing with their *Monster High* dolls, Goths and emos in pornographic poses suggesting necrophilia will be there for them on the Internet. I suppose some corrupt academic will come along and claim that's just a sexual orientation too. Part of the Illuminati plan is to normalize everything that is degenerate and corrupt.

Which leads me to the subject of anal sex. My impression is that the porn industry is pushing anal sex beyond what the typical porn consumer would like to see. In the real world, anal sex is not that popular—yet. But by pushing it on the Internet, the porn industry is trying to create a new sexual ethic revolving around anal sex. Let's be clear. Anal sex is inconsistent with natural law. It is associated with satanic rituals throughout history. Satanists believe that the act of anal sex opens up the receiving partner to be entered by demonic forces. Thus, it's reasonable to suspect that the industry itself is under the direction of Satan and his earthly representatives.

I am not a prude. Tasteful nudity does not offend me. But the porn industry goes far beyond mere nude photos and videos, taking consumers on a ride leading to their enslavement. From vagina surgery to breast implants to pole dancing for six-year-olds to twerking for teens, the porn industry is the beast devouring our culture and along with it our lives and the lives of our children. Unless we recognize the plague and all its forms, we are doomed.

"Furries" a Stepping Stone to Bestiality?

By Don

This Christmas, we had a guest, a relative who had been attending Augsberg College in Minneapolis. At dinner, she recounted a disturbing college experience.

Somehow she had been placed in a "Lesbian, Gay, Bisexual, Transsexual, Questioning, Other" dormitory with genderless showers and toilet stalls without locks. Need-

Miley Cyrus with "Furries" at MTV Music Video Awards

less to say she was upset and had to endure two weeks at the dorm before being moved.

One group in particular disturbed her. Illustrated with photos from her phone, she told us about students who dressed up as animals. Not only in the dorm but also while attending class. Some of these students dressed in full dog costumes, slept on dog beds, and ate their meals on the floor from dog dishes.

They also wore dog collars with bone medallions around their necks to identify themselves when out of costume. Although she did not go into detail, some of these students also engage in deviant sexual behavior called "yiffing."

When she tried to explain the situation to family back home, her grandmother told her not to be concerned because it was probably something related to the school's team mascot.

BACKGROUND

This was all new to me so I decided to research it. Using Google and images I was able to find labels to name this phenomenon.

The people living in the dorm belonged to the Furries or Furry community. The costumes they wore are anthropomorphic animals which are animals with human characteristics.

Furry fandom includes a range of people such as artists and costume designers, and people who live a furry lifestyle and wear fursuits.

The Furry Community also attracts people who have furry or animal related fetishes and are looking for avenues to express their sexual fantasies without condemnation. Unfortunately for the artistic types, the sexual deviants within the furry population are getting the limelight.

No doubt, it is a small step from having sex dressed as an animal, to having sex with real animals.

Living a furry lifestyle requires a fursuit. Unless a person has the skills to make their own fursuit, they will have to buy one. Fursuits can easily cost thousands of dollars for off the shelf models and even more for custom designs. Some suits have cooling fans and other modifications to provide "creature comforts" for the wearer.

The furry lifestyle is considered an alternate lifestyle and they have support groups and special housing at some colleges. They are even allowed to wear fursuits in the classroom. Some furries consider themselves to be male or female, whereas others are asexual.

Some furries engage in "yiffing" which is mostly simulated sex while wearing fursuits according to www.urbandictionary.com. Other furries actually engage in real sex while wearing fursuits.

Anyone who doubts this only needs to type "fursuit f**king" in Google or another search engine and look at the images. I would not be the least surprised if there are some furries involved in Satanism that engage in even more deviant sexual activities. Satanism is based on the assumption that people are nothing but animals.

Closely related to the furry phenomenon is animal role playing and pony play which is a variation on sadomasochism, bondage and discipline. Although some tribal societies practiced animal role playing in ceremony and dance, modern day practitioners do it more for erotic and sexual fetish purposes.

Animal role playing and pony play devotees seem to be older than those who live the furry lifestyle. Their costumes do not cover the body as much and are more bondage and discipline oriented. Many groups such as the Los Angeles Pony and Critter Club have websites and planned activities and participate in parades and other events such as fox hunts and agility contests.

Not surprisingly there is a shadow industry that supplies the props and tack for the pony players such as bridles and halters and also hoof boots. You can also get reviews of these props and equipment prior to purchase.

The question arises, will these people be treated as a minority with special "furry" rights of their own? Will they need to be protected from persecution? Are people who don't accept them intolerant "furryphobes"? Will they need their own dorms and bathrooms?

FIRST COMMENT FROM DAN:

Seeing this, I Google "furries" on YouTube and sure enough, there's a plethora of fat geeks talking about their 'preference' in all the familiar terms worked out for homosexuality. It's a legal boilerplate.

I've studied the history of human deviations and this bizarre self-identification with cartoon animals and orgiastic sex is a 20th century innovation. Now we have the music and media machine mainstreaming things that never occurred to humanity in a million years.

There's just something VERY 'Disney' about this whole 'furry' thing. Who streamed these memes into the culture in the first place? Disney studios anthropomorphic animals saturated cinema screens for decades in full length feature films of talking animals being intimate friends with humans. The animals themselves being shown having lurid romantic love affairs, with embraces and mouth kissing, and sexual innuendo. Disney animals always used a LOT of subtle sexual body language. People have noticed this really becomes obvious when you look at Disney animal movies with the sound off.

Notice that the 'furry thing' isn't being sold as a 'one on one' kind of kink. The setting is always orgiastic. There's a reason for it. Costumed public parties like Mardi Gras and Festivals conceal identity, thus lowering inhibition. Add dope and booze, and it's a 'lost weekend'. Miley told Yahoo, "If you want to smoke weed, you're going to smoke weed; there's nothing that two little girls are going to get you to do that you don't want to do."

How America Went Gay

By Charles Socarides M.D.

(Edited & Abridged by henrymakow.com)

For more than 20 years, I and a few psychiatrists have felt like an embattled minority, because we have continued to insist that gays aren't born that way.

For most of this (20th) century, we have considered this behavior aberrant...a pathology. We had patients who would seek out one sex partner after another—total strangers—on a single night, then come limping into our offices the next day to tell us how they were hurting themselves. Since we were in the business of helping people learn how not to keep hurting themselves, many of us thought we were quietly doing God's work.

Now, in the opinion of those who make up the so-called cultural elite, our view is "out of date." The elite say we hurt people more than we help them, and that we belong in one of the century's dustbins. They have managed to sell this idea to a great many Americans, thereby making homosexuality fashionable and raising formerly aberrant behavior to the status of an "alternate lifestyle."...

Charles W. Socarides, M.D., (1922-2005) was Clinical Professor of Psychiatry at Albert Einstein College of Medicine in New York.

HOMOSEXUAL REVOLUTION ORCHESTRATED

How did this change come about? Well, the revolution did not just happen...

It was all part of a plan, as one gay publication put it, "to make the whole world gay." I am not making this up. You can read an account of the campaign in Dennis Altman's *The Homosexualization of America.*

In 1982 Altman, himself gay, reported with an air of elation that more and more Americans were thinking like gays and acting like gays. There were engaged, that is, "in numbers of short-lived sexual adventures either in place of or alongside long-term relationships."

Altman cited the heterosexual equivalents of gay saunas and the emergence of the swinging singles scene as proofs that "promiscuity and 'impersonal sex' are determined more by social possibilities than by inherent differences between homosexuals and heterosexuals, or even between men and women."

Heady stuff. Gays said they could "reinvent human nature, reinvent themselves." To do this, these re-inventors had to clear away one major obstacle.

No, they didn't go after the nation's clergy. They targeted the members of a worldly priesthood, the psychiatric community, and neutralized them with a radical redefinition of homosexuality itself.

In 1972 and 1973 they co-opted the leadership of the American Psychiatric Association and, through a series of political maneuvers, lies and outright flim-flams, they "cured" homosexuality overnight—by fiat. They got the A.P.A. to say that same-sex sex was "not a disorder." It was merely "a condition"—as neutral as lefthandedness.

HATRED, INTIMIDATION & INTOLERANCE

This amounted to a full approval of homosexuality. Those of us who did not go along with the political redefinition were soon silenced at our own professional meetings. Our lectures were canceled inside academe and our research papers turned down in the learned journals. Worse things followed in the culture at large. Television and movie producers began to do stories promoting homosexuality as a legitimate lifestyle.

["For some years now, gays have been disrupting our meetings, shouting down people trying to deliver their scientific papers, threatening individual doctors like myself...The gay activists have a ferocious irrationality. They turn every scientific agreement into a political issue—which is all they can really do, since the only science they have going for them is pseudoscience." *Homosexuality: A Freedom Too Far,* pp.153-154]

A gay review board told Hollywood how it should deal or not deal with homosexuality. Mainstream publishers turned down books that objected to the gay revolution. Gays and lesbians influenced sex education in our nation's schools, and gay and lesbian libbers seized wide control of faculty committees in our nations' colleges. State legislatures nullified laws against sodomy.

If the print media paid any attention at all, they tended to hail the gay revolution, possibly because many of the reporters on gay issues were themselves gay and open advocates for the movement. And those reporters who were not gay seemed too intimidated by groupthink to expose what was going on in their own newsrooms.

And now, what happens to those of us who stand up and object? Gay activists have already anticipated that. They have created a kind of conventional wisdom: that we suffer from homophobia, a disease that has actually been invented by gays projecting their own fear on society. And we are bigots besides, because, they say, we fail to deal with gays compassionately.

Gays are now no different than people born black or Hispanic or physically challenged. Since gays are born that way and have no choice about their sexual orientation, anyone who calls same-sex sex an aberration is now a bigot. Un-American, too.

Astoundingly now, college freshmen come home for their first Thanksgiving to announce, "Hey, Mom! Hey, Dad! We've taken the high moral ground. We've joined the gay revolution."

EXCUSE ME, GAY IS NOT GOOD

Gay is decidedly not good. How do I know this? For more than 40 years, I have been in solidarity with hundreds of homosexuals, my patients, and I have spent most of my professional life engaged in a kind of "pastoral care" on their behalf.

But I do not help them by telling them they are O.K. when they are not O.K.

Nor do I endorse their "new claim to self-definition and self-respect."

Tell me: Have we dumped the idea that a man's self-esteem comes from something inside himself (sometimes called character) and from having a good education, a good job and a good family—and replaced that notion with this, that he has an affinity to love (and have sex with) other men?

In point of fact, many of my patients had character; they had an education; they were respected ad men and actuaries and actors. But they were still in pain—for one reason and one reason alone. They were caught up in this mysterious compulsion to have sex with other men. They were not free. They were not happy. And they wanted to see if they could change.

Over the years, I found that those of my patients who really wanted to change could do so, by attaining the insight that comes with a good psychoanalysis. Others found other therapies that helped them get to the bottom of their compulsions, all of which involved high motivation and hard work.

Difficult as their therapeutic trips were, hundreds and thousands of homosexuals changed their ways. Many of my own formerly homosexual patients—about a third of them—are married today and happily so, with children. One-third may not sound like a very good average. But it is just about the same success rate you will find at the best treatment centers for alcoholics, like Hazelden in Minnesota and the Betty Ford Clinic in California.

Another third of my patients remain homosexual but not part of the gay scene. Now, after therapy, they still have same-sex sex, but they have more control over their impulses because now they understand the roots of their need for same-sex sex. Some of these are even beginning to turn on to the opposite sex. I add this third to my own success rate-so that I can tell people in all honesty that my batting average is .667 out of more than a thousand "at bats."...

CAUSES OF HOMOSEXUAL DISORDER

My long clinical experience and a sizable body of psychoanalysis research tell me that most [homosexuals]are reacting, at an unconscious level, to something amiss with their earliest upbringing—over-controlling mothers and abdicating fathers.

Through long observation I have also learned that the supposedly liberated homosexual is never really free. In his multiple, same-sex adventures, even the most effeminate gay was looking to incorporate the manhood of others, because he was in a compulsive, never-ending search for the masculinity that was never allowed to build and grow in early childhood...

Once my patients have achieved an insight into these dynamics—and realized there is no moral fault involved in their longtime and mysterious need—they have moved rather quickly on the road to recovery. Their consequent gratitude to me is overwhelming. And why shouldn't it be? They were formerly caught up in compulsions they could not understand, compulsions they could not control. Now they are in charge of their own lives.

Their former promiscuity may have looked a lot like "liberation." But it was not true freedom. It was a kind of slavery. And it was not a lifestyle. With the onset of AIDS, as the playwright and gay militant Larry Kramer said in a 1993 interview, it turned out to be a death style. I have had some patients tell me, "Doctor, if I weren't in therapy, I'd be dead."

[In addition, child and youth sexual abuse is a major cause of homosexuality. A 1992 study of 1000 homosexuals found that 37% had been abused sexually by an older male. Socarides, *Homosexuality: A Freedom Too Far*, p.88)

IN WAR, FIRST CASUALTY IS TRUTH

...Gays ascribe their condition to God, but he should not have to take that rap, any more than he should be blamed for the existence of other man-made maladies—like war, for instance, which has proven to be very unhealthy for humans and for all other living things. God does not make war. Men do.

And, when homosexuality takes on all the aspects of a political movement, it, too, becomes a war, the kind of war in which the first casualty is truth, and the spoils turn out to be our own children. An exaggeration? Well, what are we to think when militant homosexuals seek to lower the age of consensual sexual intercourse between homosexual men and young boys to the age of 14 (as they did in Hawaii in 1993) or 16 (as they tried to do in England in 1994)? In the Washington March for Gay Pride in 1993, they chanted, "We're here. We're queer. And we're coming after your children."

What more do we need to know?

NOTE: DOES HOMOSEXUALITY THREATEN SOCIETY?

Socarides: "Yes, and the most troubling thing to me is that we don't know it yet. The American public doesn't understand. For more than 40 years the most basic institution in society has been under assault, while the nation's traditional watch dog, the press, has been largely unconcerned...Sexual freedoms don't give anyone the permission to destroy society. And that's what the gay rights movement is doing, destroying society, in the name of freedom, a fictive freedom." (*Homosexuality: A Freedom Too Far*, pp. 285-286)

Does Talmud Teach Bestiality, Pedophilia, Incest?

By Elizabeth Dilling

(from *The Jewish Religion: Its Influence Today, pp. 22-23*)

St. Paul, who had been a Pharisee, often bores Christians who do not know what he was arguing about, in his discourses haranguing Pharisees. But one familiar with the Talmud can appreciate his diatribe against the "uncleanness" of those, "Who changed the truth of God into a lie" and: "Professing themselves to be wise, they became fools," until "God gave them over to a reprobate mind .... Being filled with all unrighteousness, fornication, wickedness ...." (Romans 1:22, 25, 28).

Of the "sacred" Talmudic teachings of the "Sages," preserved since 500 A.D. and taught more widely today than ever before in Talmud-Torah schools in the U.S.A., perhaps nothing better illustrates "fools" with "reprobate minds" than the teaching in the Talmud book of *Yebamoth*.

Although Moses commanded that if a woman have intercourse with a beast, both should be killed (Leviticus 20:16), and that a priest must not marry a harlot or woman who is profane (Lev. 21:7), the Talmud teaches that "unnatural intercourse does not cause a woman to be forbidden to marry a High Priest," since then "you will find no woman eligible ...." (Folios 59a-59b)

Rulings of the "sages" follow: "A woman who had intercourse with a beast is eligible to marry a priest—even a High Priest." ... If she had intercourse with a dog while sweeping the floor, she is likewise reckoned to be pure, and suitable. For, "The result of such intercourse being regarded as a mere wound, and the opinion that does not regard an accidentally injured hymen as a disqualification does not regard such as intercourse either."

This alone gives a fair idea of the systematic deformation of Scripture by the Pharisees and the truthfulness of Christ's denunciations about their making God's commandments of none effect by their Tradition. (Matthew 15:6)

BABIES

Baby boys may always be used as subjects for sodomy by grown men, according to the Talmud. (The Pharisaic subterfuge here is that until a child reaches sexual maturity, capable of sexual intercourse, he or she does not rank as a person, hence Biblical laws

Illuminati 3: Satanic Possession

against sodomy (pederasty) do not apply. Throughout the Talmud "nine years and one day" is the fictitious age of male maturity.

Likewise, under "nine years and one day," the "first stage of intercourse" of a boy with the mother, or any grown woman, is harmless, Talmudically. *Shammai*, to seem more "strict," lowers the age to eight years in some cases. (See Exhibit 82 from Sanhedrin 69b of the Talmud)

A long harangue about the amount of the Kethubah (payment if divorced) a woman gets if her virginity was removed by a young boy, fills Kethuboth I lb of the Talmud. And here, the foul mother may be reckoned "pure," depending on the age of the child. Such degrading use of children was typical of paganism throughout the ancient world.

"When a grown up man has intercourse with a little girl it is nothing, for when the girl is less than this—that is, less than three years old—it is as if one puts the finger into the eye—tears come to the eye again and again, so does virginity come back to the little girl under three years." (See Exhibit 136, Kethuboth 11b of the Talmud)

This is the standard doctrine of the whole Talmud on baby girls. Sodomy and intercourse with babies is the prerogative of the adult Talmudic man, in contrast to Christ's beautiful teachings concerning little children.

The following is also typical concerning the fictitious age of sexual maturity of baby girls set by the Pharisee "sages:" "A maiden aged three years and one day may be acquired in marriage by coition ..." See Exhibit 55 (Sanhedrin 55b), Exhibit 81 (Sanhedrin 69a-69b), Exhibit 156 (Yebamoth 57b), and Exhibit 159 (Yebamoth 60b); also Niddah 44b...

INCEST

Moses ordered the priests that: "They shall not take a wife that is a whore, or profane ... for he is holy unto his God." (Leviticus 21:7) The laws against incest are most vehement: "The nakedness of thy mother, shalt thou not uncover: she is thy mother ... (Leviticus 18:7) And in the Talmud the Pharisee "sages" reverse these Biblical injunctions:

"If a woman sported lewdly with her young son, a minor and he committed the first stage of cohabitation with her—Beth Shammai say, he thereby renders her unfit to the Priesthood." Here a footnote explains that she could not marry a priest, if this made her profane and the above Leviticus 21:7 is cited precisely. (See Exhibit 82)

We then learn that the dispute concerns only the age of the son, not the lewdness of the foul mother: "All agree that the connection of a boy aged nine years and one day is a real connection whilst that of one less than eight years is not [Footnote: "So that if he was nine years and a day or more, Beth Hillel agree that she is invalidated from the priesthood, whilst if he was less than eight, Beth Shamnmai agree that she is not."] ...

Source: Elizabeth Dilling —*The Jewish Religion and Its Influence Today,* Ch 5

"Talmudic Immorality, Asininity and Pornography: The Reprobate Mind"

http://www.come-and-hear.com/dilling/chapt05.html

Book Three

"Reinventing The World"

How the Illuminati Control Culture

"No one is more a slave than he who thinks he is free without being free."
—Goethe

W. Eugene Groves was an idealistic young American who wanted to serve his country.

After winning a Rhodes Scholarship, he was a shoo-in to lead the National Student Association in 1966. But, the outgoing President Philip Sherburne let Groves in on a secret: The NSA was secretly funded by the CIA.

Until this point, Groves had been an "unwitting" member, a dupe. But as President, of course he would know the truth. He would need to become a "witting" participant.

During the Cold War, the CIA secretly funded and controlled scores of US student, labor, religious, political and artistic organizations, according to the book *"The Mighty Wurlitzer"* (2008) by Hugh Wilford.

They were modeled after Soviet propagandist Willi Munzenberg's "Popular Front" organizations which recruited earnest Westerners (socialists and liberals) in an array of "anti Fascist" causes. These seemingly spontaneous groups were secretly funded and run by Moscow (through the CPUSA) and subtly promoted Communism. Munzenberg called them his "innocents' clubs."

It's not unusual that the CIA would imitate Comintern's tactics. Behind the veil, both serve the Cabalist Jewish central bankers and their Masonic network which has now subverted all significant private and public institutions in the West.

So while Hugh Walford suggests that the CIA was fostering an "anti-Communist" Left, in fact it was controlling the post-war dialogue, fostering the illusion that the Cold War was real, and promoting a specific collectivist mentality.

As we are discovering, there isn't much difference between monopoly capitalism and Communism. Under Communism, the State owns the corporations and the Illuminati bankers own the State. Under monopoly capitalism, the corporations own the State, and the bankers own the corporations.

The Russians told a familiar joke: "Under Capitalism, man exploits man while under Communism, it's the other way round."

Both are devoted to giving the satanist bankers a political, cultural, economic and spiritual monopoly, i.e. the New World Order.

The only difference is, in the West, there is an illusion of freedom and democracy.

"Witting" servants of the Illuminati bankers are chosen to lead governments and organizations, while unwitting dupes perpetuate the illusion of a free society. The masses are also unwitting dupes kept in a coma by the education system and mass media.

Eugene Groves' dilemma was resolved when *Ramparts Magazine* and the *New York Times* exposed the CIA's student program. Now you ask, why would the controlled expose the controllers? Well sometimes the dupes throw a monkey wrench into the works. Anything that discredited the CIA and the USA was also grist for the Illuminati mill. They work both sides against the middle. But you will never see the *New York Times* attack central banking.

Groves oversaw the student association's transition to independence and then quit. "The world has lost its innocence," he said." I wanted to get out." (Wolford, 5)

KULTURE

How do we know what we know? We are taught by the mass media and the education system. But what if they were subverted by a satanic secret society, i.e. the Illuminati?

"Modernism" mirrors a gradual perversion of reality and morality by the Illuminati bankers.

The mass media and education system promote this suspension of reality. Truth is suppressed. Lies are promulgated. Negative or self-destructive behavior is portrayed in a positive light.

Modernism is a solipsism where the bankers' perversity becomes the norm. For example, the CIA actively promoted modern abstract art, an art disconnected from human identity and aspirations, an art any child or monkey could produce.

They financed the cultural magazines, (*Encounter, Partisan Review*) critics (Clement Greenberg) and art museums through a network of foundations.

"Many of the artists in the movement had radical Left backgrounds (Jackson Pollock, Mark Rothko and Franz Kline for example...) Their painting, with its gestural expression of the artist's consciousness and total rejection of representation, constituted a massive rebuke to...Soviet art..." (p.106)

Not really. While pretending to reject socialist realism, the CIA advanced the Communist agenda which is to make art discordant, irrelevant and ugly.

The same story can be applied to modern literature where the "anti-hero," i.e. the alienated outsider and misfit, (i.e. the Illuminati Jew) becomes the hero. The "hero" is not the community-builder but the Luciferian rebel, the destroyer in Cabalist doctrine. Similarly, modern literary criticism is a linguistic voodoo divorced from the author's social reality, biography or intention. Literature is treated like a self-contained artifact. Isolated words or sentences were analyzed like holy writ. Hours are spent analyzing words that turn out to be typos. When I went to university, I wondered why this placebo was presented as "truth." Now I know.

The same story can be repeated for music, TV and movies. With folks thus distracted, perverts and traitors are inserted into all positions of leadership. While we were sleeping, a satanic cult took over. For art to be relevant, it would have to address this occult cancer that is eating society.

FEMINISM

Second-wave Feminism was another Illuminati sponsored "popular front" masquerading as grass roots expression. Gloria Steinem, a Jewish misfit from a broken home was chosen to lead it. Clay Felker, who in the 1950s worked with Steinem at the CIA's "Independent Research Bureau," (another student front,) orchestrated the media campaign. Apparently Felker was not Jewish.

In 1968, Felker hired Steinem at *New York* magazine. He published the 40-page inaugural issue of *MS Magazine* as a supplement in *New York*.

In 1975, *Redstockings*, a radical feminist magazine, exposed Steinem's CIA connections. They revealed that *MS Magazine* was funded by Warner Communications and Katherine Graham, both CIA assets.

Founder of New York and Editor of Esquire, Clay Felker was one of some 600 US journalists covertly working for the CIA. He brought fellow agent and Feminist founder Gloria Steinem to prominence. Thus, the CIA secretly defined postwar culture.

In 1979, when *Redstockings* tried to put this account into a book, the publisher, Random House, was pressured to delete it by these CIA assets and the Ford Foundation. They wanted Feminism to look like natural social change instead of what it really was, elite social engineering.

At the same time, authors like myself who promote heterosexuality must self-publish and are ignored in the mass media. Kulture is contrived. We are not free.

CONCLUSION

The Cabalist bankers have subverted our political and social institutions and are using government to enslave us according to the blueprint of *The Protocols of the Elders of Zion*. The people of the world and even their governments will be "as children under-age," say *The Protocols. (15)*

There have always been two kinds of Jews: those who follow the Lawgiver Moses on the one hand; and the Baal Worshipers on the other. Unfortunately, the latter have prevailed while retaining the prestige of the former. And they have been joined by traitors from every background, willing to betray their fellow man for personal profit.

Throughout history, these Luciferians have waged a war against God, the inherent spiritual and natural design. They have sought to dethrone God and enslave humanity, and are very close to success.

This involves destroying the four sources of our human identity and meaning: race, religion (God), nation and family (gender.) They do this by creating one race, one religion, one gender and one world government.

At the same time, our kulture is increasingly rootless, depraved and meaningless. Even bacteria have culture. True culture is the quest to express and realize universal spiritual ideals like Truth, Justice and Love and Beauty, i.e. God. When God is denied, man goes in the other direction: depravity. This is what passes for culture today.

Confessions of an Ex-Luciferian Jew

"Jews don't know it but their God is Lucifer." —Harold Wallace Rosenthal

I'm talking about myself. I'm not interested in the distinction between Luciferian and Satanist. Until the age of roughly 50, I was another mass-produced Luciferian Jew —Zionist, Liberal, Socialist and Feminist.

Luciferian Jews are "revolutionaries,"— people who deny and often defy God by overturning His design, the natural and moral order of the universe. They have defined the modern world,which is built on the ruins of religious "superstition."

I was 17 in 1966 and swept up in the anti-war movement. The American invasion of Vietnam was a heinous injustice that discredited everything the US pretended to represent.

Although this obscene 1966 depiction of the seven dwarfs ravishing Snow White was a protest against the Vietnam war, it expresses the Luciferian Jew's visceral hatred of the Christian worldview.

Wally Wood's obscene "Disneyland Memorial Orgy" (shown above) published in Paul Krassner's *Realist* magazine expressed my outrage at society's fundamental hypocrisy. Snow White, the ideal of American innocence, was being ravished by the seven dwarfs. The WASP establishment were evil hypocrites.

Jewish revolutionaries like Paul Krassner and I were useful idiots. The Vietnam war was engineered by Illuminati Jews (Rockefeller, Rothschilds) partly to alienate a whole generation. The "WASP establishment" had been their errand boys for some time. I was socially engineered. My mind was moulded. They manipulated me using my youth and idealism.

Illuminati social engineers promoted a powerful Jewish meme: the universe is "unjust" if they don't run it. You see Cabalist (Illuminati) Jews believe that they channel God's will.

Throughout history, this demented ideology took the form of a desire to destroy the world and rebuild it in their own image. Thus, they fomented wars to destroy the Gentiles and concentrate money & power in their hands. They put the entire Gentile establishment in place—mostly Freemason collaborators. Collaboration is a prerequisite for success in the public sphere today. Mankind is satanically possessed.

Their goal was to undermine wholesome virtues practiced by their Christian neighbors. For example, they broke down all sexual restraint, labeling this (with their usual guile) "sexual liberation."

Even before the Vietnam war, I followed this Luciferian agenda. At age 15, I was almost thrown out of high school for buying a subscription to PLAYBOY for the school library. The story made the local newspaper, and the Principal was in hot water.

Little did I understand PLAYBOY magazine was crucial to equating sex with the meaning of life. This contributed to society's current adolescent obsession with sex, and the breakdown of marriage and family.

Although my intentions were pure, I was one of Satan's little helpers. Satan loves idealists.

"Useful idiots," he calls them. Millions have died believing satanic Judaism (Communism) really stood for "social justice and equality." These are tricks used to put their agents into power.

SATANIC CULT

Modern history and culture is the story of man's induction into Satanism, i.e. Cabala Judaism. All that nonsense about God not existing, and man's "alienation" from God, is pure Satanism.

Since when do values like love, peace, beauty, truth and justice not exist? They inspire all human beings. Of course creation is infused with Intelligence. A minor example: When I stubbed my toe, my body grew a brand new toenail. I couldn't do that!

Every time I eat an orange or drink pure spring water, I know God exists. My friend's baby is an unfolding miracle. How can we deny God?

"Modernism" was engineered by Illuminati Jewish bankers as part of a long-term conspiracy to enslave mankind.

"The modern age is the Jewish Age, and the Twentieth Century in particular is the Jewish Century, " Professor Yuri Slezkine begins his book, *The Jewish Century*.

At the beginning of the twentieth century, "Jews began to see themselves as the real bearers of the Enlightenment..."

In Vienna in 1903, Solomon Ehrmann told a B'nai Brith (i.e. Freemason) meeting that the future was going to be fundamentally Jewish. "All of mankind will have been Jewified and joined in unison with the B'nai Brith." (Lindemann, *Esau's Tears*, p. 331)

Divorced from God, like Lucifer, Cabalist Jews are metaphysical outcasts. This is the reason many Jews are so restless; they are "alienated" from God's love, i.e. their soul, or sense of Being. They constantly have to justify their existence.

In the words of Goethe, "No Jew, not even the most insignificant, but is busy towards the achievement of some worldly, temporary or momentary aim."

According to Werner Sombart, "This activity often enough degenerates into restlessness. He must forever be up and doing, forever managing something and carrying it to fruition." (*Jews & Modern Capitalism*)

Jews are over achievers because they feel unloved. In order to get love, I had to write a syndicated advice-to-parents column for 40 newspapers at age 11.

The Illuminati control the mass media and use it to induct us into their Cabalist nightmare. We become what we contemplate: violence, greed, lust (pornography,) homosexuality,and the occult.

Art and entertainment are designed to remove us from historical reality. Does anyone believe the Oscar-nominated *Lincoln*, written and directed by Illuminati Jews, tells us the true story? The real story, mankind's possession by a satanic secret society, is never told.

Like my past self, most people are unwitting collaborators. Often, they are idealists. But it's never too late to face the truth and acknowledge we were duped.

"Why do People Hate Jews?"

In May 2012, the editor of *Business Digest. com*, Henry Blodget stimulated discussion by asking the question, "Why do people hate Jews?"

Scandals at Goldman Sachs had created anti Semitism; Blodget wanted to give the subject an airing.

But the largely negative reaction made Blodget amend the question to "some" people and then to "What are the sources of anti Semitism?"

Finally he issued a retraction:

"Some people I like and respect told me they felt insulted by and uncomfortable with the post...I am very sorry to anyone I offended. I sincerely apologize."

This is an example of how Jews control discourse and make sure they are not part of it.

In an article, "Does Henry Blodget Hate Jews?" Jewish writer Foster Kamer commented:

"The only possible motivation for writing a headline like that is to attract attention, and page views, and it ... will only inflame parties on all sides (be they Jews, Jew Haters, Self-Loathing Jews, and so on.) You can rest assured that whatever genuine intellectual curiosity Blodget has about this issue—and compassion towards marginalized and/or persecuted peoples, ...was made a moot point by that headline. And as a Jew, I can tell Blodget, this does not necessarily help our cause."

Stereotypically, Kamer thinks this discussion is about "helping the Jewish cause." His reply reflects the Jewish delusion that they are "marginalized and/or persecuted" rather than dominant and exclusive. He thinks any Jew who is self-critical must be "self loathing"—an attitude indicative of a closed, authoritarian society.

PLEASANTVILLE

The 1998 movie *Pleasantville* illustrates that secular humanism is occultism. Writer and director Gary Ross illustrates the harm Jewish liberal crusaders do while imagining they are our benefactors. His father, the screenwriter Arthur Ross, was a Communist blacklisted during the 1940s and 1950s. (Communism is an Illuminati creation.)

Gary Ross recently co-wrote and directed the Illuminati film, *The Hunger Games.*

Pleasantville is Luciferian propaganda in the form of science fiction. David and his sister Jennifer are transplanted from 1998 into an 1950s American idyll like *Father's Knows Best* or *Ozzie and Harriet.*

The tagline of the movie is "Nothing is as Simple as Black and White." In other words, there are no moral absolutes. This is Satanism (secular humanism.)

Sheltered White conservative robots waiting to be liberated by Illuminati Jews

The two streetwise teenagers introduce promiscuous sex, modern art, jazz and literature to the sheltered robotic denizens of *Pleasantville,* who resemble Christian Conservatives.

As these innocent White robots are exposed to the wonders of modern CULT - ure, they change from black and white into color. This is especially true when they partake in sex.

David's "mom" changes into color after she is taught to masturbate BY HER CHILDREN! We see mom masturbating in the bathtub; it is portrayed like the Second Coming. This film was rated "Parental Guidance."

Remember when "as American as mom's apple pie" denoted goodness and innocence?

Mom immediately rejects her role as housewife and enters into an illicit relationship with the soda fountain owner who takes up impressionist art.

Needless to say all these black and white people are now seen in living color.

Meanwhile dad is like the Exercizer bunny in black and white repeating, "Where's my dinner?"

There is a conservative "authoritarian" reaction but David soon quells it with breathless talk of "kids making out in the streets" and "women working and men staying home to cook."

Can you see how these Illuminati Jews are Luciferians, and reverse good and evil? Metaphysical misfits, they wage relentless war on what is innocent, natural and healthy. Can you see how they preach rebellion? How they spread their dysfunction? (See also online, "Hollywood Hypes Lesbian Jewish Parable")

The irony is Gary Ross yearned for a "normal life" like the ones he witnessed on TV.

"My '50s were different than other people's '50s," Ross says. "The myth didn't permeate our world, 'Donna Reed' and all that. I longed for that, I wanted to be like other normal families on TV."

Yet the first thing he does is destroy that vision.

FINALLY

Modern society is a solipsism created by Illuminati (Cabalist) Jewish bankers and their Masonic minions.

The word "solipsism" means a self-created reality that has little or no relation to Truth.

The word was coined in 1874 from the Latin solus "alone" and ipse "self."

It is the view that self is the only object of real knowledge or the only thing that is real. This is why modern art is personal and subjective to the point of absurdity as opposed to universal and true. This subjectivity implies that every artist is divine.

The New World Order is dedicated to replacing Truth with a solipsism created by the same people who create money from nothing and charge interest.

What is Truth? On the material plane, it is the natural design, the most efficacious functioning of the natural realm. On a spiritual plane, it is God, who is the ultimate reality, another name for *absolute truth, beauty, love, harmony and justice,* what all human beings naturally crave.

While nature may be red in tooth and claw, our mission is to mitigate nature by applying these spiritual ideals.

Television Psy Op Ruined My Life

We must introduce into their education all those principles which have so brilliantly broken up their order. —Protocols of Zion,16

Television is the Satanic family altar. Television is the major mainstream infiltration for the new satanic religion. —Anton Lavey

In the 1950s, when I was a child, television was pretty wholesome. That's how I got hooked.

I was naive and idealistic and assumed I lived in a benevolent and free society that was attempting to raise everyone to a higher level, materially and spiritually. I looked to mass media and schooling for information, insight and guidance.

After watching *America in Primetime*, (2011) a four-part documentary history of TV, I realize that TV is not entertainment. It is social engineering and occult indoctrination. It made me dysfunctional and depressed. It has done this to millions of people.

America in Primetime consists of interviews with dozens of TV writers and producers, and excerpts from their shows. Although homosexuals and Jews make up perhaps 5% of the US population, they are about 70% of TV writers and producers. They hold up a mirror to life. If 70% were Irish Catholics, I'd feel the same way if they were degrading society.

What Jews and gays have in common is that they are outsiders who want everyone to see the world from their perspective.

Most of my fellow Jews don't know that Judaism is a Luciferian cult, a rebellion against God. Cabalist (Illuminati) Jewish leaders wish to supplant God and redefine reality according to their perversity and self interest. This is the New World Order.

They deny there is the natural and moral order, the Creator's instruction manual in our soul, that is required reading for health and happiness. They pay lip service to morality and do whatever they want.

The documentary pretends contemporary TV presents reality more truthfully. In fact, it is creating this reality in its own perverted image. Television is an indoctrination. It has deliberately undermined what is healthy and inverted normal and abnormal. They now have a show called have *The New Normal*. Another is called *The Modern Family*, which includes a gay couple raising a baby.

Then, TV convinces us that there is something redeeming, ennobling and quintessentially human about being weird, sick and miserable. I've been in this humanistic space. It's mostly self-pity.

Nurse Jackie, who is addicted to prescription drugs, torn between family and work and infidelity, has her consolations. The heroes of *Weeds* and *Breaking Bad,* normal middle class people who become drug dealers and mobsters, have their moments of redemption. Jack Bauer, the hero of "24" does evil to protect us all from evil, but hey! Life is complicated. Tony Soprano, a mobster who lives in a New Jersey suburb, wants the same things as we all do. *Dexter* is a serial killer who kills serial killers but don't judge him. When he was five, he saw his mother cut to pieces with a chainsaw! (At least, he wasn't sexual abused.)

"Audiences are more sophisticated," the writers tell us, "people want moral ambiguity." Really? They are normalizing immorality. It's pure Cabala.

We've reached the point where amoral and violent delinquents, misfits and weirdos are the norm. They have made the world conform to them.

The documentary is quite explicit: "Whether they are oddballs, losers, or just plain weird, misfit characters have grown beyond comic stereotypes and are taking center stage with a vengeance, refusing to apologize for who they are."

Thus in HBO's *True Blood,* the vampires demand "human rights." They want to be treated like any other minorities. One character is incensed when someone judges all vampires based on the behavior of a few. That's prejudice!

Freaks and Geeks. Six Feet Under. Seinfeld. Glee. Arrested Development. The Office. Self absorbed misfits are the "new normal."

HOW WE GOT HERE

In the 1950s they had to rebuild, so the Illuminati gave us healthy values. They dealt with moral dilemmas. An episode of *Ozzie and Harriet* dealt with whether the oldest son would put himself out to take a visitor to a dance.

The documentary asks: "In 1950s television, the man of the house was king of his castle. Was it an illusion to begin with?" *Father Knows Best. Leave it to Beaver. My Three Sons.*

Was it an illusion? I don't think so. Some things are hard wired. Most men want to rule their own roost. That doesn't mean we want to lord it over anyone. But every successful organization is a hierarchy and that applies to families as well. Only a monster has two heads. The division of labor made a lot of sense. If you want a man to shoulder responsibility for a family, he has to lead it. It must be his.

There was no moral or gender ambiguity in the 1950s Westerns. Good versus evil. *Gunsmoke. The Lone Ranger. Have Gun Will Travel.* Men were men. They put their lives on the line to build a just society. Women supported and loved them for it.

Then, almost by clockwork, having set up this target, the Illuminati got to work destroying it. Birth control allowed women to be sexually independent. Why not be financially independent too?

New shows made women feel being wives and mothers was not fulfilling.

America in Primetime: "Far removed from the model housewife of yesterday, women today on TV care less about pleasing others, and more about being true to themselves." (An euphemism for selfish.)

Why sacrifice for love when you can be selfish? Sounds like Satan again doesn't it? Love is sacrifice. As if devotion to husband and family wasn't "being true to themselves?" As if career success is the path to fulfillment for most women.

Mary Tyler Moore was the prototype of the "independent woman." When her mother asks her father, "Did you take your pill?" Mary thinks she is talking to her.

"Yes" both father and daughter reply. Thus, the show taught young women to go on the pill and have extramarital sex.

Women modeled themselves on *Mary Tyler Moore,* just like they mimed *Sex in the City* 20 years later.

Lauren Hutton said *Sex and the City* portrayed "women acting like gay men;" not surprising given its gay Jewish creator, Darren Starr.

In the 80s, men started being portrayed as wimps. Someone wrote *Thirty Something* should be called "Whine and neuroses." The only exception to this trend was *The Bill Cosby Show* where the father was the head of the family.

Like men, women are also hardwired to belong to one man who returns their devotion. Most women want to put motherhood before career. Yet the freaks that control popular culture mess them up by telling them their natural biological instincts are wrong.

Mary Tyler Moore

In a 2008 Amazon review of Kevin MacDonald's *Culture of Critique*, E. Baumgartner, a former scriptwriter, wrote: "As a Jew myself, I Can Tell You That Dr. MacDonald Is Correct."

"As a former leftist Hollywood Jew (I wrote TV shows), I can say from personal experience that Prof. MacDonald is 100% correct in this book. The shows I worked on: *Mary Tyler Moore* Show, *That Girl*, & *Love American Style*, among others, were nothing more than Jewish tools (for the most part) to undermine the innocence of American WASP culture, ("Cultural Marxism" as Prof. MacDonald calls it.)

I became disturbed with the studio editorial "rule" that children should be portrayed as sassy and disrespectful towards their parents. A few times I presented a script to my editor (also a Jewish guy) in which I had the child character behaving politely and respectfully towards his parents. The editor changed the lines to make the child bratty/sassy and then told me ."... that's the way it should be done from now on, unless I tell you otherwise." That's when I started to see that something else was going on besides just making TV shows. I could see the changes in American society resulting from all this TV propaganda. I eventually left writing and became a teacher."

CONCLUSION

Because television and movies were my reference point, I was dysfunctional until almost 50. I was obsessed with relationships and sex as a panacea. I didn't know how to be a man. I idealized women and called it love. There were no models of true masculinity. When dysfunctional sick people are your role models, you become dysfunctional. Arrested development. Immaturity. Three failed marriages. Confusion. Periods of depression. (I do take responsibility for being so trusting and gullible.)

Why are there so few positive role models on TV? Why so few examples of healthy, happy life?

My rehabilitation began when I started to listen to my own instincts instead of the mass media.

Liberals like to think the social trends of the last 50 years represent spontaneous social change. Rather, we were being degraded and inducted into a satanic cult. The Illuminati bankers are waging a diabolical war on us, and we don't even know it.

Home Movies Spread Hollywood Jewish Nightmare

There is a special schadenfreude you get from watching other people degrade themselves.

Judd Apatow's productions which include the HBO series *Girls* and movies like *Knocked Up* (2007) and *This is Forty* (2012) specialize in this kind of train-wreck voyeurism.

In 2007, I wrote: "*Knocked Up* is a trip down a psychic rabbit hole populated by perverts, creeps and losers. Hollywood wants us to emulate them. Judging from the rave reviews, we are willing to oblige."

It is no exaggeration to call *This is Forty* "a home movie." Apatow wrote and directed it. Although Paul Rudd plays Apatow's character "Pete," Apatow's wife, Leslie Mann plays wife "Debbie," and

his two daughters, Maude and Iris, play the children. As Malcolm Forbes said, "There is nothing wrong with nepotism as long as you keep it in the family."

Leslie Mann actually turned 40 in 2012 and this movie obviously was lifted from Apatow's domestic life, including what passes for witty pillow talk. The only fictional element concerns the family facing financial distress.

They sold this movie with the tagline: "This is the way we all are." Judd Apatow mainstreams the dysfunction of Hollywood Jews, the only people he knows.

Before I get to the family dysfunction, let me harp one more time on Apatow's vulgarity and adolescent obsession with bodily functions. As I have said, the Luciferian defines "courage" not in terms of standing for truth and justice, but in breaking norms of decorum, good taste and style.

LUCIFERIAN VISION OF MAN

Since man is an animal with no divine soul, there is no need to restrain his basest appetites and functions. (That would be "repression.") Therefore "comedy" no longer is defined as being "funny" but as being disgusting. Since man cannot aspire to be godlike, all that remains is a race to the bottom.

The litany of vulgarity and tastelessness crammed into the first hour of this movie include Pete sitting on the toilet; Pete getting a colonoscopy; Pete farting in bed; Pete examining his hemorrhoids in a mirror; Pete looking up an woman's skirt.

Apatow has a woman expatiate for five minutes on how her vagina is numb from an operation and two gays talking about blow jobs. Apatow displays his wife's breasts, has her feel Megan Fox's breasts (to see if they are real,) give Rudd a blowjob and get a vaginal exam. Mercifully, he doesn't reference his daughters' genitals this time around.

After an hour of cataloging bodily functions, the film settles down to an inventory of the dysfunction facing rich Hollywood Jewish families. These include foulmouthed children who defy their parents and take their cues from social media; parents of parents who start second families when they are too old and poor; people living way beyond their means and feeling life is a treadmill, and a general inner emptiness which defies definition or solution. Gatherings with family and friends are toxic with everyone starved for a crumb of encouragement or, failing that, a chance for recrimination.

The problem is the abdication of the father. The father fails to set down the law. Thus the family is in a state of anarchy.

Rudd's Apatow is a weak man who is lost in the world. His record company is floundering. He can't keep his diet. He can't control himself so how can he control his family? Debbie is the usual melange of insecurities and they bicker constantly.

"What are we even doing?" Debbie says. "This is not making me happy. You're not happy. You don't like me. I can feel that. I'm not blind. Jesus. We're like business associates. We're like brother and sister. There's no passion there."

The problem is not passion, it is power. Pete has to take possession of his wife and children. They have to obey him. He is the leader. He must have a vision. When the man is emasculated by the wife, the result is anarchy.

PETE: "Don't be such a ball buster."

DEBBIE: I am not a ball buster. You make me one! I am a fun girl! I am fun-loving! I am a good time Sally! I dance hip-hop. I cannot believe I've wasted my whole life busting the balls of people who have no balls. I am the only one here who has any balls."

Hollywood Jews are very good at creating and spreading dysfunction but they never present the solution. For them, the human condition is to wallow in sickness and derive solace from self pity or sentimentality. Imagine if this story were about the husband reasserting his authority and his wife supporting him? But that would be "sexist."

In general, Hollywood was hydrochloric acid to Christian civilization. It corroded every form of social coherence: marriage and the nuclear family, racial homogeneity, and religion. It promoted homosexuality. Now all that is left to destroy is human dignity and self respect.

Dog's Breakfast at Tiffany's

In retrospect, the movie "classic" *Breakfast at Tiffany's* (1961) was a major salvo in the Illuminati's war on heterosexual society. We can now clearly see their goal is not "gay rights" or "equality" but making homosexuality the societal norm.

While passed off as a "romance," this movie was poison to heterosexuals. It set the 1960s template where women were allowed to lose their minds and men were forced to rescue them. From that point on, it was all about their needs.

With a danish and coffee in hand, Holly taught modern women to chase a chimera and eat on the run.

The movie was written by Truman Capote, a product of a broken family who became a homosexual. Like Tennessee Williams, he was championed by our Illuminati Jewish cultural controllers. And like Tennessee Williams, his crippled, perverted vision was held up to the goyim as the last word in sophistication.

In the movie, the heterosexual Adam and Eve are portrayed in homosexual terms. Essentially they have to navigate a gay obstacle course to find heterosexual love and marriage, just as we do today. For 1961, this movie is sick, sick, sick. Let me count the ways:

1. Holly Golightly, played by Audrey Hepburn, is a prostitute. Her appeal is strictly based on "beauty" and occasional repartee. The prostitute part is glossed over and she is portrayed as a "party girl." She is looking for financial security symbolized by the store *Tiffany's*. She spends her time trolling for a rich husband. Are we supposed to find this woman attractive?

2. Her suitor, Paul Varjak, played by George Peppard, is a writer. He is also a prostitute, supported by a rich older woman played by Patricia Neal as though she were still acting in *The Fountainhead.*

In other words, heterosexuals are rent boys who must get used to selling their souls in order to survive. "I need money and I'll do whatever it takes to get it," Holly vows.

3. Everything Holly does is designed to emasculate Paul. She wants him as a "friend" only. Sleeps in his arms. Whistles down a cab when he can't. Throws his "arrangement" in his face. She gives mixed signals and blows hot and cold. This became the typical neurotic behavior of modern women.

4. There is a sick subplot where we learn Holly is really from Texas and was married at age 14 to "Doc," a vet played by Buddy Ebsen, a man easily 40. She claims the marriage was "annulled" but obviously they had sex.

5. In order to make this crap palatable to heterosexuals, Holly and Paul must overcome their moral lapses and find their way to each other. But Holly is a royal pain-in-the-ass to the end. Even after Paul dumps his gigolo gig, finds a real job and declares his love, Holly is set on going to Brazil with a rich heir. When the heir dumps her, she is still intent on hunting "the 50 richest men in South America." She tells Paul that she doesn't want "to belong to anyone" or to be "put in a cage."

"I don't know who I am," she says. She is a mental case, modeled after Capote's mother who also pursued adolescent values.

7. This is the way the novel ends. But in order to sell the movie to unsuspecting goyim, they tack on a romantic finale. We have 110 minutes of homosexual dysfunction followed by five minutes of heterosexual romance. Paul tells her she is "afraid of reality" and walks away. She find rejection irresistible and chases after him. Passionate kisses in the rain.... Not one minute of truth.

CONCLUSION

The reason my generation had to "search for our identity" is because our primary identity as men and women (protectors and providers, wives and mothers) was constantly under attack by the Illuminati.

In 2012, *Breakfast at Tiffany's* was deemed "culturally, historically, or aesthetically significant" by the United States Library of Congress and selected for preservation in the National Film Registry. Considered "iconic," it set an example for the 1960s generation. Women wanted to be Holly Golightly just as a generation later they wanted to be *Sex and the City's* Carrie Bradshaw.

Thanks to Illuminati (feminist) mind control, women exchanged a socially secure and honored position as wives and mothers to raise children alone, often in poverty. Truly a dog's breakfast.

Yes Virginia, we are satanically possessed.

A Touch of Crass

In a fit of nostalgia, I watched one of my favorite movies again, *A Touch of Class* (1973.) I had fond memories of a sophisticated romantic comedy starring George Segal and Glenda Jackson that had influenced me.

What a shock! I quickly realized why I was so messed up as a young man.

The movie presented a man betraying his wife and children as the height of sophistication and fun. It presented random sexual intercourse as if it were the Holy Grail. As an impressionable 23-year-old, I stupidly assumed society was not run by psychopaths and perverts. I adopted these attitudes which ultimately undermined my ability to form healthy relationships with women. (I am now on my third and I hope final marriage.)

Then, I happened to see a trailer for an upcoming movie, *No Strings Attached* which teaches young people that promiscuous sex is the ultimate in modern thinking.

Both these movies were made by Jews. Although almost 40 years apart, Hollywood Jews are pumping out socially destructive agitprop in the guise of sophisticated comedy. If *A Touch of Class* hurt me, I can't imagine the damage Hollywood is doing to the new generation.

Illuminati Jews Melvin Frank and Ivan Reitman directed the two movies respectively. Their sex for sex's sake dogma is hardly the "latest thing." The Illuminati are a continuation of the Sabbatean-Frankist Jewish heresy dating back to the 17th and 18th century.

The Sabbatean-Frankists were Satanists who believed in "redemption through evil." They believed the Messiah would return when the world had descended into chaos. They advocated the destruction of marriage and family, and engaged in adultery, orgies, incest and pedophilia.

They have enormous power because the Rothschild banking syndicate belong to this cult. Sabbatean-Frankist (Illuminati) Jews were behind Communism and Zionism. Long story short, Satanism and Communism is spewing from our movie theaters and TV's, and no one has a clue.

MORE ON THESE MOVIES

Illuminati Jews who own Hollywood have been making home movies for decades and passing them off as entertainment.

In a *Touch of Class*, George Segal plays a typical narcissistic Jew yet the "J" word is never mentioned. There is no explanation of why anyone would find him attractive, except for his money. His friend "Walter Menkes" played by Paul Sorvino, is also a Jew. The movie oozes self-serving "Jewish humanistic" values yet the audience is totally unaware.

Glenda Jackson plays the Gentile divorcee looking for uncomplicated sex on the side. Since Segal is married, there is no danger of "falling in love."

Which of course always happens. But on Menkes advice, Segal summons up the strength to end it for her sake, because he really loves her and doesn't want to hurt her any more.

Based on the trailer, *No Strings Attached* follows the same line. "Uncomplicated sex" leads to "wanting more."

"Monogamy goes against human nature," *No Strings* star Jewish actress Natalie Portman exclaims. "Why can't we just have sex?" In fact, it is promiscuity that is against human nature. They want "more."

It seems like Illuminati Jews are obsessed with having sex as long as it is out of wedlock. The "falling in love" part is a fig leaf to cover making sexual promiscuity pervasive and socially acceptable.

People who have developed a habit of promiscuity do not stop when they marry. Combined with feminism, it effectively kills the institution of marriage.

Promiscuity includes homosexuality as Kutcher, in the trailer, awakes and wonders if in his drunken stupor, he had sex with the guy.

Recently, I walked in on someone watching *Hot Tub Climate Change*, directed by another Cabalist, Steve Pink. The scene was pure porn, interracial at that. A naked white girl with ample jugs is having intercourse with a black guy in a hot tub. Mainstream movies today would be banned as obscene as recently as 20 years ago.

Some of these home movies are just Jewish navel gazing. Recently I rented *Greenberg* with Ben Stiller, directed by Noah Baumbach. The title character is a self-obsessed middle-aged Jew at loose ends. The tiniest thing he does for anyone is treated as earth shattering. He is of no interest to anyone yet his sense of self-importance is staggering. He says he's the "funniest person he knows" yet there is zero evidence of this. Nothing happens except that he has sex with a Gentile girl, avoids commitment and helps her get an abortion.

When you own Hollywood, you can inflict your vulgar home movies on the world, even if they are derived from Sabbatean Satanism.

NOTE:

To be fair, Baumbach's *The Squid and the Whale*, about a dysfunctional Jewish family in Brooklyn, is excellent.

The Conspiracy to Defile

By Christine

I try to warn others about what has happened and what IS happening. A few of my family members are in the "Jew media" and one is directly responsible for promoting the sort of ideals that people like you and I warn others about.

When I try to explain to people what's going on, they laugh—oh no it can't be a "conspiracy" as I claim. What proof do they need?

Years ago, my uncle and his long-time friend Joan Rivers (Rosenberg) made a horrible, offensive film. Title is *Rabbit Test*. It's very bad—it's now on YouTube in sickening entirety.

The sick "humor" in the film is exactly what is promoted in media today, although it came out in '78, way ahead of it's time.

It thinks pedophilia jokes, bathroom and fecal matter jokes are swell. I believe my uncle was inadvertently warning us of things to come. He became a media big wig later. If you want to be disgusted, watch it (midgets in blackface?? scene where little girl is implied to be giving oral sex to an old man from under a table?? Black African nationals serving watermelon... Joan Rivers picks up a shit with her bare hands...) but be spiritually prepared.

I use that film as an example, a "template" as it were, an icon of horrible-ness that is seeping into mass media. Every joke in that film has been used and re-used many times in TV shows and movies in the last 30 years with some variations.

Seth Macfarlane has a "cutesy" pedophile character "Herbert" on *Family Guy*. MacFarlane may not be Jewish but the entertainment industry is.

Secret Communist Goals Near Fruition (http://www.henrymakow.com/secret-goals-of-communism.html)

25. "Break down cultural standards of morality by promoting pornography and obscenity in books, magazines, motion pictures, radio, and TV.

26. Present homosexuality, degeneracy and promiscuity as "normal, natural, healthy."

INSIDIOUS

If made by the "cabal," movies give a little hint they are "one of THEM" by inserting a reference, maybe an old Jewish joke in the first few minutes of the show that most people won't see unless they are in the "know." This identifies the filmmaker as a person on the "inside."

These members of the cabal do ANYTHING to sneak in a dirty reference, a nasty innuendo, a lie, outright propaganda into everything they produce in order to sully the "good."

For people that are honestly trying to keep their homes spiritually "clean" it is almost impossible now, as the monsters creep into any crevice, like cockroaches getting into a new apartment.

Since we are trying to stay away from direct offense, the cabal needs to SNEAK it in through various ways.

The object is to shock, like a flasher who gets off on women's surprised disgust. Just when you thought you were safe watching an cooking show, the ads for vaginal mesh failure come on.

SUBVERSION - ONE PERSON AT A TIME

My aunt has a funny way of introducing herself to people—she asks LOTS of probing questions. She is trying to get you to open up, admit to things you may regret.

Another "trick" to finding out how game you are is to tell some filthy joke. If you laugh, you're pegged as a possible player. A righteous & fearless person won't fall for it.

This is how they work, trying to get dirt on a person to be used against you later. This is the same way the pedophile intel agents work. They find out your worst secrets to be used against you later.

This is what set up David Petraeus. Most if not all of those political offices vacated by persons "needing to resign to spend more time with family" are in reality given the option to quit or get exposed.

Don't get yourself into a situation like those guys. Don't get drunk or high with people. If you find yourself making friends with a new person and they seem *very interested* in you, don't let them into your life.

They ARE out to get you.

The Way We Live Now

Starved for entertainment that describes "the way we live now?"

You may have to return to 1875, when Anthony Trollope's novel by that title was published.

A four-part BBC miniseries (2001) depicts the depredations on British society of a Jewish banker, "Augustus Melmotte." It shows his effect on people eager to protect their values, yet vulnerable to temptation (i.e. greed.)

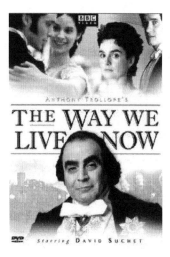

Melmotte is a shady figure, recently arrived from Frankfurt via Vienna trailing rumors of bank collapses and swindles. He quickly establishes himself in London as the go-to man for investment and profit.

His emotionally-needy daughter Marie attracts spendthrift aristocrats. Sir Felix Carbury, a laughable wastrel is first in line for Marie's affections.

Paul Montague, an earnest young English engineer seeks Melmotte's backing for a railroad running from Salt Lake City to Vera Cruz in Mexico.

Melmotte floats the company on the London Stock Exchange without any intention of actually building the railway.

There is a marvelous scene where Melmotte lectures his (Gentile) Board of Directors on the profit motive, which "moves mountains and changes the world." He advises them to put their last shilling in railway shares for they will quadruple!

"Just trust me!" he says. The effect on them is intoxicating.

Melmotte runs for office and his hustings speech is both intoxicating and prescient:

"We have had the Austrian Empire, and the Ottoman Empire. These will all be replaced by the Empire of Trade. The result will be untold wealth for all of you!"

Melmotte is elected to Parliament where he champions free trade to the detriment of local industries.

Screenwriter Andrew Davies marveled at the novel's timeliness: "It's so dark and so modern in its tone, and centered around a city scam that reminds one of the dot-com collapse or the recent Enron scandal. And in the middle is this huge monster, Melmotte, sitting like a fat spider, drawing all the other characters into his great scheme."

Paul Montague returns from Mexico disgusted that no work has been done. Melmotte assures him that maintaining "public confidence is the main thing." We see the recurring Cabalist theme that "saying is believing," not seeing.

Rob Byrdon plays "Mr Alf" a crusading Gentile newspaperman who confronts Melmotte: "You don't move mountains. All you move is money, from other pockets into your own!"

There are many romantic subplots that involve marrying for love vs. money, a Victorian preoccupation. In one, the daughter of a struggling English aristocrat is about to marry another Jewish banker when he drops her.

"I've been jilted by a Jew!" she exclaims in disbelief.

Generally speaking, the miniseries is not anti Semitic although it pokes fun at the Jews' lack of grace and manners. However, it is just as scathing in its criticism of the decadent English aristocracy.

In the end, Melmotte's love-starved daughter, Marie, is quite sympathetic. And Melmotte's Jewish associates Breghert and Croll are also seen as honorable men.

Ultimately, the novel/miniseries is an inspired preview of the overthrow of traditional values by the reductionism championed by Jewish finance. It is hard to believe that this novel was written before the Panama Scandal of 1892 and the Marconi Scandal of 1912.

David Suchet (of Hercules Poirot fame) is convincing as Melmotte and Mathew Macfadyen is a hoot as the wastrel Felix Carbury.

I highly recommend this miniseries as an heartening reminder of art when it upheld truth and enduring wisdom. *The Way We Live Now* is available on Netflix.

"Anti Semitic" Movie Flew Under the Radar

I was prepared to pan this movie which I thought treated an affair between a teenage girl and an older man as "An Education." But I had badly misjudged.

The movie is a brilliant metaphor for the corruption of Christian (Western) civilization by organized Jewry, as projected in the *Protocols of the Elders of Zion.*

Carey Mulligan and Peter Sarsgaard in *An Education*

The majority of critics missed this and gave the film an 84% positive rating. It was nominated for Best Picture and Best Actress Oscars in 2009. However, it won neither as the largely Jewish Oscar committee must have recognized its real message.

An Education is a rare movie that doesn't patronize Jews. It's well aware that, while many Jews are decent and honest, a segment consists of pathological liars, Satanists, thieves and perverts. Unfortunately these Illuminati (Masonic) Jews seem to have leadership positions.

The only other movie I've ever seen that depicts an unattractive Jewish character is *The Upside of Anger* (2005) featuring another cradle robber.

An Education is based on a memoir by Lynn Barber. The brilliant screenplay is by novelist Nick Hornby. The Director is a Danish woman, Lone Scherfig. Amazingly, it was made partly by BBC Films.

SEDUCTION ISN'T ONLY SEXUAL

Art captures the universal in the particular. Here, the seducer is a Jewish petty crook, David Goldman, played by Peter Sarsgaard. He is the classic smooth talker,

Jenny is a bright, precocious non-Jewish schoolgirl played by Carey Mulligan. She and her parents see marriage to the flamboyant Goldman as a path to security, sidestepping an arduous and expensive Oxford education.

Jenny doesn't just give her body for the "glamorous" life he offers; she gives her soul. Her mother and father also compromise themselves.

Goldman's behavior is a reminder that Jews were on the vanguard of crime in England. They have been called "gypsies with Ph.Ds." Jenny witnesses how Goldman and a friend steal a painting.

Jenny is ready to leave him but he wins her over by saying, "People like us (Jews) aren't as sharp as you and we have to cut corners in order to finance the night clubs and trips to Paris."

She agrees to look the other way, anxious to escape her stifling 1961 London suburban lifestyle. Later, when he betrays her, she reproaches his Jewish friend.

"Why didn't you tell me?"

"Well if you want to have that conversation," he says. "You saw us stealing and you looked the other way." (You are complicit in your own corruption. Ouch.)

She lies to her parents but they can't reproach her either. "Goldman" had compromised them with gifts and flattery as well.

Jenny's fall symbolizes a society seduced by money, sex, and lies.

The only people Goldman didn't take in were her teacher and headmistress. The teacher refuses her gift of Chanel perfume saying that she could not condone Jenny's degradation.

The Headmistress, played by Emma Thompson, is portrayed as an "anti Semite" but she is the moral center of this film.

"The Jews killed Jesus," she tells Jenny.

"But Jesus was a Jew," Jenny replies.

"Yes. Jews betrayed themselves by rejecting Jesus and now we imitate them," the headmistress should have replied but didn't, indicating the Christian's own confusion.

Art finds the universal in the particular. *An Education* lays bare the plight of a civilization cut adrift from its spiritual moorings. It's inspiring that such a movie still could be made in 2009.

Satire on Homosexual Adoption is Exhilarating

The Illuminati are imposing homosexuality by whitewashing its image. Therefore, we need constant reminders of how dysfunctional this "lifestyle" actually is. *Buyer's Remorse* is one of five stories by a homosexual Christopher Landon in the 2010 movie *Burning Palms*. A work of genius, it presents a realistic view of two gay men adopting a little Black girl.

Seven-year-old "Mahogany" is left in car alone while gay parent leaves for bondage sex.

The truth is exhilarating and, God knows, we rarely find any truth in the mass media.

Like Jews and anti Semitism, gays are the only people allowed to criticize without being smeared as "homophobic." Nevertheless, for *Buyer's Remorse*, Landon has been labeled homophobic and racist to boot!

"Buyer's Remorse" is notable for confirming many unflattering "prejudices" about gays and gay adoption. The gay couple is totally promiscuous, flirt with every male in sight, and have extramarital sex whenever possible. Sex has become jaded and requires drugs, in this case crystal meth.

It's based on real life. "I had a great deal of fun watching the two most irresponsible gay men on earth adopt a child that they had no business caring for," Director Landon said in an interview.

The couple parody male-female roles with the "female" taking it up the ass. There is actually a sex scene which conveys the disturbing character of homosexual intercourse.

The female character, who assumes the mother role, is irresponsible. He jokes about "finger-f**king" Mahogany, in her presence. The male role-character is forced to shut him up saying that child protection agencies are on the look-out for this kind of talk.

The female character cranks up on Chrystal meth and goes out for bondage sex, leaving Mahogany sweating in the car on a hot day. She finds the meth and tries some. When the male character comes home from work, the child is drugged and tearing her dolls to shreds.

One suspects the other of infidelity and they get into a wrestling match.

Mahogany appears at the door and utters her first word: "Faggots!"

At this point, the couple realize they are not cut out for parenting. Since the child appears to be feral, a Zulu warrior, they decide to abandon her in a national forest with a supply of energy bars. She seems happy to be set free. They adopt a dog instead.

This is a refreshing dark comedy which Stalinist America cannot understand, condone or forgive. The film got 29% from *Rotten Tomatoes* and went directly to cable and DVD. Ironically its only theater venues have been in Romania.

Movies today are a place for propaganda, pornography, disinformation and maudlin sentiment. They are not an honest reflection or comment on our reality.

Without honesty, there can be no inspiration. But occasionally something honest slips through the filters. When it does, it's exhilarating.

Japanese Children's Cartoon Lifts the Spirit

Recently my wife introduced me to a Japanese animated feature called *My Neighbor Totoro.* (1988)

Although made for children, this movie reminded me of the power of art to reassure, refresh and inspire. It was a reminder of what we are being denied.

Written and directed by Hayao Miyazaki, the film describes the interaction between two sisters, Satsuki and Mei, and "wood spirits" in a rural area near Tokyo in 1957.

Many things about this picture amazed me. I can't remember when I have last seen innocence portrayed. These children are innocent, especially the youngest, Mei. The child's wide-ranging emotional reactions deftly conveyed in her facial expressions reminded me that art makes us more human by revealing what is universally human. The feelings of a child resonated in me, a man of 64.

Rarely do I see recognizable wholesome human emotions portrayed in the movies—loss, yearning, hope, love. I'd list more but I have forgotten what they are. Everyone is becoming dehumanized and jaded.

The girls' father, Mr. Kusukabe, an archeology professor, is acting as a single father. Mrs. Kusukabe is in the hospital. I loved the way this father treated his children, with such patience and respect. I loved the world they inhabited, where he could bathe with his two girls without neighbors snooping and Family Services breaking down the door.

This world is innocent. The culture is intact. People know the difference between what is healthy and what is sick and evil.

When Mei sets out alone to visit her mother, we don't have to worry about her being abducted or sexually molested. When Satsuki goes to find her, everyone is courteous, concerned and helpful. Despite what Japan went through in the last war, the culture remained intact.

Satsuki calls upon the wood spirit Totoro for help. In turn, he enlists a giant cat (above) who doubles as a bus. I loved that these creatures were benign. There was no sense of menace.

Compare this with the trauma or filth found in many children's movies. Take *Bambi* where the mother is killed by hunters or *Finding Nemo* where his family is eaten by a shark. *Madagascar* is full of homosexual references.

If we want a healthy society, the mass media has to uphold healthy values. Call me Ayatollah, but I would ban porn, depravity and violence. Why is it that they can impose immorality on us, but we can't impose morality on them?

We have been brainwashed to reject the notion of Satan and Satanism, but our society is satanically possessed. You can see it in the obsession with sex and money and the acceptance of depravity, obscenity and violence. This is not accidental. It is the deliberate policy of the Illuminati, a satanic cult that controls the mass media and much more.

Environmentalists object to pollution but are oblivious to the toxic bilge they pump into our minds and souls. We can't seem to stop this pipe either.

A FM-radio jazz announcer used to sign off with the words: "Think nice thoughts." That's half the battle to saving our souls. It's all in where we focus our attention.

I was amazed by how much *My Neighbor Totoro* invigorated me. I felt cleansed and uplifted. It reminded me that my soul needs nourishment, not just mind and stomach.

Book Four

Hidden History (World Wars)

Does History Follow Rothschild Messiah Script?

The ideology behind the New World Order may be Jewish Messianism, the view that God has chosen "the King of the Jews" to rule the world. This "Messiah," or antichrist, will be selected from the ranks of the Rothschild family.

Edmund de Rothschild on Israeli 50 shekel note.

This argument is espoused in a rare, suppressed book entitled *Elijah, Rothschilds and the Ark of the Covenant* by Tom Crotser & Jeremiah Patrick (Restoration Press, 1984.) It is consistent with the *Protocols of Zion* (23-24) which says the dynastic heir of King David, the "King of the Jews" will be "king of the world."

Rooted in Biblical prophesy, this bizarre vision is behind economic and political events today. The Zionist vision is much larger than a Jewish homeland. "The Messianic hope promises the establishment by the Jews of world power in Palestine to which all the nations of the earth will pay homage." (p. 29)

"This glorious age can only be affected by a man, a scion of the House of David" who will lead the Jews to "righteousness" and "regenerate" the human race.

In *The Jewish Utopia* (1932) Rabbi Michael Higger writes, "All the treasures and natural resources of the world will eventually come in possession of the righteous."

Obviously, the majority of Jews are not informed of this plan, the easier to manipulate them.

MESSIAHS

As early as 1836, Anselm Meyer Rothschild received a letter from rabbi Hirsch Kalischer, who revealed the divine plan: "Let no one imagine that the Messiah will appear suddenly and amid miracles and wonders, lead the Israelites to their ancient inheritance. The beginning of the redemption will be in a natural way, by the desire of the Jews to settle in Palestine, and the willingness of the nations to help them in this work."

There would be no Israel were it not for the Jewish holocaust. The holocaust likely prepared the groundwork for Israel and the appearance of a Jewish Messiah.

After Jews return to Palestine and the Temple was rebuilt, "then will God show them all the miracles in accordance with the description given by the prophets and the sages... God will send His prophet and his anointed king," Kalischer wrote Rothschild.

Albert Cohen, Edmund de Rothschild's tutor, shared Kalischer's views and imbued them in his pupil. As a result Edmund de Rothschild funded the Jewish colonization of Palestine in the 19th century.

Edmund de Rothschild engineered the famous Dreyfus Affair in order to create anti Semitism and force Jews to support Israel as a refuge.

DEBT

The Rothschilds bend the nations to their will by means of debt. Moses relates the basic principle in *Deuteronomy* 15:6: "Thou shalt lend unto many nations, but thou shalt not borrow; and thou shalt reign over many nations, but they shalt not reign over thee."

The authors write: "Note that this is not a suggestion given in the scriptures. It is a command from the God of Israel. Lending upon usury is how to possess the land." (175)

"Lending on interest for consumer and emergency needs became a virtual Jewish monopoly in Western Europe between the 12th and 15th centuries...As security, real estate was most preferred. In this way Jews acquired in pledge houses, vineyards, farms, villages, castles, towns, and even provinces." (177)

"The rise of absolute monarchies in Central Europe brought numbers of Jews into the influential position of negotiating loans for the various royal courts. The phenomenon of court Jews now continued into Europe. The most famous included Lehmann, Oppenheimer and Goldschmidt in Germany and Austria." (180)

"Jean Izolulet, a member of the Jewish *Alliance Israelite Universal* wrote in 1932: 'The meaning of history of the last century is that today 300 Jewish financiers, all masters of lodges, rule the world.'" (183)

"Vatican City came under Rothschild influence in the early 19th century...Pope John Paul II admitted the Roman Catholic Church is still tied to the Rothschilds...In Sept. 1979, the Pope revealed the Church had $50 billion invested in various Rothschild banks..." (191)

CONCLUSION

Edmund de Rothschild was playing a role in a larger drama which would see his successor finally become the antichrist. This required that Jews return to Palestine, and that required a holocaust, the huge Rothschild-organized pogrom in Europe. (see Makow, *Hitler was a Godsend for Israel*.)

The author of *The Protocols of the Elders of Zion* repeatedly refers to world conquest in terms of "when we have come into our kingdom." I suspect he was a Rothschild.

We can already see this agenda taking shape in the way the US and other Western nations finance Israel and pledge to guarantee its security.

The Jewish Conspiracy:
Last Moment of Lucidity

After the Bolshevik Revolution, Christian nations briefly stirred in their sleep and recognized that the "Jewish Conspiracy" was not the figment of a bigot's imagination but rather the key to understanding the human condition.

History is the product of a long-term occult plan by Cabalist (satanist) bankers to subjugate the human race using war (genocide), revolution and financial collapse as their main instruments.

In his book *The Decline of the West* (1918) Oswald Spengler noted that almost an entire generation of the ruling classes of Germany and England had perished in WWI.

"Thus the Anglo Saxon race had entered a period of irreversible decline in which it would inevitable give way to another more vigorous race, probably from the east."

With the rise of Communism and the mass migration of Jews to the United States, many identified the Jews as this race.

In July 1920, the staid Tory newspaper, *The Morning Post* published a series of 18 articles saying there has long existed, "like a canker at the heart of our civilization, a secret revolutionary sect, mainly of Judaic origin, bent on the destruction of all Christian empires, altars, and thrones."

In the first article, an expert on the occult, Copin Albancelli, stated that "the occult power which works behind Revolutionary Freemasonry is the secret government of the Jewish nation."

The article quoted a Jewish convert to Christianity, Abbe Joseph Lehman, as saying that "Hebraic antagonism to Christianity had led the Jews to utilize secret societies."

From the time of Moses, a secret cabal was the custodian of the "most sublime truths of the Hebraic religion" and, unlike the average Jew, was hellbent on world domination.

The Morning Post then affirmed that the *Protocols of the Elders of Zion* is not a hoax. Its goal was to establish "government of the world by a king of the blood of David."

The *Protocols* linked Jews with Freemasonry. There was "an inner or Jewish Masonry, the true governing power, and an outer or Gentile Masonry which blindly follows [the direction of the former.]"

According to the *Post*, the *Protocols* took credit for the French Revolution: "On the ruins of the natural aristocracy of the goyim, we have set up the aristocracy of our educated classes, headed by the aristocracy of money."

The Morning Post tied the *Protocols* to the Russian Revolution. It acknowledged Cabalist Jewish backing of socialists, communists and anarchists under the ruse of the bankers' "alleged ardent desire to serve the working classes."

After an engineered financial crash, the goyim "will be compelled to offer us international power that will enable us to gradually absorb all the great forces of the world and to form a super-government."

Sound like the NWO? The Gentile cattle will work for their Cabalist Jewish masters. A system of education will erase "any recollection of their former state" from the minds of the goyim, and "establish the Jewish religion as the universal faith."

The alarm sounded by *The Morning Post* echoed another by the *Times of London*. In May 1920, Lord Northcliffe, a part-owner of *The Times*, printed an article about the *Protocols of Zion* entitled *"The Jewish Peril, A Disturbing Pamphlet, A Call for an Enquiry."* It concluded:

"An impartial investigation of these would-be documents and their history is most desirable...Are we to dismiss the whole matter without inquiry and to let the influence of such a book as this work unchecked?"

But the alarm largely fell on deaf ears. As Hillaire Belloc explained in his book *The Jews* (1922), the British Empire was the product of an alliance between Jewish Finance and the British aristocracy under the rubric of Cabalism i.e. Freemasonry. The Cabalist "Jew" World Order is nothing but an extension of British imperialism. American imperialism is a subset.

As Douglas Reed described in his book *A Controversy of Zion*, Lord Northcliffe was declared insane and poisoned in 1922. Howell Gywnne, the editor of the *Morning Post* survived until 1937 when the paper was bought by Rothschild allies and merged into *The Telegraph*. With the upcoming ruse called World War Two, the Rothschilds were taking no chances.

CONCLUSION

At present, the world represents the near-consummation of plans laid centuries ago and voiced in *The Protocols of the Elders of Zion*.

We can't even acknowledge our calamity without being "politically incorrect." It makes us nostalgic for that brief shining moment 90 years ago when the mainstream media could still mention the most pressing issue of all time.

NOTE

This article is indebted to the book, *On a Field of Red—The Communist International & the Coming of WWII*, 1981 by Anthony Cave Brown & Charles MacDonald. pp. 202-204

First World War:
First Christian Holocaust

Like millions of others, my wife and I have been enjoying the TV series, "Downton Abbey."

Set in an English Manor House during World War One, the costume drama depicts the prevalent attitude that a man's virility and honor are measured by his willingness to die or be maimed for his country.

The war's legitimacy is assumed. There is no hint that it might be a sinister ruse.

Lord Ronald Grantham, Matthew Crawley and Lady Sybil Crawley, in "Downton Abbey."

The only cynical character is the villain, Thomas, who engineers a minor injury to escape service.

The young heir to the estate, Matthew Crawley is paralyzed from the waist down. This happens when you run into a maelstrom of machine gun fire. He seems surprised by the consequences of his "heroism." He may never be able to walk, or to father a child.

This is what the Illuminati (Masonic) bankers wanted, to destroy Europe's Gentile best.

There were only a few hundred Masonic bankers, and many were getting old. They were more adept at making deals, having gay sex and performing satanic child sacrifices. They were not capable, all by themselves, of slaughtering millions of strong young men.

So they concocted a world war which was also highly profitable. They owned the companies that made the machine guns and bullets.

Illuminati Jews and Masons hate Christianity first and foremost. "Christianity is our only real enemy since all the political and economic phenomena of the bourgeois states are only its consequences," insider C. Rakovsky, told his NKVD interrogator in 1937. (See *Rothschilds Conduct Red Symphony* on my website.)

The overall goal of WWI was to bring down Christian civilization and destroy the German, Austrian and Russian monarchies.

Out of the old Christian order would emerge the (satanic) New World Order. This is the real meaning of the terms "revolution" and "progressive."

"The lamps are going out all over Europe; we shall not see them lit again in our lifetime," said the British Foreign Secretary Edward Grey, a Freemason who played a major role in engineering this catastrophe.

He made a secret treaty with France and Russia that if Germany or Austria-Hungary attacked, they would unite. Sir Edward concealed this treaty, and lied to Parliament when asked about it. If Germany had known about this pact, it would have backed down.

The goal of the war was to kill the new generation of white Christian males on both sides. They succeeded: 10 million men were killed and 21 million more were maimed.

Sixty thousand Allied soldiers died in one day at the Battle of the Somme in 1916. The Commander of the British Army was the Freemason Douglas Haig. The Commander of the US Expeditionary Force in 1917 was the Freemason John Perishing. Old Satanists sent young men to die.

HOW THEY MADE THE WAR

This needless war was concocted by Illuminati.

On the British side were Lord Robert Cecil, a wealthy banker; Lord Herbert H. Asquith, British Prime Minister 1908-1916; Viscount Haldane, Secretary of State for War; Lord Nathan Rothschild and Lord Alfred Milner, the second most powerful man in the British government after 1916.

A French observer wrote, "for some time a group of financiers whose families for the most part are of German Jewish origin...exerts a dominant influence over Lloyd George [Prime Minister 1916-1922.] The Monds, the Sassoons, Rufus Isaacs, representatives of the International Banking interests, dominate England, own its newspapers and control its elections."

Conditions in Germany were similar. "...Since the beginning of Kaiser Wilhem II's reign, the Illuminati Jews had been the real rulers of the German empire. For the last fifteen years, those in immediate personal contact with the Kaiser were the Hebrew financiers., Hebrew manufacturers and Hebrew merchants such as Emile and Walter Rathenau, Ballin, Schwabach, James Simon, Friedlander-Fuld, Goldberger etc. (Andre Krylienko, *The Red Thread*, p.153)

All that remained was to light the fuse. The First World War began August 14, 1914, after the Jewish Mason Gavrilo Princep assassinated the Austrian heir Archduke Franz Ferdinand on June 28.

Kaiser Wilhelm believed the Masons were responsible for the Great War. He wrote:

"I have been informed that an important role was played in the preparation of the World War directed against the monarchical Central Powers by the policy of the international 'Great Orient Lodge'; a policy extending over many years and always envisaging the goal at which it aimed..."

"In 1917, an international meeting of the lodges of the 'Great Orient' was held, after which there was a subsequent conference in Switzerland; at this the following program was adopted: Dismemberment of Austria-Hungary, democratization of Germany, elimination of the House of Hapsburg, abdication of the German Emperor, ... elimination of the Pope and the Catholic Church, elimination of every state Church in Europe."

Thus, Max Nordau, co-founder of the World Zionist (i.e. Masonic) Organization was able to predict WWI in 1903: "Let me tell you the following words as if I were showing you the rungs of a ladder leading upward and upward: Herzl, the Zionist Congress, the English Uganda proposition, **the future world war**, the peace conference—where with the help of England a free and Jewish Palestine will be created."

With Freemasons controlling both sides, it was easy to manipulate the Kaiser into attacking Belgium. The "mediator" was Albert Belan, a prominent Illuminati Jewish businessman and friend of the Kaiser. Together with the English, he managed to mislead the Kaiser as to England's real intentions.

To quote Andrei Krylienko (*The Red Thread*): "An unambiguous statement by the British on the side of France and Russia, could still, as the French ambassador to Germany reported, have led Germany to decide against aggression...In short, war was not decided upon by Wilhelm II...but by the occult powers...by whose intrigues [it] was made to seem ineluctable." (155)

Wilhelm quickly recognized that he had fallen into a trap.

In *A Child of the Century*, Ben Hecht wrote, "the Twentieth Century was cut off at its knees by World War One."

The same can be said of mankind. A cancer, Cabalism, gnaws at its vitals. We are at the mercy of a multi-generational satanic conspiracy which is nearing consummation. Modern history, properly understood, is the story of this process of subversion.

Hitler and Bormann Were Traitors

In the past, I have presented evidence that Martin Bormann, the man who signed Hitler's paycheck, was a Soviet, i.e. Illuminati agent; but I was not sure if Hitler was also a conscious traitor.

The testimony of General Reinhard Gehlen, Abwehr Chief Intelligence for Russia, suggests that he was.

Reinhard Gehlen

In his memoirs, *The Service* (World Pub.1972) Gehlen says that he and Admiral Canaris, head of the Abwehr, suspected there was a traitor in the German Supreme Command.

Both had noticed that the Soviets were receiving "rapid and detailed information... on top level decision-making."

They suspected Martin Bormann, the Deputy Fuhrer and Head of the Nazi Party.

"Our suspicions were largely confirmed when, independently of one another, we found out that Bormann and his group were operating an unsupervised radio transmitter network and using it to send coded messages to Moscow.

When OKW monitors reported this, Canaris demanded an investigation;but word came back that Hitler himself had emphatically forbidden any intervention: he had been informed in advance of these Funkspiele, or 'fake radio messages,' and he had approved them" (p.71.)

GEHLEN CONFIRMED BORMANN TRAITOR

Despite the fact that vital information continued to leak, Gehlen and Canaris left it at that. "Neither of us was in any position to denounce the Reichsleiter [Bormann] with any prospect of success."

In his book *Hitler's Traitor,* Louis Kilzer estimated that Bormann was worth fifty divisions to the Soviets.

After the war, Gehlen, who headed the BND (West German Intelligence Agency) was able to confirm Bormann's treason. "During the 1950s, I was passed two separate reports from behind the Iron Curtain to the effect that Bormann had been a Soviet agent..."

The fact that Hitler shielded Bormann confirms that he also was an active traitor. Both served the Illuminati (Masonic) bankers, i.e. the Rothschild syndicate, based in London. The Illuminati were also behind Stalin and Communism, not to mention Churchill, and FDR.

By fabricating war, the Illuminati wage war on humanity with the ultimate goal of a veiled world government dictatorship.

Think 9-11, "The Patriot Act," FEMA, NSA surveillance. Behind the veil of democracy and fighting "terror," they have constructed a police state.

HITLER'S DELIBERATE BLUNDERS

In the winter of 1941-42, Gehlen and fellow generals had concluded that the Russian campaign was doomed "not because it could not be militarily or politically won, but because of Hitler's continued interference, that resulted in such elementary blunders that defeat was inevitable." (98)

Despite the fact that Hitler had covered for the traitor Bormann, Gehlen didn't come to the obvious deduction, that Hitler's "elementary blunders" were deliberate.

In his book, Gehlen details some of these blunders.

The General Staff wanted to concentrate resources on capturing Moscow. Hitler insisted on dissipating the effort on three fronts.

The General Staff saw that the Soviets were going to entrap the Sixth Army at Stalingrad and demanded a strategic withdrawal. Hitler vetoed this with the result that 200,000 of Germany's best troops (and irreplaceable weaponry) were killed and captured.

To replace these losses, the General Staff wanted to recruit millions of willing volunteers from anti-Communist ranks, i.e. Russians, Ukrainians, Lithuanians etc.

"After 20 years of arbitrary injustice and terror, the re-establishment of elementary human rights such as the dignity of man, liberty, justice, and the sanctity of property united every inhabitant of the Soviet empire in a common readiness to support the Germans." (81)

The Wehrmacht began to build a nationalist regime around the charismatic Russian defector, General Vlasov.

Indeed, such an appeal was Stalin's worst nightmare, according to his son, who became a POW.

"The one thing my father dreads is the emergence of a nationalist regime opposed to him. But that is a step you'll never take." Yakov told his Nazi interrogator. "Because we know you have not set out to liberate our country but to conquer it." (80)

Stalin knew he could trust Hitler, a fellow Illuminati agent, to take a fall. Hitler didn't even try to deceive the Slavs about his grim intentions for them, and instead of being welcomed, won their implacable hate.

CONCLUSION

World War Two was the most egregious hoax in history. A cult of satanic (Sabbatean) Jews and Masons, financed by the Rothschild syndicate, is responsible for destroying more than sixty million lives.

Hitler proved by his actions that he was a traitor. He was installed by the Illuminati to geld Germany so that it would slip neatly into the NWO.

Hitler was catastrophic for Germany. But what did the German people expect from a Viennese vagrant and male prostitute?

A comparison with Barack Obama is pertinent. Like Hitler, he is not native born and has a shady homosexual past. He works for the Illuminati. Is his assignment also to destroy the US, so Americans too will meekly accept world government?

Hitler's example reveals the unexpected dimensions of treason. If we fail to learn the lessons of the past, we will repeat them.

NOTE:

See also in previous editions, or online: *Did Bormann Run Hitler for the Illuminati?* and *Bormann Was a Rothschild Agent-Damning Evidence.*

FBI Ignored Hitler's Post-War Life

A recently declassified document reveals that the FBI knew Hitler had not committed suicide and was living in Argentina. The document can be found on the FBI website. (See url below article.)

The report presents the testimony of an informant who approached the FBI in Los Angeles August 28, 1945 offering information on Hitler in exchange for asylum. He said he was given $15,000 for his role in arranging Hitler's reception.

The documents states, '███ claimed to be one of four men who met Hitler and his party of about 50 when they landed from two submarines in Argentina approximately two and a half weeks after the fall of Berlin May 2, 1945.'

'███ explained that the subs landed along the tip of the Valdez peninsula in the Gulf of San Vatias. ███ told ███ that there are several tiny villages in this area where members of Hitler's party would eventually stay with German families. He named the towns as San Antonia, Videma, Neuquen, Muster, Carmena, and Rason.'

He describes a surreal scene of top Nazis' climbing the Andes Mountains on horseback:

'By pre-arranged plan with six top Argentine officials, pack horses were waiting for the group and by daylight all supplies were loaded on the horses and an all-day trip inland toward the foothills of the southern Andes was started. At dusk the party arrived at the ranch where Hitler and his party, according to ███, are now in hiding.'

This part is unclear since it is more than 500 km from the coast to the Andes.

The informant gave specific physical details about Hitler. 'According to ███, Hitler is suffering from asthma and ulcers, has shaved off his mustache and has a long "but" on his upper lip.'

He offered to identify the three other men who assisted him, and to locate Hitler. 'If you go to a hotel in San Antonia, Argentina, I will arrange for a man to meet you there and locate the ranch where Hitler is.'

The FBI never took up his offer. The informant also gave an interview to the *Los Angeles Examiner* on July 29, 1945. The story was not published.

HITLER IN ARGENTINA

The FBI had many more sightings of Hitler in Argentina which they also ignored.

Many books have been written on this subject. They include *Hitler's Escape* (2005) by Ron T Hansig; *Grey Wolf* (2013) by Dunstan and Williams and *Hitler in Argentina* (2014) by Harry Cooper.

Arguably the best is *Hitler's Exile* (2010) by Argentine journalist Abel Basti. He visited German compounds surrounded by security guards, interviewed witnesses in nearby villages, and collected hundreds of media reports and government documents in Argentina that state matter-of-factly that Hitler was laying low within their borders.

In an interview on *Deadline—Live*, an Argentine news program, Basti said, "Hitler escaped via air from Austria to Barcelona. The last stage of his escape was in a submarine, from Vigo, heading straight to the coast of Patagonia. Finally, Hitler and Eva Braun, in a car with a chauffeur and bodyguard—a motorcade of at least three cars—drove to Bariloche.

"He took refuge in a place called San Ramon, about 15 miles east of that town. It is a property of about 250,000 acres with a lake-front view of Lake Nahuel Huapi, which had been German property since the early twentieth century, when it belonged to a German firm by the name of Schamburg-Lippe.

"I was able to confirm the presence of Hitler in Spain thanks to a—now elderly—Jesuit priest, whose family members were friends of the Nazi leader. And I have witnesses that allude to meetings he had with his entourage at the place where they stayed in Cantabria.

"In addition, a document of the British secret services reveals that in those days, a Nazi submarine convoy left Spain, and after stopping in the Canary Islands, it continued its journey to the south of Argentina.

"Hitler lived as a fugitive with his wife and his bodyguard. His first years were in Patagonia, and then he lived in the more northern provinces [of Argentina].

"In Argentina, I have interviewed people who had seen and met with Hitler. In the Russian archives, there is abundant documentation that shows that Hitler had escaped.

"The U.S. has just reclassified [under national security auspices] for 20 [more] years all official material related to this story, and when that deadline is met, it will probably be reclassified. "The British reclassified all related documentation for 60 more years. The researchers cannot access that information."

SOVIETS ALSO COVERED UP ESCAPE

Colonel W. J. Heimlich, Chief of U.S. Intelligence in Berlin, concluded, "There is no evidence beyond that of hearsay to support the theory of Hitler's suicide. On the basis of present evidence, no insurance company in America would pay a claim on Adolf Hitler."

In his book *Speaking Frankly* (1947), Secretary of State Jimmy Byrnes wrote; "While in Potsdam at the conference of the Big Four, Stalin left his chair, came over and clicked his liquor glass with mine in a very friendly manner. I asked what was his theory about the death of Adolf Hitler and he replied—Hitler is not dead. He escaped either to Spain or Argentina." (Quotes are from *Hitler in Argentina*)

In the immediate aftermath of Hitler's disappearance, the Soviets made a series of contradictory statements, bizarrely claiming they had found his remains one day and that he had escaped the next.

First, they said his body wasn't found. Then, they proclaimed Hitler's remains had been discovered on May 4th 1945. However, Marshall Zhukov, the head of the Soviet army, announced on the 9th June, "We did not identify the body of Hitler. I can say nothing definite about his fate. He could have flown away from Berlin at the very last moment."

The only evidence that Hitler committed suicide are skull fragments that the Russians insisted were Hitler's. This lie was blown apart in 2009 when an American researcher carried out tests and found the skull belonged to a young woman.

The Russians have never got their story straight and presented false evidence. Did the Illuminati Soviet leadership protect one of their own?

Their actions certainly aided Hitler's escape. Nürnberg Judge Michael Mussmanno wrote in his book *Ten Days to Die* (1950) that, "Russia must accept much of the blame that Hitler did not die in May 1945."

CONCLUSION

Although the informant offered to identify the others involved, and to locate Hitler, the FBI determined "it would be impossible to continue efforts to locate Hitler with the sparse information to date."

The fact that neither the FBI nor Mossad nor the mainstream media had any interest in Hitler's whereabouts suggest that he was an Illuminati agent and that the official narrative of WW2 is bunk.

Hitler protected Martin Bormann who was definitely a Soviet agent. The implication is that Hitler was also a traitor and this is the real reason neither the Russians nor the West were concerned with his post-war career.

FBI website: http://vault.fbi.gov/adolf-hitler/adolf-hitler-part-01-of-04/view

Basti quotes: http://beforeitsnews.com/conspiracy-theories/2011/09/nazi-expert-i-have-proof-hitler-died-in-1960s-1163749.html

Identity Theft:
England's Jewish Aristocracy

In 1941, Friedrich Wilhelm Euler, Nazi Germany's leading expert on Jewish genealogy, published a lengthy article entitled "The Penetration of Jewish Blood into the English Upper Class."

Euler asked how modern Britain became the "protecting power of Jewry" despite the relatively small size of the Jewish community there.

He claimed too much emphasis had been placed on Jewish economic and

Daughters of Downton Abbey had a Jewish mother.

intellectual influence, and not enough on the penetration of the English aristocracy by Jewish blood.

Well before British Jews were emancipated in the 19th Century, baptized members of financially successful Jewish families had married into the English nobility.

Virtually all of his 148-page article consisted of a catalog of Jewish conversions and subsequent marriages with non-Jews, starting in the fourteenth century.

Euler said the English aristocracy had literally sealed a "marriage with Jewry" in terms of its "blood substance."

This information, cited from Alan Steinweis, *Studying the Jew: Scholarly Anti-Semitism in Nazi Germany* (2006) p. 107, has important implications.

The New World Order is an extension of the British Empire, which has always represented the rapacity, greed and satanism of a mixed-race caste of Masonic (Cabalist) Jews and Gentiles called the Illuminati.

If Euler is correct, it's no exaggeration to say that the English elite is crypto Jewish. This is consistent with the conclusions of Leslie Pine, editor of the renowned *Burke's Peerage*. (See *England's Jewish Aristocracy* in Illuminati2 or online.)

The "Jewish Conspiracy" is the British Empire. So are the American Empire and the NWO.

The "Jewish Conspiracy" is the "Establishment," founded on the power of the London-based central banking cartel.

IMPLICATIONS FOR WORLD WAR TWO

History needs to be rewritten from this perspective. We can begin with Dunkirk (May 1940) when Hitler let 330,000 British and Allied soldiers escape, ostensibly as a peace gesture.

Hitler's desire to make a "Nordic" pact with England doesn't make sense. He knew that in terms of its elite, England was not an Aryan nation. He was a British (i.e. Illuminati) agent.

England was the bastion of Illuminati Jewish power. If Hitler had been genuine, England's invasion would have been his first priority. He would have incarcerated the 330,000 soldiers at Dunkirk. Instead, he let them escape, and carried out *British policy* by attacking Russia.

As I have shown in my book *Illuminati*, Hitler was placed in power to do exactly what he did, *destroy Germany* and pave the way for one world government. Hitler, Stalin and Churchill were all Illuminati Jews who colluded. (For e.g. see *Stalin's Complicity in Operation Barbarossa* online or in Illuminati2.)

Hitler persecuted Jews because the Illuminati wanted to trauma-brainwash them in order to set up Israel, and for future use as pawns of the NWO.

At the same time, Nazi persecution served to discredit opposition to their Jewish pawns, giving them immunity as victims. This allows the Illuminati to criminalize freedom of speech, better to protect themselves.

Look at the *modus operandi* of Marranos, Crypto Jews, Communists and Freemasons. It is the same as Hitler's: *Conceal your real identity and true aims; infiltrate, subvert and eventually destroy Christian civilization.* This involves subverting every individual, nation and group, including non-Illuminati Jews.

NOTE: Hermann Goetsche (1815-1878) was a German "anti Semite" credited with inserting a chapter in his novel *Biarritz, (1868)* entitled *In the Jewish Cemetery of Prague.* The chapter consists of a speech by a rabbi which is thought by some (not me) to be the inspiration for the *Protocols of Zion.* It includes the following passage which might shed light on how Illuminati Jews regard intermarriage:

"We must encourage marriages between Jews and Christians for the people of Israel lose nothing by the contact and can only gain from these marriages. Our race, chosen by God, cannot be corrupted by the introduction of a certain amount of impure blood, and by those marriages our daughters will secure alliances with Christian families of some influence and power. It is right that, for the money we give, we should obtain the equivalent in influence over everything around us. To be related to gentiles shall not imply a departure from the path we have chosen to follow; on the contrary, with a little skill it will make us the arbiters of their fate." —Quoted in Norman Cohn, *Warrant for Genocide*, p. 272

Illuminati Betrayed British Agents in World War Two

In the wake of D-Day June 6, 1944, hundreds of acts of sabotage were committed by the French Resistance—with one exception.

There were none in the north and north west where they mattered most.

There, the "Prosper" and related "Scientist" networks had been mopped by the Gestapo in 1943. Prosper's courageous young leader, Francis Anthony Suttill, 34, was languishing in a concentration camp.

He and scores of British agents were later executed, along with over 10,000 members of the French Resistance. One hundred and sixty plane loads of armaments—2600 containers—including tons of sten guns and explosives, were seized by the Nazis. (193)

Who was responsible for this debacle?

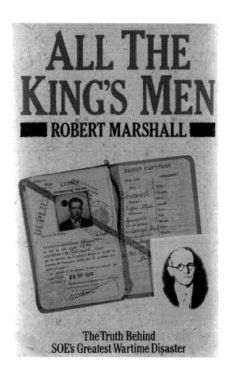

The Truth Behind
SOE's Greatest Wartime Disaster

According to BBC Producer Robert Marshall's thoroughly documented book, *All The King's Men* (Collins, 1988) the culprit was none other than the homosexual and Freemason, Deputy Head of MI-6, Sir Claude Edward Marjoribanks Dansey (1876-1947.)

Dansey deliberately placed a double agent, Henri Dericourt, at the heart of the Prosper organization. Dericourt, a French pilot, was responsible for organizing the nighttime shuttling of agents and materiel in and out of France.

He kept his handler, SS Sturmbannfuhrer Karl Baumelburg, head of counter sabotage in France, apprised of all the comings and goings, including the mail that passed back and forth. In return, the Gestapo allowed the operation to unfold which made Dericourt look very good indeed.

MI-6 placed their own man Nicolas Bodington in SOE to vouch for Dericourt and block all efforts by SOE to uncover the traitor. Bodington actually met with Baumelburg on a visit to Paris in 1943. They had known each other before the war. It was Bodington who introduced Baumelburg to Delicourt.

After the war, Dericourt confirmed that he worked for Dansey/Baumelburg. (151)

Why would MI-6 engage in this kind of treason?

Marshall offers this explanation. When Churchill formed a coalition government in 1940, Labour was promised ministerial control of one of the Intelligence Services. As a result, Special Operations Executive (SOE) was carved out of MI-6 and given responsibility for sabotage.

Henri Dericourt

In revenge, Dansey and MI-6 decided to sabotage SOE by placing Dericourt (left) at the heart of its primary network, and instructing him to betray it to the Gestapo.

After Prosper collapsed, Dansey and his superior, Sir Stewart Menzies lobbied to have SOE dissolved. In 1946, it was folded back into MI-6.

Since the network was doomed anyway, they had Illuminatus Winston Churchill summon the heroic Francis Suttill to a private meeting where Churchill confided that D-Day would take place at Calais in September 1943.

They were confident that Gestapo torture methods would suffice to extract this juicy tidbit from Suttill or his confreres. (It did but the Nazis weren't fooled, and actually transferred divisions from France to Russia.)

THE REAL MOTIVE

I don't believe MI-6 would sabotage the war effort over bureaucratic rivalry.

My hypothesis is that the Illuminati infiltrated and controlled the top ranks of *all* the wartime adversaries. The real war was not between the Allies and the Axis but rather between this satanic cult and humanity.

The war was just a pretext to destroy the genetic elite: the natural leaders, the patriots and the idealists. It was a Genocide of the Best, who might in future offer resistance to their plans for Luciferian one-world government.

And who were better than these highly trained SOE agents who were prepared to sacrifice their lives for their country?

SATANIC SLAUGHTER

Henri Dericourt had immense respect for the man he betrayed. He called Francis Suttill "magnificent, strong, young, courageous and decisive, a kind of Ivanhoe." (133)

When Suttill (left) was arrested June 23, 1943, the Nazis showed him Dericourt's file. They knew *everything* about the Prosper Network. All that was left for Suttill was to try to save his agents' lives.

He negotiated a deal whereby, in exchange for treating his agents and the French resistors as prisoners of war, he would reveal where the arms caches were located. He even got Heinrich Himmler to sign the agreement.

Francis Suttill

The Gestapo "swept through the countryside like a scythe through ripening wheat. At first scores, and then hundreds of French men and women were delivered to the prisons around Northern France. At Fresnes, people were crowded, sometimes five or six to a cell." (192)

Of course, the Nazis did not keep their bargain. The Illuminati could not allow Suttill and his kind to live. That was the point of the war. They could not allow them to discover that the Illuminati, including the Prime Minister, had betrayed them and the war effort.

Francis Suttill was hanged at Sachsenhausen concentration camp March 24, 1945.

Andree Borrel, 25, Suttill's second-in-command, was given a lethal injection and then incinerated at Natzweiler in July 1944.

Noor Inyat Khan

Agents Gilbert Norman, John MacAllister, Frank Pickersgill, Johnny Barrett and Robert Benoist were hanged at Gross Rosen in Sept 1944.

Noor Inyat Khan, 30, their radio operator, was kept in chains at Pforsheim and then sent to Dachau where she was shot.

There is no account of the fate of hundreds of other agents, British and French. "Frances Suttill had 144 full agents within his network, but when you count everyone officially connected to Prosper, the number rises to 1015." (192)

After the war, Gestapo officers confirmed that Henri Dericourt was their agent, responsible for the implosion of the resistance networks in Northern France.

Nevertheless, an investigation and trial were stymied by MI-6 and Dericourt continued his career as a pilot. He became involved in the heroin trade and died in a plane crash in Laos, November 22, 1962.

WHO WAS CLAUDE DANSEY?

In June 1943, Patrick Reilly, an assistant to MI-6 Chief Stewart Menzies was shocked when Dansey came bounding in clapping his hands.

"Great news Reilly!" he exclaimed. "One of the big SOE networks in France has just blown up!"

Reilly naturally thought him "a wicked man, undoubtedly." One of his colleagues actually claimed, "Dansey was the only truly evil man I met." (193)

Born in 1874, Dansey had a long distinguished career maintaining the Illuminati (aka "British") Empire.

According to Anton Chaikin, in 1911, William Rockefeller, (JD's brother, President of Standard Oil and founder of Citibank,) employed, "in a private capacity *through his elite social club*, a high-ranking British secret intelligence service officer named Claude Dansey... [to reorganize] the U.S. Army intelligence service into an adjunct of the British secret service."

Claude Dansey

Dansey went on to organize the Freemason executives of the Freemason corporations controlled by the Illuminati bankers into an informal intelligence service called "Z Section."

When MI-6 was mortally wounded by the capture of two agents at Venlo Holland in 1939, Z-Section became the backbone of MI-6.

Thus, we see why MI-6 and the CIA, as well as most intelligence agencies, have always served the Illuminati bankers and their design for one world tyranny called "world governance," "internationalism" and "globalism."

The Illuminati traitors didn't just sacrifice thousands of agents. They endangered the Allied war effort and the lives of millions of soldiers. This leads me to wonder if the Nazi war effort wasn't also sabotaged, and the Allies allowed to succeed in Normandy.

It's hard to speak about treason when the dominant forces in society are engaged in the recolonization of independent democratic nations by a Masonic international banking cartel.

NOTE:

The same thing happened to the Dutch Resistance. See '*"British" Betrayed 56 Dutch Resistance Agents*' on my website.

Nazis Knew About Normandy

Six weeks before D-Day, the Nazis crashed a dress rehearsal for Utah Beach at Slapton Sands in Devon where the terrain was identical to Normandy. Yet, we are supposed to believe they didn't know the invasion was coming in Normandy?

This is additional evidence that wars are orchestrated. They are meat grinders that allow Illuminati leaders on both sides to kill "patriots"—part of their long-term war on humanity.

In his CIA interrogation, Gestapo Heinrich Mueller claimed that an agent alerted them to a massive exercise involving 30,000 men at Slapton Sands.

In the middle of the night, April 27-28, 1944, nine Nazi torpedo boats attacked eight heavily laden LST (tank transports.)

Two were sunk and a third disabled at a cost of about 1000 lives.

"Mistakes" were made by the Nazis. Mueller claims that the Nazis returned to base with the invasion plans taken from the corpse of a US army officer.

"This information which indicated Normandy was the main target was sent on to higher commands but was not acted upon." (*Gestapo Chief: The 1948 Interrogation of Heinrich Meuller*, ed. Gregory Douglas, p. 142)

On the Allied side, the disaster was compounded by *a long list* of highly suspicious "failures."

These include:

1. US naval commanders did not establish liaison with counterparts in Royal Navy.

2. Royal Navy radar picked up movement of the Nazi S-Boats but did not pass it along.

3. Escort Corvette HMS Azalea knew about S-Boats but didn't tell LST's

4. Radio frequencies given to Americans were changed without notice.

5. The one-sided battle had been watched by Royal Artillerymen at Blacknor Fort, high on Portland's western cliffs. The men had the E-boats in their sights, within range, but were ordered not to fire by an American officer, because of the number of Allied personnel fighting for their lives in the water.

6. There was no emergency training so life jackets were not put on properly. They flipped the wearer upside-down with his head in the water.

ON THE BEACH

As many as 500 additional men were killed on the beach April 27 from "friendly fire." Due to a "screw up," the beach was bombarded just as troops were landing. In addition, American soldiers "defending" the beach were using live ammunition and inexplicably did not aim above the heads of the "invading" troops as they were supposed to.

The roughly 1500 American fatalities from both mishaps were thrown into mass graves with a quantity of quicklime to hasten decomposition. After D-Day they were dug up and loaded on to trains:

"Detailed records kept by the station master at Kingsbridge, five miles away, reveal that three trains were secretly loaded with the bodies of GIs under military guard between July and August 1944. The trains, each able to carry at least 100 corpses, 'were crammed with men dug from mass graves', said local rail historian Ken Williams.

The historian's father, George, who served in the Royal Navy during the war, saw the bodies of dozens of men killed by friendly fire washed ashore on the sands.

'He told me how the sea turned red,' Ken said.

The families were told that their loved ones had died in Normandy.

According to historian Charles MacDonald: "It was a disaster which lay hidden from the World for 40 years ... an official American Army cover-up."

Generals Omar N. Bradley and Eisenhower watched "the murderous chaos" and "were horrified and determined that details of their own mistakes would be buried with their men."

"Relatives of the dead men have been misinformed—and even lied to—by their government."

It was "a story the government kept quiet ... hushed up for decades ... a dirty little secret of World War II."

Admiral Donald Moon was made the scapegoat and committed suicide Aug. 5, 1944.

CONCLUSION

Despite the fact that Slapton Sands resembled Normandy, and not the Pas de Calais, we are told that the Nazis didn't know where the invasion was coming. We are fed the line that Hitler slept in on June 6, and when he awoke prevented a concerted response because he was still sure the invasion was coming at Calais.

The Nazis knew about Normandy just as Stalin knew about Barbarossa. Churchill, Stalin, Hitler & FDR were all Freemasons and Illuminati. Both sides in WW2 were sabotaged by these traitors. When are the sheep going to realize that their shepherds are wolves in disguise?

Historian Brought Freemasons to Heel

For a brief moment, during the Nazi occupation of France, (1940-1944), Freemasonry met its nemesis. He wasn't a mighty warrior but rather an intellectual.

Harvard-educated historian, Bernard Fay, a member of the College de France and Director of the National Library, headed an investigative unit that rooted out Freemasons.

Working for Vichy President Philippe Petain and the Gestapo, Bernard Fay compiled a list of 170,000 Freemasons, of whom 989 were sent to concentration camps where 549 were shot. In addition, about 3000 lost their jobs. All Freemasons were required by law to declare themselves to authorities.

Bernard Fay

Fay also seized the secret archives from the Grand Orient in Paris and from Masonic lodges throughout the country. He compiled the information at the Biblioteque National and edited a monthly Journal, *Les Documents Maconniques*.

The lead articles had titles like *Freemasonry and the Corruption of Morals. Freemasonry Against the State,* and *The Masonic Lie.*

In 1943, Fay produced a film entitled *Forces Occultes* which depicted Masonic subversion world wide. The film recounts the life of a young Député (Congressman) who joins the Freemasons in order to relaunch his career. He thus learns of how Illuminati Jewish finance in England and the US used Freemasonry to involve France in a war against Germany. The Director Jean Mamy was executed as a collaborator in 1949. The film with English subtitles can be seen on YouTube.

LIBERATION

Of course, after France was "liberated" by the Masonic powers in 1944, the tables were turned.

Fay was arrested and sent to a concentration camp. When he finally came to trial in 1946, he was unrepentant and defiant.

"My great imprudence was to remain in France from 1940 to 1944, to dream of its regeneration, to consecrate all of my forces to it, to risk my life for it, and to believe in it, " he said.

According to Barbara Will, author of *Unlikely Collaboration*, "perhaps the most striking aspect of his trial was the unwillingness of prosecutors to argue with Fay about the political opinions he still freely expressed."

For example, he stated to the court that "for many years I have considered Masonry a dangerous institution, and on this point for some twenty years I have changed neither opinion nor language. The presence of the Germans had no effect on my ideas." (p. 181)

It is a measure of the vice-like grip Freemasonry has on the liberal mind that Barbara Will, an English professor at Dartmouth College, persists in describing Fay's views as "paranoid" and "bilious."

Fay had access to the secret archives of the Grand Orient. If he said their goal was a Luciferian world tyranny, he was anything but uninformed.

After the war, the French Masonic power investigated more than 300,000 cases of collaboration. 6783 sentences of death were handed down in France and 1600 carried out. In contrast, only 200-300 Nazis were hanged in Germany.

Fay didn't have much faith in his trial. The judge, he noted, was an "Israelite and Freemason." Surprisingly, he was not hanged. On Dec 6 1946, at the age of 54, he was sentenced to hard labor for life.

In 1951, while convalescing in a prison hospital, he escaped to Switzerland with the help of fellow anti-Masons. Two years later, he was pardoned by Charles de Gaulle. Nevertheless, he remained in Switzerland where he continued to teach and write books until his death in 1978.

CONCLUSION

Bernard Fay belongs to the France of the *ancien regime*, the true France of Monarchy, Church and army. This France was rotted out and destroyed by Illuminati Jewish finance and their Masonic lackeys who sponsored the French Revolution.

Modern history is an account of how power and wealth has been transferred from the church and aristocracy to Illuminati finance using liberal and democratic ideals as pretexts.

Nazi Germany had to make a show of being anti-Masonic since its enemies were controlled by Freemasonry. Bernard Fay seized this brief moment to try to save his beloved France. Of course, this window closed quickly since the Nazis also were also financed and controlled by the Illuminati.

War is a Racket

When the United States and England loaned Mexico money in 1903 using its customs revenue as collateral, Illuminati banker Jacob Schiff cabled his English counterpart, Ernest Cassel:

"If they don't pay, who will collect the customs?"

Cassel replied: "Your marines and ours." (*The Life of Otto Kahn*, p. 22)

Marine General Smedley Butler (1881-1940) confirmed that he was "a high class muscle man for Big Business, for Wall Street and the bankers."

In *War is a Racket* (1935) he wrote: "I helped make Mexico, especially Tampico, safe for American oil interests in 1914. I helped make Haiti and Cuba a decent place for the National City Bank boys to collect revenues in. I helped in the raping of half a dozen Central American republics for the benefits of Wall Street. The record of racketeering is long. I helped purify Nicaragua for the international banking house of Brown Brothers in 1909-1912. I brought light to the Dominican Republic for American sugar interests in 1916. In China I helped to see to it that Standard Oil went its way unmolested."

Flash forward to 2011 when NATO fomented and led a "revolution" in Libya, one of only four countries that didn't have a Rothschild central bank. Now Libya does.

They don't call it *imperialism* anymore. They call it "Our mission in Libya." Soldiers aren't mercenaries; they are "missionaries."

WORLD WAR TWO

While we were losing fathers and sons, Allied and Nazi central bankers were huddled together in Basel at the *Bank of International Settlements* financing the Nazis.

The BIS handed over to the Nazis the national treasure of Czechoslovakia, Holland and Belgium to ensure the war could go on. This gold, worth $378 million at the time, was the basis of loans to the Nazis and was never returned.

The BIS accepted and stored Nazi plunder—art, diamonds and precious metals including dental gold and wedding rings from concentration camp inmates.

The US Federal Reserve, the Banks of England, France, Italy, Japan and the Reichsbank were all members of the BIS. The Nazi Reichsbank had most seats but the BIS President was a Rockefeller factotum Thomas H. McKittrick (1889-1970). (Significantly he has no Wikipedia entry.)

"CHANGING THE WORLD" MEANS HAVING A WORLD WAR

Questioned by a US Treasury Dept official in March 1945, McKittrick said that the war had been a charade all along, with Germany taking the fall.

Asked why the BIS worked with the Nazis, he replied, "In the complicated German financial setup, certain men who have their central bankers' point of view, are in very strategic positions and can influence the conduct of the German government..."

Thomas McKittrick

Then he spelled it out, albeit in an euphemism. The war's purpose was to reposition Germany for the banker New World Order:

"McKittrick went on to say that there was a little group of financiers who had felt *from the beginning* that Germany would lose the war; that after defeat they might emerge to shape Germany's destiny. That they would "maintain their contacts and trust with other important banking elements so that they would be in a stronger position in the postwar world to negotiate loans for the reconstruction of Germany."

This quotation is from Charles Higham's mind blowing book, *Trading With the Enemy*, 1983, p. 37.

A *Who's Who* of corporations controlled by these bankers had factories in occupied Europe that underpinned the Nazi war effort and profited handsomely.

Ford, General Motors, Standard Oil and ITT provided the Nazis with essential trucks, airplane engines, materiel and technology, often giving the Nazis preference during shortages. In a telling example, the Allies bombed a ball bearing plant in Germany only to have the stock replaced by a factory in Pennsylvania (via Sweden.)

Higham refers to these bankers as "the fraternity." They are the Illuminati.

An earlier set of bankers masterminded World War One and kept it going. But I think you get the picture. All wars are really waged by the Luciferian central bankers against humanity, i.e. "the goyim."

NOTE: STALIN FUNDED HITLER'S RISE

After Hitler took charge of the fledgling Nazi Party on July 21, 1921, he spent lavishly on propaganda and recruitment. There was no shortage of funds during this critical stage.

Wall Street and German industry funding didn't kick in until the late 1920's. The German Army was financing the Nazis, but didn't account for the seemingly unlimited money at Hitler's fingertips.

In the book, *A Field of Red: The Communist International and the Coming of World War II* (1981, pp. 245-246)) the authors, Anthony Cave Brown and Charles MacDonald report that in 1923, Hitler returned from Zurich "with a steamer trunk stuffed with Swiss Francs and American dollars." There were other mysterious sources of funds in Czechoslovakia, Hungary and Latvia.

After World War II, US Army intelligence officers took an affidavit from industrialist Arnold Rechberg who maintained that General Kurt Von Schleicher told him in 1933 that Stalin had provided Hitler with "substantial funds."

Von Schleicher was head of the Black Reichswehr program before becoming Chancellor and Defence Minister in 1932-1933. The Black Reichswehr program was dedicated to rebuilding the German army, contrary to the provisions of the Versailles Treaty.

According to Walter Schellenberg, Chief of SS Foreign Intelligence, Von Schleicher also advanced Hitler 42 million Reichsmarks during this formative period on instructions from Stalin! (*Memoirs,* p.43) This is probably why the Gestapo murdered Von Schleicher and his wife in the 1934 purge.

Supposedly Stalin hoped Hitler would cause a civil war after which the Communists would take over Germany.

The truth is that Stalin and Hitler were both Illuminati. The Illuminati created Nazism as the dialectical opposite of Communism. In other words, the Illuminati created the "Jewish Marxist" world conspiracy and then created its antithesis, its supposed arch enemy, the Nazi movement, destined be annihilated.

While seemingly opposed to each other, they represented the same group of billionaire Satanists determined to enslave humanity in a world government. While the evil twins duked it out, millions of potential opponents of world government would be killed in a false cause.

In April 1922, the Treaty of Rapallo began a massive German military build-up in Russia designed to evade the provisions of the Versailles treaty. It included training and factories for production of munitions, poison gas, tanks and aircraft. In return for Communist cooperation, the Germans provided know-how and investment. The two prizefighters were training in the same gym for the future world conflagration. Thus, the Illuminati economized.

According to Schellenberg, from 1929 on, Stalin directed the German Communist Party to regard the Social Democrats and not the Nazis as their enemy. There is no question the Communists assisted the Nazis in attaining power. (p.43)

Hitler's First Murder

To say Adolf Hitler was a psycho- path and killer might seem re- dundant, but few know that he murdered his first victim with his own hands. It was swept under the carpet and has yet to see the light of day. Western historians are as determined as Nazis to protect the Fuhrer's reputation.

On Sept 18, 1931, he shot his beloved niece Geli Raubal, 24. The murder was ruled a suicide by the Bavarian Minister of Justice, a political ally.

However, Raubal's body was badly bruised and her nose was broken. An unfinished letter indicated she was leaving her uncle's apartment to go to Vienna. She was buried in a Catholic cemetery that would bar suicides. (*The Münchener Post*, 20th September 1931)

The bisexual love triangle that led to Raubal's murder reveals the true perverted char- acter of a man that many "patriots" still worship.

Although a homosexual, Hitler still enjoyed the company of buxom young blonds and brunettes that fit the Nazi mold. Raubal was the daughter of Hitler's half-sister and cook. Nineteen years his junior, she was an unselfconscious extrovert who brightened every room she entered. Hitler seemed to relax when she was around.

"I love Geli and could marry her," Hitler told his friend Heinrich Hoffman. [But] "I want to remain single. So I retain the right to exert an influence on her circle of friends until such a time as she finds the right man." (Hoffman, *Hitler Was My Friend*, 1955.)

Hitler's rival was his own bisexual, Jewish chauffeur and bodyguard, Emil Maurice. In December 1927, Hitler prevented his niece from marrying Maurice and fired him. The following year, Raubal wrote to Maurice:

"Uncle Adolf is insisting that we should wait two years. Think of it, Emil, two whole years of only being able to kiss each other now and then and always having Uncle Adolf in charge. I can only give you my love and be unconditionally faithful to you. I love you so infinitely much. Uncle Adolf insists that I should go on with my studies." (Dec. 24,1928)

EMIL MAURICE (1897-1972)

In Mein Kampf, Hitler describes a fracas at a beer hall when Communists tried to break up an event. He marveled at how his "storm troopers," although bloodied, "swept the enemy literally out of the hall...at their head, my splendid Maurice."

Maurice was a pioneer member of the SA and later the SS. He and Hess took Hitler's dictation of *Mein Kampf;* and like Hess, Maurice was one of Hitler's lovers. After their release from prison, Maurice became Hitler's personal bodyguard and chauffeur. He accompanied Hitler during the 1934 Purge and personally dispatched people who had become liabilities.

"It is absolutely inconceivable that Maurice was not known as Jewish," Dr. Judith Reisman writes. [Considering] "his appearance, his family, and the very high probability of his circumcision...homosexual lust easily overpowered anti Semitic hate."

When it later emerged that Maurice had a Jewish great grandfather, Hitler made an exemption for him and his family. Since one-sixteenth Jews were already exempt from the Nuremberg Laws, Maurice, who became an SS general, was probably more Jewish than that. Nazi race laws were a matter of expediency, mostly designed to persecute non-Zionist Jews and justify the formation of the Jewish State.

Despite his prowess as a bouncer, Maurice, a watchmaker by training, had an artistic temperament, and played the guitar at Nazi gatherings. Raubal, also a musician, took a fancy to him during her visits to Landsberg Prison in 1924, at age 16. Thus began a passionate romance that blossomed over the years.

HITLER'S DEPRAVITY

For his book, *Hitler and Eva* (1974) Glen Infield interviewed Wilhelm Stocker, a SS Guard at Hitler's apartment. Stocker said that when Uncle Adolf was away, Geli had many suitors.

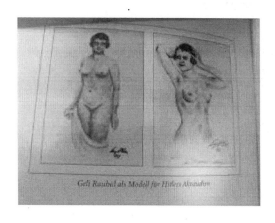

Geli Raubal als Modell für Hitlers Aktzeichen

Because he kept her secrets, Geli told him "that at times Hitler made her do things in the privacy of her room that sickened her but when I asked her why she didn't refuse to do them, she just shrugged and said that she didn't want to lose him to some woman that would do what he wanted."

Gregor Strasser, a Nazi leader who had a fling with Geli said she told him the Nazi dictator forced her to urinate and defecate on him. Strasser was one of the Nazi leaders who met in Hitler's apartment after the murder to decide on a story. Hitler wanted to call it an "accident." But the word had already gone out that Raubel had committed suicide using Hitler's gun.

Strasser was murdered in the 1934 Purge.

Michael Dean reports that after leaving Hitler's service, Maurice sued the Nazi Party for unlawful dismissal and won a tidy sum. He opened a watchmaker shop a few blocks from Hitler's apartment and resumed his affair with Raubal.

Apparently she became pregnant by him and wanted to go to Vienna to have the baby. Hitler was furious at this betrayal and refused permission. When she defied him, he killed her.

It is not clear which betrayal was greater to Hitler since he had feelings for both Raubal and Maurice.

In any case, Hitler's relationship with Maurice proved resilient. Maurice became an SS general and Hitler protected him against rivals resentful of accepting orders from a Jew. Maurice was actually the second member of the SS after Hitler himself, and was considered a founder.

The take-away is that before Hitler indirectly killed millions of people, Jews and non-Jews alike, he bloodied his hands on the young niece he supposedly loved. Millions of people chose to follow a murderer and psychopath. Nothing has changed.

The Fraud that Begets all Others

This fraud is the establishment of the Federal Reserve Bank in 1913.

In 1913, Congressman Charles Lindbergh said: "When the President signs this bill; the invisible government by the Monetary Power will be legalized...The greatest crime of the ages is perpetrated by this banking and currency bill...The day of reckoning is only a few years removed."

Prophetic words.

The establishment of the Federal Reserve Bank in 1913 set off a chain of events that blighted the 20th century and darkens our prospects for the 21st. It began with World War One and the Great Depression, and continues with 9-11 and the wars on Afghanistan, Iraq, Libya, Syria and possibly Iran.

In 1913, America's leaders were bribed and bamboozled by mostly foreign bankers and their US agents. Our leaders committed treason by giving these bankers the power to create money out of thin air backed only by the credit, i.e. taxes, of the American people.

The U.S. government now borrows its own money from international bankers and pays them interest to the tune of $220 billion per annum for the privilege.

If you hoodwinked the United States in this fashion, what would you do?

You would either give the magical power back to its rightful owner, the US government.

Or, you would use it to take over the world, to own everything and to control everyone.

Guess which choice the bankers made?

FDR EXPOSED BY SON-IN-LAW

FDR was a pawn of the Illuminati bankers. This conviction is reinforced by Col. Curtis Dall's book, *FDR: My Exploited Father-in-Law* (1970). Dall, who was married to Franklin Roosevelt's daughter Anna, spent many nights at the White House and often guided FDR around in his wheelchair. He was also a partner at a Wall Street brokerage.

Dall portrays the legendary president not as a leader but as a "quarterback" with little actual power.

The "coaching staff" consisted of a coterie of mostly Jewish handlers (his "brain-trust" like Louis Howe, Bernard Baruch and Harry Hopkins) who represented the international banking cartel. For Dall, FDR ultimately was a traitor manipulated by "World Money" and motivated by conceit and personal ambition.

For Dall, FDR's main perfidy was suppressing information about the Japanese attack on Pearl Harbor at the cost of almost 3,000 lives. He did this because the bankers needed US involvement in WWII, something 85% of Americans opposed. The Japanese had instructions to call off the attack if they lost the element of surprise.

Dall relates a less known but more telling anecdote. In 1956, George Earle, a former governor of Pennsylvania, told him that in 1943 the Nazis tried to surrender. Earle was Naval Attaché in Istanbul when Admiral Wilhelm Canaris, Chief of the German Secret Service, approached him personally.

Canaris told him that the German generals felt Hitler was leading Germany to destruction. They could not accept Roosevelt's policy of "unconditional surrender," but if FDR would offer "honorable surrender," the army was prepared to stage a coup d'etat.

They believed that Russia represented a threat to Western Civilization and they were ready to present a non-Nazi German bulwark against Communist designs in Eastern Europe.

To make a long story short, FDR repeatedly ignored this proposal which could have ended the war in 1943 and saved millions of lives. Canaris and hundreds of other decent German officers were tortured and killed by the Gestapo.

The German generals were naïve about the bankers' secret world government agenda. The bankers' demand for unconditional surrender both prolonged the war and ensured that Soviet Russia would occupy Eastern Europe and become a major world power.

The banking cartel acted as if Communist Russia was their personal fiefdom, which it was. One of FDR's first acts in office was to recognize the Soviet regime. FDR advisers Henry Morgenthau and Harry Dexter White arranged for U.S. treasury printing plates to be sent to Russia so the Communists could print their own US money.

They arranged $8 billion in lend lease aid to Russia *after the war was over.* Col. Dall personally confronted Louis Howe over Russian agents he saw him meeting at the White House.

During the war, Major George R Jordan was a lend lease control officer at Gore Field Air Force base in Great Falls Montana. In 1952, he published a book, *Major Jordan's Diary* in which he revealed that the United States supplied Russia with both the know-how and raw materials for the atomic bomb. Clearly the Rosenberg spy scandal was designed to cover up this high-level treason.

Hitler Tested Nuclear Bombs

Did you know that the Nazis tested three nuclear bombs in 1944 and 1945?

I didn't either and I consider myself reasonably well informed. The information is out there but few people are aware of it.

This, and the fact that details are still kept secret, makes me suspicious.

They don't want anyone to ask this question: "If the Nazis had this game-changing technology, why didn't they perfect and use it?"

Why are they afraid of this question?

Because the answer potentially leads to the "ugly secret" of the Second World War: Hitler was an Illuminati agent. His mission was to lead Germany to annihilation.

Admittedly, these were small "dirty" bombs, combining conventional & nuclear explosives, but they produced shock waves and blinding light. One killed 500 Russian POWs used as guinea pigs. 126,000 barrels of wartime nuclear waste recently were found in a German salt mine.

The question remains. Did Hitler delay or sabotage the development of nuclear weaponry until it was too late? I have not found the "smoking gun" but there are precedents with other war-winning technology.

THE V-2

For example, in 1944 the SS took over the production of the V-2 ballistic missile. Werner Von Braun was actually arrested and charged with delaying its development. He was released when Himmler was shown that Hitler had vetoed Von Braun's requests for additional resources in 1943. (source: *Assignment for Mussolini* documentary film.)

In his memoirs, Albert Speer wrote: "...in the late fall of 1939 Hitler crossed the rocket project off his list of urgent undertakings and thus automatically cut off its labour and materials. By tacit agreement with the Army Ordnance Office, I continued to build the Penemunde installations without his approval—a liberty that probably no one but myself could have taken."

Over 5,000 V-2s were fired on Britain. However, only 1,100 reached Britain. These rockets killed 2,724 people and badly injured 6,000. Obviously, there was a disconnect between the delivery system and the "payload." What if V-2s carried these rudimentary nuclear bombs?

JET FIGHTERS

Germany had jet fighters before anyone else. The Messerschmidt 262 could fly almost twice as fast as conventional airplanes. Germany produced 1400 of these but only 300 were used in battle. They might have thwarted the Allied bombing campaign.

But Hitler had other plans. In his *Memoirs,* Albert Speer claimed that Hitler originally had blocked mass production of the Me 262 before agreeing in early 1944. He rejected arguments that the aircraft would be more effective as a fighter against the Allied bombers, and wanted it as a bomber for revenge attacks.

According to Speer, Hitler felt its superior speed meant it could not be attacked, and so preferred it for high altitude straight flying. (p.363.)

TRAITOR

Hitler's failure to support game-changing technology adds to our suspicion that he was an Illuminati agent and traitor. If Hitler was sincere about conquering the world, what could be more important than nuclear weapons? Especially when they potentially had the missile technology to reach New York City.

One of Hitler's reasons for conquering Russia was to convince Britain to make peace. You'd think a nuclear threat would have done the job faster and easier.

World War Two, all wars in fact, are orchestrated. Hitler's mission was not to win the war, but to extinguish the German spirit. His mission was to discredit everything he represented, especially race and nation.

At that, he was a resounding success.

NOTES

Der Spiegel cites *Hitler's Bombe* by Rainer Karlsch

"Another piece of evidence Karlsch cites is a March 1945 Soviet military espionage report. According to a "reliable source," the Germans "detonated two large explosions in Thuringia." The bombs, the Soviet spies wrote, presumably contained uranium 235, a material used in nuclear weapons, and produced a "highly radioactive effect." Prisoners of war housed at the center of the detonation were killed, "and in many cases their bodies were completely destroyed."

Luigi Romersa, a former war reporter for a Milan newspaper, *Corriere della Sera* visited Hitler in October 1944 and then was flown to an island in the Baltic Sea. Romersa says that he was taken to a dugout where he witnessed an explosion that produced a bright light, and that men wearing protective suits then drove him away from the site, telling him that what he had witnessed was a "fission bomb."

http://www.spiegel.de/international/spiegel/the-third-reich-how-close-was-hitler-to-the-a-bomb-a-346293.htm

Book Five

Hidden History II
(Communism, Freemasonry & Other)

The Red Terror:
Does this Fate Await America?

By James Perloff

The Illuminati bankers responsible for the Bolshevik Revolution and the greatest mass murder in history control the United States today.

Is America on the precipice of another "Red Terror"? There are some disturbing signs:

- Empowered by the "Patriot" Act, the Dept. of Homeland Security could become a Cheka, (secret police) and FEMA's detention camps a gulag archipelago. Last year DHS ordered 1.6 billion rounds of ammunition—enough to kill every American five times.

- Edward Snowden's revelations of NSA spying on everybody.

- Executive Order 13603 gives the President the power to take control of all national resources, public and private, and to impose martial law.

- NDAA 2014 gives the military the power to indefinitely detain American citizens without charge and without trial.

- To facilitate enslavement, the Bolsheviks outlawed gun ownership. Their war on the people was "machine guns against pitchforks." Although Americans aren't disarmed yet, the pressure to ban weapons has never been greater, as staged "lone gunman shooting sprees" have increased. In general, false flag terrorism like 9-11 and Boston Marathon point to a general contempt for the public.

- We aren't razing churches yet, but the media relentlessly demonize Christians while courts increasingly suppress religious expression.

- The US military is trained to view Christians as extremists and potential terrorists.

- The elites' comments about population control reveal a genocidal agenda behind legalized abortion, HAARP, GMOs, and mandatory vaccination.

None of this should surprise us: the Rothschild-Illuminist-Masonic network that ruled in 1917 still rules in 2014.

THE RED TERROR

In 1992, the newspaper *Literaturnaya Rossiya* estimated that Soviet Communism left 147 million dead. Even accepting the more moderate claim of Harvard University Press's *Black Book of Communism*—that Communism murdered "only" 100 million worldwide —what these numbers represent is beyond comprehension. Stalin reportedly said: "One death is a tragedy; a million is a statistic."

By December 1917, the Bolsheviks established their instrument of terror, the Cheka (the KGB's precursor.) Jyri Lina writes: "Lists of those shot and otherwise executed were published in the Cheka's weekly newspaper. In this way it can be proved that 1.7 million people were executed during the period 1918-19. A river of blood flowed through Russia. The Cheka had to employ body counters." (*Under the Sign of the Scorpion.*) In contrast, under the Czars, 467 people were executed between 1826 and 1904.

Trotsky declared: "We must turn Russia into a desert populated by white Negroes upon whom we shall impose a tyranny such as the most terrible Eastern despots never dreamt of... It will be a red tyranny and not a white one.

"We mean the word 'red' literally, because we shall shed such floods of blood as will make all the human losses suffered in the capitalist wars quake and pale by comparison. The biggest bankers across the ocean will work in the closest possible contact with us.

"If we win the revolution, we shall establish the power of Zionism upon the wreckage of the revolution's funeral, and we shall became a power before which the whole world will sink to its knees. We shall show what real power is.

"By means of terror and bloodbaths, we shall reduce the Russian intelligentsia to a state of complete stupefaction and idiocy and to an animal existence... At the moment, our young men in their leather jackets, who are the sons of watchmakers from Odessa, Orsha, Gomel and Vinnitsa, know how to hate everything Russian! What pleasure they take in physically destroying the Russian intelligentsia—officers, academics and writers!..."

(*Memoirs of Aron Simanovich*, cited in Vladimir Stepins in *The Nature of Zionism*, Moskva, 1993, translated from Russian to English by Clive Lindhurst.)

Lina writes: "1,695,604 people were executed from January 1921 to April 1922. Among these victims were bishops, professors, doctors, officers, policemen, gendarmes, lawyers, civil servants, journalists, writers, artists..."

The Bolsheviks considered the intelligentsia the greatest threat to their dictatorship. This sheds light on the Marxist buzzword "proletariat." The Illuminati knew nations are easier to enslave if only peasants and laborers remain. But even the proletariat wasn't spared. The Cheka brutally suppressed hundreds of peasant uprisings and labor strikes, executing victims as "counter-revolutionaries."

Satanic torture often accompanied killings. Many priests were crucified. Some victims had eyes put out, or limbs chopped off, or were otherwise mutilated, while the next victims were forced to watch.

Although Russia had been "the world's granary," over five million died of starvation during the famine of 1921-22 . This wasn't "socialist inefficiency," but genocide from grain confiscation.

In the Holodomor (1931-1932), Stalin murdered seven million Ukrainians, including three million children, by ordering all foodstuffs confiscated as punishment for resisting farm collectivization. Communist brigades went house to house, ripping down walls with axes searching for "hoarded" food.

In Soviet gulags (concentration camps) millions perished. Aleksandr Solzhenitsyn estimated that during Stalin's "great purge" of 1937-38 alone, two million died in gulags.

'CHAMPIONS OF THE PEOPLE'

The Bolsheviks meanwhile lived royally. Lenin, who occupied Grand Duke Sergei Alexandrov's estate, placed 75 million francs in a Swiss bank account in 1920. Trotsky, who lived in a castle seized from Prince Felix Yusupov, had over $80 million in U.S. bank accounts. Top Cheka officials ate off gold plates. Communism was plunder masked by ideological slogans. Money and jewelry were stripped from homes at gunpoint.

Illuminati Jew, Secretary of State John Kerry makes Communist clenched fist salute at NAACP conference in 2008

Lenin and Trotsky repaid their bankster masters. Jyri Lina writes: "In October 1918, Jewish bankers in Berlin received 47 cases of gold from Russia, containing 3125 kilos of gold." The Masonic *Grand Orient de France* refurbished its Paris Lodge with money Lenin sent in 1919. In New York, Kuhn, Loeb received, in the first half of 1921 alone, $102 million in Russian wealth." (*Under the Sign of the Scorpion*, 278)

Bolsheviks were predominantly Jewish—unsurprising given the long linkage of cabalistic Jews to Freemasonry and revolution. (Robert Wilton, *Les Derniers Jours des Romanofs* (1920) I state this objectively, without anti Semitism. I am half-Jewish; my paternal grandparents emigrated from Russia in 1904.

Under Lenin, anti Semitism became a capital offense. The Bolsheviks destroyed 60,000 churches; many became latrines or museums of atheism. Yet Russia's synagogues went untouched.

Jews dominated the Cheka. Lina lists 15 Jewish gulag commandants (*Under the Sign of the Scorpion*, p. 310). The Cheka targeted classes and ethnicities: the "bourgeoisie;" "kulaks" (landowning farmers); and Cossacks, whom the Central Committee declared "must be exterminated and physically disposed of, down to the last man." They tried to eradicate Russian culture, renaming Petrograd and Tsaritsyn after the revolution's psychopaths. In Ukraine, the Bolsheviks seized traditional national costumes. Obliterating nationalism is a precursor to the Illuminati world order.

Despite claims that Jewish dominance ended under Stalin, in 1937, 17 of 27 Presidium members were still Jewish, and 115 of 133 Council of People's Commissars. Stalin did turn against the Zionists in 1949, heavily persecuting Jews during 1952, after which he was poisoned.

From Hungary's Bela Kun, to Germany's Rosa Luxemburg, to America's Rosenbergs (atomic spies), to Karl Marx himself, Jews were undeniably disproportionate among Communists. This observation is not meant to stigmatize Jews. But why are Communism's victims forced to sit in the back of the holocaust bus?

Why are we constantly reminded of Kristallnacht, but never the Bolsheviks' destroying 60,000 churches and murdering over 300,000 priests?

Why was historian David Irving imprisoned for challenging the Shoah's official version ("hate crime"), whereas *New York Times* correspondent Walter Duranty denied the Ukrainian Holocaust and received a Pulitzer Prize?

Why are no Ukrainian Anne Franks honored in films? They are all God's children. The answer to these questions point to the already stated fact: the political descendants of the people responsible for these atrocities control the world today.

CONCLUSION

We need to hope for the best but be prepared for the worst.

With the hindsight of the Gulag, Alexander Solzhenitsyn's wrote:

"And how we burned in the camps later, thinking: What would things have been like if every Security operative, when he went out at night to make an arrest, had been uncertain whether he would return alive and had to say good-bye to his family?

Or if, during periods of mass arrests, as for example in Leningrad, when they arrested a quarter of the entire city, people had not simply sat there in their lairs, paling with terror at every bang of the downstairs door and at every step on the staircase, but had understood they had nothing left to lose and had boldly set up in the downstairs hall an ambush of half a dozen people with axes, hammers, pokers, or whatever else was at hand?...

The Organs would very quickly have suffered a shortage of officers and transport and, notwithstanding all of Stalin's thirst, the cursed machine would have ground to a halt! If...if... We didn't love freedom enough. And even more—we had no awareness of the real situation.... We purely and simply deserved everything that happened afterward."

James Perloff is author of *Truth Is a Lonely Warrior,* an expose of the satanic drive for a New World Order.

Totalitarian Judaism is Template for NWO

"Some may call it Communism, but I call it what it is: Judaism." —Rabbi Stephen Wise

"Anti-Communism is Anti Semitism." —Jewish Voice, July-August 1941.

Recently we learned that the NSA is monitoring our every word and movement.

Since most terrorism is state-sponsored, "security" is just a pretext.

Where does this drive to spy upon and dominate others originate?

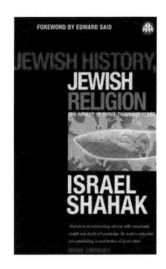

Israel Shahak's book, *Jewish History, Jewish Religion* (1986) provides the answer. This is the way satanic cults behave. From the second century until roughly the eighteenth, Jews were under the heel of their rabbis and wealthy leaders. They were a "closed society... one of the most totalitarian societies in the whole history of mankind." (14-15)

Shahak (1933-2001) was a retired professor of chemistry at the Hebrew University in Jerusalem. He arrived in Israel in 1945, served in the Israeli army and studied Jewish history and religion in Hebrew

His book suggests to me that Cabalist Judaism is the template behind Communism and the NWO, only now everyone is going to be enslaved.

Since the late Roman Empire, Judaism was enforced by physical coercion. Rabbinical Courts ordered fines, flogging, imprisonment and even death for Jews breaking any of the myriad trivial laws governing daily life.

"Jewish women who cohabited with Gentiles had their noses cut off by rabbis...In religious disputes ... 'heretics' had their tongues cut out."

The rabbis and rich Jews were in alliance with the Gentile aristocracy who enforced this tyranny and shared in the spoils. They were arrayed against poor Jews and peasants alike. The rich Jews always flourished in oppressive feudal regimes because, as bureaucrats, bailiffs and tax farmers, they "mediated the oppression" of the peasants.

CLOSED SOCIETY

According to Shahak, classical Judaism was inspired by the image of Sparta as it appears in Plato's *Laws* 942. Judaism adopted the objectives Plato described in the following passage.

"The principal thing is that no one, man or woman, should ever be without an officer set over him, and that no one should get the mental habit of taking any step, whether in earnest or in jest, on his individual responsibility. In peace as in war, he must always live with his eyes on his superior officer...In a word, we must train the mind to not even consider acting as an individual or know how to do it." (Shahak, p.13)

Shahak says "rabbi" and "officer" are interchangeable. In Communism, the sons of rabbis built a new worldly religion that mirrored the fanaticism and oppression of classical Judaism.

After visiting Bolshevik Russia in 1920, Bertrand Russell wrote to Lady Ottoline Morrell: "Bolshevism is a closed tyrannical bureaucracy, with a spy system more elaborate and terrible than the Tsar's, and an aristocracy as insolent and unfeeling, composed of Americanized Jews. No vestige of liberty remains, in thought or speech or action." (*The Autobiography of Bertrand Russell*, paperback ed. 354)

Shahak says Israel is also a "closed society" frankly dedicated to Jewish supremacy and hatred of non-Jews. Jewish culture evinces little honest self-examination lest Judaism's true malevolent character be exposed.

Shahak writes: "Classical Judaism had little interest in describing or explaining itself to its own members ... The first book on Jewish history proper (dealing with ancient history) was promptly banned and repressed by the highest rabbinical authorities... As a consequence, 200 years ago, the vast majority of Jews were totally in the dark about ... Jewish history and Jewry's contemporary state; and they were quite content to remain so....Jewish studies are polemics against an external enemy rather than an internal debate...When a whole society tries to return to totalitarianism, a totalitarian history is written." (p. 20-22)

Similarly, the West is a mini-Israel where mainstream discourse is tightly controlled. Pundits who stray from the party line are fired or forced to atone. We have become Jews under the yoke of Judaism (i.e. Communism.)

According to Shahak, Judaism is concerned with meaningless observances and legalities rather than morality or faith. Communism is Talmudic. The Talmud regulates "every aspect of Jewish life, both individual and social...with sanctions and punishments provided for every conceivable ...infringement of the rules." (Shahak, p. 40)

Far from being monotheistic, the Old Testament implies the existence of many Gods. The Cabala includes many prayers and duties designed to propitiate Satan.

WHAT IS COMMUNISM?

Illuminati insider Christian Rakowski said the illuminati bankers created the Communist state as a "machine of total power."

In the past, due to many factors, "there was always room for individual freedom. Do you understand that those who already partially rule over nations and worldly governments have pretensions to absolute domination? Understand that this is the only thing which they have not yet reached."

"Communism" is devoted to concentrating all wealth and power in the hands of the central banking cartel (the Rothschilds and their allies) by disguising it as State power.

The central banking cartel is the ultimate monopoly. It has an almost global monopoly over government credit. Its object is to translate this into a monopoly over *everything*— political, cultural, economic and spiritual. One world government = Rothschild monopoly = Communism.

CONCLUSION

The New World Order is about inducting humanity into Judaism, which is Satanism disguised as "secularism." A satanic cult is the template governing change. It is the explanation for the invasion of privacy by the NSA, and inventing reality which includes staged "massacres" aimed at disarming Americans.

Organized Jewry is a Trojan Horse for this agenda, but thanks to Freemasonry, most other governments, religions and organizations have also been subverted. Anti Semitism is a red herring designed to deflect blame from the Illuminati bankers and high ranking Freemason onto innocent Jews. Most everyone today is duped, manipulated and compromised.

For most of their history, Jews were held in mental and physical bondage by Judaism. The NWO is a recrudescence of this satanic tyranny not only for Jews but for humanity as a whole. In Shahak's words: "Israel and Zionism are a throw-back to the role of classical Judaism, writ large on a global scale..."

"The road to a genuine revolution in Judaism—to making it humane, allowing Jews to understand their own past, thereby re-educating themselves out of its tyranny—lies through an unrelenting critique of the Jewish religion." (p.74)

Illuminati Banker Unveiled Method of Control

Otto Kahn, (1869-1934) was a partner with Jacob Schiff and Paul Warburg in America's most influential investment bank Kuhn Loeb.

Thus, what he said about the Illuminati Jewish strategy is worth revisiting.

In his book *Geneva Versus Peace* (1937) the Comte de St. Aulaire, who was French ambassador to London from 1920-24, recalled a dinner conversation with Otto Kahn which took place shortly after WWI. This shocking expose has disappeared down the memory hole.

Asked why bankers would back Bolshevism, a system supposedly inimical to private ownership, Kahn tugged on his cigar and explained that the bankers create apparent opposites to "remake the world" according to their specifications:

Otto Kahn

"You say that Marxism is the very antithesis of capitalism, which is equally sacred to us. It is precisely for this reason that they are direct opposites to one another, that they put into our hands the two poles of this planet and allow us to be its axis. These two contraries, like Bolshevism and ourselves, find their identity in the International. [Presumably, he means the Comintern.]

"These opposites ... meet again in the identity of their purpose and end in the remaking of the world from above by the control of riches, and from below by revolution.

"Our mission consists in promulgating the new law and in creating a God... by identifying it with the nation of Israel, which has become its own Messiah....

"Bolshevism is the accelerator and the League is the brake on the mechanism of which we supply both the motive force and the guiding power...We are a League of Nations which contains the elements of all others...Israel is the microcosm and the germ of the city of the future."

People who presume to supplant God are Satanists. Satanists redefine reality and morality, turning them upside down. They seek a worldwide political, economic and cultural monopoly institutionalized in a world government.

This is achieved by a Hegelian dialectical process of creating adversaries (thesis-antithesis) and achieving a synthesis which corresponds to their goals. In the process, potential opponents are eliminated.

COMMUNISM-CAPITALISM

In the *Red Symphony* revelation, insider Christian Rakovsky showed how Communism and Capitalism were part of this dialectical process. In each case, the Illuminati Jewish banking cartel controls all wealth and power.

"In Moscow there is Communism: in New York capitalism. It is all the same as thesis and antithesis. Analyze both. Moscow is subjective Communism but [objectively] State capitalism. New York: Capitalism subjective, but Communism objective. A personal synthesis, truth: the Financial International, the Capitalist Communist one. 'They.' "

In the USSR, the State owned the corporations and the bankers owned the State, i.e. State Capitalism. The US also has Communism objectively because the same bankers control most of the corporations, and the corporations control the State.

Of course, this is consistent with the famous 1954 statement by Rowan Gaither, President of the Ford Foundation to Reece Committee investigator Norman Didd: "We operate here under directives which emanate from the White House... The substance of the directives under which we operate is that we shall use our grant making power to alter life in the United States such that we can comfortably be merged with the Soviet Union."

Kahn says Jewish nationalism dissolves all others: "We are a League of Nations which contains the elements of all others. It is the fact which qualifies us to unite the nations around us. We are accused of being the agent which dissolves them. **It is only at points which are impervious to that synthesis of national elements, of which ours is both the example and the means, that we act as dissolvent.** Israel is the microcosm and the germ of the City of the Future."

FINALLY

We are in the final stages of a long-term conspiracy by Cabalist Jewish bankers and their Masonic lackeys to erect a world police state, and to control us by fraud and force (their watchwords.) This has been achieved by a contrived "dialectical process" best exemplified by World War Two and the Cold War where they fabricated and financed the adversaries.

Domestically, the illuminati dialectic is mirrored by George Soros who funds the left, and the Koch Brothers who fund and control the right. Both are Illuminati Jews. The radical Left and Islam are also funded by corporations through the Tides foundation. You can bet that this funding extends to media control through ownership or advertising. It also extends to universities, foundations and think tanks.

Mass protests like Occupy Wall Street are part of this false dialectic. This would be real if they demanded 1. Nationalizing the Fed, creation of debt-free currency and disowning that portion of the national debt created by book entry. 2. Independent investigation of 9-11 and prosecution of those responsible for the attack and the cover-up. 3. All national political campaigns be publicly funded. For the price of one battle cruiser, we could have real democracy. 4. Media monopolies be broken up. 5. NATO (Rothschild) Interventions be stopped. As is, popular resistance is a banker Punch and Judy Puppet Show.

I hope I'm wrong but I suspect Putin's Russia is part of this strategy of control. Remember Hitler was also Illuminati-sponsored. Russia has a Rothschild central bank. You need two sides to justify war and arms expenditures.

The 2014 conflict over Ukraine is really a dispute between two Masonic branches. The Russian branch refuses to accept a subordinate role, i.e., it refuses to be exploited by the Zionist branch (US, UK, EU.) It wants equal status with the West in the NWO and to restore some of the USSR's former power and glory.

Geneva Versus Peace Online:

http://ia701207.us.archive.org/11/items/LesDerniersJoursDesRomanof/Geneva-Versus-Peace.pdf

See online: *US Corporate Elite Funds radical Left and Islam*

http://www.henrymakow.com/americas_corporate_elite_funds.html

The Zionist Billionaires
Who Control Politics

The best way to control the opposition is to lead it—Lenin

The plan, I think, is the old one of world dominion in a new form. The money-power and revolutionary power have been set up and given sham but symbolic shapes ('Capitalism' or 'Communism') and sharply defined citadels ('America' or 'Russia'). Such is the spectacle publicly staged for the masses. But what if similar men, with a common aim, secretly rule in both camps and propose to achieve their ambition through the clash between those masses? I believe any diligent student of our times will discover that this is the case.—Douglas Reed

Bloomberg News has a story on how the Zionist Koch brothers bankrolled the campaigns of Governors (like Scott Walker) who are cutting union powers. Whether we agree or not, these billionaires continue to define the political discourse in Left-Right terms when they should be defined as people versus the Illuminati both Left and Right disguise.

The Sept 20, 2010 issue of *The New Yorker* had a profile of David and Charles Koch, entitled "The billionaire brothers who are waging a war against Obama."

According to the article by Jane Mayer, the Koch's bankroll a plethora of Libertarian and "right-wing" lobbies, think tanks and foundations which, in turn, fund and direct the "grass roots" Tea Party movement.

"The anti-government fervor infusing the 2010 elections represents a political triumph for the Kochs," she writes. "By giving money to educate, finance, and organize Tea Party protesters, they have helped turn their private agenda into a mass movement."

Mayer neglects to mention that the Kochs are crypto Jews; instead she tries to give them a "goy gloss."

Patriarch Fred Koch, a founding member of the John Birch Society, was a "real John Wayne type." He was the son of a "Dutch" printer who emphasized "rugged pursuits.' He took his four sons "big game hunting in Africa" and made them do "farm labor at the family ranch."

Surprising then to learn that Fred and his sons are on lists of Jewish billionaires, and "free-enterprise-Fred" made his fortune building refineries for the genocidal Communist Jewish dictator Josef Stalin in the 1930s. The Birch Society was an Illuminati Jewish front.

Liberals whinge about these nefarious "red necks" who oppose Obamacare and climate change, and lobby for less taxes and government interference. But that's not the real story here.

The real story is that Jane Meyer works for another Illuminati Jewish billionaire, publisher Sam Newhouse. Her job is to create the illusion of free democratic discourse. Between the Sam Newhouses and George Soros' on the Left, and the Koch's and the Rupert Murdochs on the Right, a half dozen Illuminati (Masonic) Jewish billionaires are able to define political discourse in America.

So while we're busy arguing about government intervention, we ignore the long list of things these billionaires apparently agree on: the Masonic NWO, Masonic Jewish power, Israel, 9-11, the bogus war on terror, the wars in Iraq and Afghanistan, trillion dollar bank bailouts, liberal immigration policy and "equal rights" for gays and lesbians, i.e. undermining marriage and family by promoting homosexual norms. You can bet they also agree on the private money creation which cost the US taxpayer $220 billion in interest in 2013 alone, or 6% of tax revenue. You can also be sure they agree on world government to ensure this never changes.

This is why crack dealer and bathhouse boy Barack Obama is our President. Why the "conservative" alternative was the Zionist-created Mormon Mason Mitt Romney. The billionaires of Zion are laughing up their sleeves at the dumb goyim.

THE KOCH EMPIRE

Koch Industries is the second-largest private company in America after Cargill.

According to *The New Yorker,* "the company has grown spectacularly since their father, Fred, died, in 1967, and the brothers took charge. The company expanded at an unreal rate: its revenues increased from $100 million in 1966 to $100 billion in 2008—that's 1,000-fold growth. The Koch's operate oil refineries in Alaska, Texas, and Minnesota, and control some four thousand miles of pipeline. Koch Industries owns Brawny paper towels, Dixie cups, Georgia-Pacific lumber, Stainmaster carpet, and Lycra, among other products."

According to researcher Yasha Levine, part of this growth was fueled by corruption: "William Koch, the third brother who had a falling-out with Charles and David back in the '80s over Charles' sociopathic management style, appeared on *60 Minutes* in November 2000 to tell the world that Koch Industries was a criminal enterprise:

"Charles Koch's racket was very simple," explained William. "With its extensive oil pipe network, Koch Industries' role as an oil middleman—it buys crude from someone's well and sells it to a refinery—makes it easy to steal millions of dollars worth of oil by skimming just a little off the top of each transaction, or what they call "cheating measurements" in the oil trade. According to William, wells located on federal and Native American lands were the prime targets of the Koch scam."

It is estimated they stole $230 million.

FRED KOCH AND THE JOHN BIRCH SOCIETY

Rich Illuminati Jews and Masons not only created Communism in Russia; they created anti-Communism in the USA.

Fred Koch (1900-1967) was a chemical engineer who invented a new process for refining oil. Supposedly, he was shut out of the US by the Rockefellers and had to go to work for Stalin. He built many refineries in Soviet Russia and trained Russian engineers to operate them. Supposedly, he became disillusioned with Communism and became a founding member of the John Birch Society in the 1950s.

The trouble is that according to the 1964-65, Edition of *Who's Who*, this militant "anti-Communist" went on building refineries in Russia and Eastern Europe well into the 1960s. Moreover, the John Birch society was founded by members of the Council on Foreign Relations, many of whom were Masons, and staffed by former Communist writers.

For example, the founder Robert Welch had been a member of the Communist front "League for Industrial Democracy." William Grede, for many years Chairman of the Executive Council of the JBS was a Fed banker. Robert Love, member of the Governing Council was a 32nd Degree Mason. William Macmillan was a member of the CFR. Writers Eugene Lyons and Harold Varney used to work for the Communist "Workers World." (Helen Peters, *Is the JBS Subversive?* July 1970)

Ralph Epperson was on their speaker's bureau. But they expelled him from the JBS when he mentioned Freemasonry in one of his speeches somewhere. The JBS does not want Freemasonry mentioned.

According to Eustace Mullins, the founder Robert Welch was a 32nd Degree Mason.

POLITICS IS A CHARADE

Illuminati insider Harold Rosenthal explained how they pit labor (Left) versus management (Right):

"In modern industry ... capital, which force we represent, is [at] the apex. Both management and labor are on the base of this triangle. They continually stand opposed to each other and their attention is never directed to the head of their problem."

"At first, by controlling the banking system we were able to control corporation capital. Through this, we acquired total monopoly of the movie industry, the radio networks and the newly developing television media. The printing industry, newspapers, periodicals and technical journals had already fallen into our hands. The richest plum was later to come when we took over the publication of all school materials. Through these vehicles we could mold public opinion to suit our own purposes. The people are only stupid pigs that grunt and squeal the chants we give them, whether they be truth or lies."

Thus the Illuminati have a monopoly over our minds. By controlling both Left and Right, education and the mass media, the Masonic Jewish billionaires ensure that the masses are tractable. As the late great Alan Stang warned, the Tea Party is a psy-op meant to channel the Patriot Movement into the Left VS Right matrix.

Politics is like a House League in sports. The different teams all are Masons or are beholden to them. Thus, there's little chance of democratic change. Anyone who wants to play must abide by the "rules."

It's amusing to see "progressives" rail against the Tea Party and their sponsors. They are as much billionaire puppets as the rednecks they condemn. George Soros' puppets instead of Charles Koch's.

See also on my web site: *Proof Libertarianism is an Illuminati Ploy* by Anthony Migchels

"House of Cards:"
Media Mask Masonic Control

I devoured the second season of *House of Cards* like a box of chocolates. I was surprised to learn that the main character, Francis Underwood, played by Kevin Spacey, is a Freemason. What? You didn't see that?

Neither did I. That's my point. Most congress critters belong to this satanic secret society, but you can watch a series that pretends to unveil Washington politics, and not hear the word "Freemason" mentioned once. (The second season also avoids any mention of Jews and Zionist influence.) Actually there is one Masonic reference, the upside down flag

Cognitive dissonance

in the series logo is a Masonic sign of distress, perhaps a wink to people in the know.

Search "How many congressmen are Freemasons?" on Google and you'll find practically no information. Just a story about the honest Congressional stenographer who broke down in October, 2013, and blurted out about Freemasons and the devil controlling Congress. There's no reminder of the 2004 Bush-Kerry election where both men confessed to being members of the Masonic Skull and Bones, but couldn't talk about it because "it's a secret."

How gullible can people get? Both Presidential candidates belong to a secret society. Nothing happening here. Move along folks. The watchdogs of freedom, the mass media, didn't even tug on their leashes. (Another deception in *House of Cards* is that the mainstream media actually pursues the truth.)

The pioneer work on the subject of US Freemasonry is a 1996 book entitled *Unholy Alliances* by a Florida dentist, James Wardner... Here are 10 facts about Masonic control of Congress and the Judiciary in the recent past. You can bet that things have only gotten worse.

1. Wardner lists 75 congressmen who were Freemasons in the 1980s but there were probably many more. These included both liberals and rednecks: Bob Dole, Jesse Helms, Mark Hatfield, Lloyd Bentsen, Robert Byrd and Arlen Specter. Presidents who were Freemasons include: George Washington. James Monroe. Andrew Jackson, James Polk. James Buchanan. Andrew Johnson, James Garfield, William McKinley. Theodore

Roosevelt, Howard Taft, Warren Harding, FDR, Harry Truman, LBJ, Gerald Ford, G.H.W. Bush, Bill Clinton, George W. Bush and Barack Obama.

In 1987, Freemason and Senator Alan Simpson bragged that "Forty one members of the Federal Judiciary are presently Masons." (67)

3. Masonic authority Henry Clausen boasted in the early 90s that Masons include "14 Presidents and 18 Vice-Presidents of the United States, a majority of the Justices of the United States Supreme Court, of the Governors of the States, of the members of the Senate, and a large percentage of Congressmen. Five Chief Justices of the United States were Masons and two were Grand Masters." (67) Wardner adds that these two Grand Masters were John Marshall and Earl Warren who effectively ended prayer in schools.

4. This is nothing new since Thaddeus Stevens, Pennsylvania's delegate to the 1830 Anti Masonic Convention noted that "though but one hundred thousand of [Americans] are Freemasons, yet almost all the offices of high profit and high honor are filled with gentlemen of that institution."

5. Freemasons in Dwight Eisenhower's Cabinet included the Secretary of State, the Secretary of Defense, the Secretary of the Interior, Secretary of Commerce and Ike's Chief of Staff, Sherman Adams.

6. Apart from President Truman himself, Masons in his Cabinet include the Secretary of State, Commerce, Defense, Attorney General and his four Supreme Court appointments. Truman said, "Although I hold the highest civil honor in the world, I have always regarded my rank and title as a past Grand Master (of the Grand Lodge of Missouri) as the highest honor that has ever comes to me." (61-63)

7. FDR was an ardent Scottish Rite Mason. Masons in his Cabinet included the Vice President, the Secretary of the Treasury, War, Commerce, Attorney General and six of his eight Supreme Court appointments. No surprise that *Empire State Mason* boasted in Feb 1953 that if "World Masonry ever comes into being, historians will give much credit to when FDR was President."

8. President Warren Harding (1921-1923) was a Mason and by 1923, 300 of the 435 members of the US House of Representatives (69%) and 30 of the 48 Senators (63%) were Freemasons. In 1929, 67% of Congress were Masons. (p. 56)

9. Leon de Poncins wrote that the First World War was contrived to create a Masonic Super State in the form of the League of Nations. The Treaty of Versailles deliberately led to revolutionary unrest in Germany, the Civil War in Spain and finally to the Second World War. "It is a frightening thought that an occult organization ...can direct the course of European politics, without anyone being aware of the fact." (p.55)

10. In 1834, the Massachusetts Legislature concluded that Freemasonry was "a distinct independent government within our own government, and beyond the control of the laws of the land by means of its secrecy and the oaths and regulations which its subjects are bound to obey." (p.54)

Wardner concludes that the tentacles of the Masonic lodge pervade society. There are at least 160 different organizations that require its members to be Masons, including the higher ranks of the US military.(p.70) In 1950, Masons estimated that nearly 10 million adults were directly linked to Freemasonry through the nation's three million Master Masons.

CONCLUSION

Clearly, Freemasonry is a conspiracy to give its member unfair and even criminal advantages. This is the real party and we're not invited. Instead we have an ersatz of democracy, freedom and culture.

No wonder vapid white men with pinched pussy faces run the country; no wonder people are so artificial and false and we have constant scandal, corruption and war.

Clearly, the whole Gentile establishment is complicit in the subversion of humanity. Anti Semitism is a diversion. But how many of the Internet anti Semites ever mention Freemasonry? Of course the Jewish leadership is also guilty. Almost all leadership is. How much easier for Freemasons to slough off the blame on ordinary Jews who are just as clueless as ordinary Gentiles.

Clueless because they watch *House of Cards* and think it portrays political reality.

Must See YouTube lectures by Dr. Wardner:

http://www.youtube.com/playlist?list=PLF776EEC5D6A6A3C0

Communist Takeover of US Began Long Ago

In 2005, KGB generals were given important positions in the Dept. of Homeland Security run by Lenin look-alike Zionist Michael Chertoff.

I described this development as the "stealth Communist takeover of the USA. We don't recognize what has happened because we think Communism was an idealistic but discredited "working class" experiment, tried mainly in Russia and China.

The Illuminati bankers created Communism to harness the working class to their program of a comprehensive world dictatorship (now known as "globalization.") The Illuminati and Communists are Masonic secret societies that celebrate the same anniversary, May 1, 1776 and share the same satanic symbols. Coincidentally, "Chertoff" means "devil" in Russian.

AN EX-COMMUNIST SPEAKS

Many high-ranking former-Communists risked their lives to alert their fellow Americans. In her shocking book *School of Darkness* (1954) Bella Dodd describes how Communists morph into liberals, feminists and socialists, and myriad front groups (identifiable by the words like "human rights," "equality," "international" and "peace") to divide and subvert society. (Search Makow, *Bella Dodd's Exposure of Communism*.)

In *Return to My Father's House* (1972), Maurice Malkin provides more revelations which I will list below. He was a leader of the American Communist Party (CPUSA) in the 1920s and 30s, and part of the Soviet secret service (GPU.) When he left the CPUSA, he testified before Congress and suffered a stabbing attack as a result.

Malkin, a Jew, had been involved in the Bolshevik underground in Russia. His older brother Joseph, a devoted Marxist later killed by Stalin, taught him that by overthrowing the Czar, workers could "eliminate all injustices and create a heaven on earth." All problems were due to the "class war."

The dogma of the duped went like this: "The capitalist bourgeoisie owned everything yet the working class did all the work. The mission of the working class was to take through violence what rightly belonged to them...[Only Marxism] could relieve the human race of brutality, discrimination [i.e. anti Semitism] and injustice, of hunger, poverty and the drudgery that filled the lives of ordinary working people everywhere." (27-29)

Malkin immigrated to New York and took the ersatz religion of a workers' heaven on earth with him. Lev Bronstein (Leon Trotsky), a close family friend taught him "bullets, not ballots would liberate the workers." (50)

"ELITE" SUBVERSION

Thus, for most of the last century, the United States has tolerated a party openly dedicated to the violent overthrow of the US government and the enslavement of its people.

This party, the CPUSA, was funded and directed by a hostile foreign government. It engaged in industrial and military espionage, trained guerrilla units on American soil, forcibly took over unions, raided their treasuries and controlled whole industries. It slandered, harassed and killed opponents; bribed police and judges and infiltrated the military.

Yet all the while, our highest elected officials defended it as a harmless idealistic enterprise. "Some of my best friends are Communists," FDR famously said.

Malkin reports that Adlai Stephenson (as Assistant to Navy Secretary Knox) sabotaged efforts to curtail Communist activities. In 1956, Eisenhower "liquidated all anti-subversive sections in the Immigration Dept. and halted deportation and prosecution of known alien Communists. [He] stopped prosecutions of Communists under the Smith Act, giving the Party a chance to regroup and organize new mass fronts." (191)

The Liberal media marginalized and ridiculed as "right wing fanatics" people who warned of the Communist threat. To this day, people don't accept that the Rosenbergs were indeed Russian spies. The House Un-American Activities Committee is portrayed as a "witch hunt."

Communism is nothing but a sugarcoated goon squad for the Illuminati bankers. Malkin reports that the CPUSA even had a formal alliance with the Mafia, another Masonic sect.

Moscow provided the Mafia with heroin to sell in the USA. The Mafia "lent" money to the Communist Party, provided muscle for taking over the labor movement, and disposed of enemies or members who woke up. (One Communist leader, Juliet Stuart Poyntz, was kidnapped, killed at sea and thrown overboard.) The Mafia also distributed counterfeit US dollars printed in Moscow.

Following Stalin's example, American Communists robbed banks, calling it "expropriation." In his book, Left Wing Communism (Vol. 30) Lenin counseled: "Communists are to be ready to cheat, lie, perjure and do everything possible to gain their ends." Thus, when evidence of their skulduggery surfaced, it was little matter to denounce it as a "forgery" and smear the messenger.

The Communist Party infiltrated the Negro Civil Rights movement and got Ralph Abernathy and Martin Luther King to work with their Moscow-trained Negro mercenaries. W.E.B. BuBois and Ralph Bunche were among their "black" front men but they hardly had any black followers. American Negroes were too patriotic.

"The Reds realized that the only way to weaken our country is by dividing it through anarchy and chaos," Malkin writes.

They had more luck with women. The Communist attitude to women is instructive since second-wave feminism is Communist in origin. Feminism is recycled "class war" adjusted for gender. (See *Red Feminism* on my website.)

Young female members were used on the waterfront to recruit sailors and longshoremen and bring them to party functions. "Girls would always be found in the Communist summer camps doing the party's bidding plus offering a little enjoyment on the side. The Party believes that the only laws and morals are Communist morals. ....Communists do not believe in family institutions or morals so everything is free." (239)

The Communists had a department dedicated to "the destruction of the morale of the American people by undermining their faith in their moral and social patterns." (71) You can bet that something like this is behind same-sex marriage.

CONCLUSION

When Hitler and Stalin made a pact in 1939, Malkin quit the Party. He devoted the rest of his life to defending American institutions, working for the U.S. Dept. of Justice from 1948-1956. He realized belatedly that his religious father's condemnations of Communism were correct, hence the title of the book.

Although this book was published in 1972, the Communist (Satanist) conspiracy is more active than ever. Conscious and unconscious agents abound especially in homosexual, feminist, socialist, zionist, neo-con and liberal circles. "Human Rights" commissions, "employment equity" and diversity officers are modern political commissars. "Hate speech" is censorship applied selectively. "Politically correct" is a longtime Communist Party term.

Once, a lesbian running for the head of my English Department gave a long speech saying she believed in "peace." What did this have to do with English literature? "Peace" is code for the end of resistance to the NWO, i.e. Communist global tyranny. She was elected Chair of the Department.

The New World Order is full of empty platitudes about "peace" "tolerance" and "human rights." But in light of the NWO's murderous Communist (and Fascist) pedigree, these platitudes are not convincing.

Western elites (including the intelligentsia) suffer from a peculiar death wish. We would be slaves already were it not for the fact that ordinary Americans own firearms. This, the Internet, and the inherent self-destructiveness of evil, are my main reasons for hope.

Rosa Parks & Our Communist Corporate Elite

Rosa Parks was not a simple seamstress whose lonely act of defiance in December 1955 sparked the beginning of the Civil Rights Movement. In fact, she was a trained Communist Party (CPU-SA) activist.

Her refusal to move to the back of the bus wasn't a spontaneous gesture, but a provocation organized by her employer, the National Association for the Advancement of Colored People (NAACP.)

In 2005, Rosa Parks' body lay in state under the Capitol Rotunda; an honor accorded only 29 times in US history, to people like Abraham Lincoln, John Kennedy, and most recently Ronald Reagan.

Rosa Parks' refusal to go to the back of the bus was a typical Communist publicity stunt.

This treatment illustrates how the American public is routinely lied to and betrayed by its political leaders and mass media. The *New York Times* obituary said her arrest "turned a very private woman into a reluctant symbol and torch bearer." President Clinton said her action "ignited the most significant social movement in American history."

While I support the ostensible aims of the Civil Rights movement, I have to ask, given its Communist sponsorship, "What is the hidden agenda?"

THE PATTERN OF ELITE DECEPTION

The portrayal of Rosa Parks as an ordinary citizen triggered my alarm bell. Betty Friedan, the "founder" of feminism and long-time Communist activist was also depicted as an average mother and housewife. Thanks to a well informed Internet forum, *Daily Kos. com*, I quickly discovered Rosa Parks began working as a secretary for the NAACP in 1943 and still held that position when she was arrested.

In July 1955, five months before the famous incident, she attended "Highlander Folk School" in Monteagle, Tennessee. Myles Horton and James Dombroski, both Communist Party members, started this school in 1932 to train Communist subversives. Betty

Friedan was another alumnus. The school was cited for subversive activities and closed by the State of Tennessee in 1960.

Highlander Folk School

Rosa Parks and many others had defied the bus segregation laws on numerous occasions since the 1940s. The Montgomery bus boycott was planned in advance. Martin Luther King was brought in to lead it. Rosa Parks was chosen to kick it off. (See Aldon Morris, *The Origins of the Civil Rights Movement*)

A member of *Daily Kos.com* who works for the CPUSA newspaper said a CPUSA executive member told him Rosa Parks was a member of the Communist party. (This is something Communists don't advertise.) David Horowitz writes in *Radical Son* that his Communist Party parents also claimed Rosa was a member.

The testimony of numerous defectors leaves no doubt the US Communist Party was directed from Moscow. Despite what idealistic dupes ("useful idiots") like Parks and Friedan thought, its goal is to subjugate the American people.

The Women's Liberation Movement was patterned on the Civil Rights Movement. They are off-the-shelf Communist psycho-social operations. To be effective, they must appear to reflect a popular groundswell rather than an elite agenda imposed from above.

While these movements may have rectified some genuine injustices, their hidden purpose was to destabilize American society.

NAACP & MARTIN LUTHER KING: THE DARK SIDE

Banker Jacob Schiff, the Rothschild's agent in the US, and later the funder of the Bolshevik Revolution, started the NAACP in 1909.

In his book, *My Awakening* David Duke paints a picture of the NAACP that suggests a typical Banker-Communist front . (pp.282-284) Although founded in 1909, it didn't have a black president until the 1970s. Until then, its president and board were mainly drawn from the ranks of Communist Jews.

Martin Luther King may have been a typical front man. Privately, he declared himself a Marxist. He attended the Highlander School and his personal secretaries Bayard Rustin and Jack O'Dell were Communists. Another Communist, Stanley Levinson, wrote his speeches and managed his fund raising.

King's integrity has also been called into question. King plagiarized large sections of his doctoral thesis. He also had liaisons with white prostitutes, which were taped by the FBI and confirmed by his successor Ralph Abernathy. (*And the Walls Came Tumbling Down*, 1989)

CONCLUSION

The sanctification of the Communist Rosa Parks proves again that the American political and cultural elite is irredeemably corrupt.

Social change doesn't take place in the USA unless the central bankers and their media assets sponsor it. Their long-term plan for world dictatorship is disguised as spontaneous grassroots revolt.

Increasingly as traitors are treated as heroes, the mass media, government and education reveal that success today requires complicity in the destruction of our country and its Christian heritage.

FIRST COMMENT FROM RICARDO, A BLACK READER:

Before the civil rights movement there were many economically viable black communities. Segregation forced black people especially black man to take care of business. The civil rights movement destroyed that.

Harry Belafonte said Martin Luther King was killed after he realized that he was a pawn, that he was duped. Martin Luther King saw that de-segregation would impoverish the black community. Now there is no black community; we have no real leadership and we have no collective economic power. Put together we have a lot of money but we are the targets of corporations. This is what the civil rights movement has brought us. And the Nation of Islam was started by the Jesuits to foment race war.

Nelson Mandela Was a Terrorist

Terrorism is not terrorism when the Illuminati Jewish banking cartel is behind it.

From 1961-1990, the Illuminati-sponsored African National Congress waged a terrorist war against the Apartheid government of South Africa. It was characterized as a "people's struggle" in the Zionist-controlled mass media.

However, when the Palestinians employ terror against the Apartheid regime of Israel, they are "terrorists." Never mind that Israel was built on Zionist terror against the British. When the Illuminati bankers or their shills use it, terrorists are "freedom fighters" and "activists." (Syria today is another example.)

Nelson Mandela and Joe Slovo in Moscow give the clenched fist salute in front of the blood-drenched Hammer and Sickle flag of Illuminati Jewish Bolshevism.

In South Africa during the 1960s and 70s, barely a week went by without terrorism—dynamite at a fuel depot, a car bomb outside Air Force headquarters in a city center. The ANC's guerrilla force known simply as MK, or more formally as *Umkhonto we Sizwe* translated «Spear of the Nation» was founded in 1961 by Nelson Mandela and his handler, the Communist Jew Joe Slovo.

At first, the targets were infrastructure but two decades later MK was killing civilians without compunction—grenades would be bowled into a hamburger joint, or a trip-wired limper mine planted in an arcade—and Mandela did not object.

"Notable among these attacks were the January 8, 1982 attack on the Koeberg nuclear power plant near Cape Town, the Church Street bombing on May 20, 1983, killing 19, and the June 14 1986 car-bombing of Magoo›s Bar in Durban, in which 3 people were killed and 73 injured." (Wikipedia)

Of course, Mandela had been in jail since 1963 when captured in a raid on MK headquarters at a farm outside Johannesburg. The ANC was funded and run by Communist Jews who in turn were shills for the Illuminati bankers. Mandela posed as a farmhand.

The farm was purchased and run by the Jewish Communist Arthur Goldreich.

In 1985, when the government offered to release Mandela if he would repudiate terrorism, he refused. In 1990, he was let out anyway and vowed the MK would continue to wreak havoc. It was not necessary.

The government was ready to negotiate a handover of power. In 1994, Mandela and F.W. de Klerk shared a Nobel Peace Prize. Queen Elizabeth II in her 1996 Christmas message hailed Mandela as a great statesman. (The account of MK terror above is indebted to Philip Gourevitch's review of the novel *Absolution* in *The New Yorker*, April 30, 2012, p.70)

ANC IS A COMMUNIST JEWISH FRONT

Thanks to Michael Hoffman II, we know: "The African National Congress (ANC) in South Africa was guided by two Communist Jews, Albie Sachs, "one of its foremost intellectuals"(*London Sunday Times,* August 29, 1993) and Yossel Mashel Slovo (Joe Slovo, 1926-1995.)

Slovo was born in a shtetl in Lithuania and grew up speaking Yiddish and studying the Talmud. He joined the ANC's terrorist wing, the *Umkhonto we Sizwe,* in 1961 and eventually became its commander. He was named Secretary General of the South African Communist Party in 1986. ("Joe Slovo," *Jewish Chronicle,* January 13, 1995.)

Slovo had been the "planner of many of the ANC terrorist attacks, including the 1983 car bomb that killed 19 people and injured many others... Slovo, who had traveled to the Soviet Union many times, was awarded a Soviet medal on his 60th birthday...Slovo was a dedicated Communist, a Marxist Leninist without morality of any kind, for whom only victory counts, whatever the human cost, whatever the bloodshed...Slovo disputes little of his image as 'the Communist mastermind' behind the ANC's armed struggle.

'Revolutionary violence has created the inspirational impact that we had intended, and it has won for the ANC its leading position,' Slovo said." (*"Rebel Strategist Seeks to End Apartheid,"* L.A. Times, Aug. 16, 1987, p. 14.) When Nelson Mandela's ANC took over South Africa, Slovo was named Minister of Housing.

COMMUNISM IS A RUSE

Wrapped in bogus idealism, Jewish social & political activism largely serves the Illuminati's secret satanic agenda. Jewish activists are dupes or opportunists. The ANC, like Communism in general, deceived the masses into overthrowing the government and installing Illuminati puppets like Nelson Mandela.

The plight of blacks in South Africa is much worse under the "peoples' government." The number of people living on $1 a day doubled from two to four million. The unemployment rate doubled to 48% from 1991 to 2002. (It was 28% in 2011.)

In 2006, only 5,000 of the more than 35 million black South Africans earned more than $60,000. A quarter of the entire population lived in shacks without running water or electricity. A quarter have no access to clean water. 40% have no telephone.

The HIV/AIDS/TB infection rate is 20%. Life expectancy dropped by 13 years. 40% of schools have no electricity.

Where is the ANC'S concern for the people? Obviously it was a ruse that enabled the bankers to gain control over South Africa's resources, just as they took over Russia's 70 years before .

(Source: http://www.spainvia.com/leftwingdisaster.htm)

CONCLUSION

Terrorism is an instrument of the Illuminati Jewish central banking cartel based in London.

Ninety five percent of the world's terror, including 9-11, can be traced to this source via the world's intelligence services, especially the CIA, Mossad and MI-6. These intelligence services serve the Illuminati agenda, which is world communism.

In his book, *MI-6: Fifty Years of Special Operations,* Stephen Dorril named Nelson Mandela as an MI-6 agent who allowed UK spying operations to be based in South Africa.

We live in a society that is breathtaking in its hypocrisy. But that is the strategy, to pretend to be one thing while doing the opposite.

Cristeros: Armed Resistance to Judeo Masonic Tyranny

In the 1920s, hundreds of priests were tortured and murdered in Mexico when the Freemason President Plutarco Elias Calles ordered the suppression of the Catholic Church.

For Greater Glory, a superb film released in 2012, now available on Netflix, documents the Cristeros uprising where thousands of Christians took up arms against

Sr. Dn. Francisco Vera, anciano Sacerdote fusilado an Jalisco por celebrar la Santa Misa. 1927.

the Government of Mexico and forced it to compromise. The rebellion, from 1926-1929, claimed 57,000 government soldiers and 30,000 Cristeros "insurgents" plus civilians.

Never heard of this rebellion? Neither have Mexicans. Freemasons, who espouse freedom and tolerance (for their own evil), don't want you to know about armed resistance to their tyranny.

American Christians are facing persecution from the Judeo Masonic (Illuminati) government of Barack Obama. They may get inspiration from this story which defines the true occult nature of the tyranny enslaving mankind. Freemasons pretend that they stand for a secular society. But their consistent bloody persecution of Christians proves that secularism is just a mask for a satanic agenda.

The following are excerpts from *20th Century Mexico's Catholic Uprising* by Olivier Lelibre:

"In 1924, Plutarco Elias Calles became President. For this descendant of Spanish Jews, a 33rd degree Mason, the Church is the unique cause of all Mexico's misfortunes." For him, too, she had to disappear. Plutarco-Elias-Calles and his clique launched a new offensive which they hoped to be definitive:

"Now there must be a psychological revolution," Calles declared. "We must penetrate and take hold of the minds of the children and the youth because they must belong to the revolution.

"The Catholic schools were shut down, the congregations expelled, Christian trade unions forbidden, numerous churches confiscated and profaned (turned into stables or

186   Illuminati 3: Satanic Possession

halls) or destroyed. Public school attendance became mandatory, atheism was officially taught, and religious insignia (medals, crucifixes, statues, and pictures) were forbidden, even at home. God was even chased from the language! The use of such expressions as Adios, "If God wills," or "God forbid," was subject to a fine....

"In January 1927, Catholic Mexico rose: 20,000 combatants (30,000 by the end of the year, and 50,000 in 1929); few arms (a few rifles and carbines, but mostly hatchets, machetes, and sometimes simply sticks); few horses; but all the people supporting them, offering them their money, and necessaries.

"A Cristero peasant recounted how they set out with songs and prayers on their lips: 'We were 1,000, then 5,000, then more! Everyone set out as if to go to the harvest.... We firmly intended to die, angry or not, but to die for Christ.'

"Against them were 100 mobile columns of 1,000 men each, veritable 'infernal columns' financed by the US (light armored cars, tractor-drawn artillery, combat aircraft....) The first clashes were bloody massacres. An officer of Calles wrote: 'They are more like pilgrims than soldiers. This isn't a military campaign, it's a hunting party!" The president himself predicted: 'It will be wrapped up in less than two months.'

A CRUSADE!

"But when a pilgrimage takes up arms, it becomes a crusade! The Cristeros were able to equip themselves from the adversary, profiting from their cowardice or their corruption. The 'Federales' were more like pillagers, drunk on tequila and marijuana, rather than soldiers worthy of the name. On March 15, 1927, they were defeated at San Julian; at Puerto Obristo, they left 600 dead.

"In November, the military attache of the US began to worry about the success of the 'fanatics,' 40% of whose troops were now equipped with excellent Mausers recuperated from the enemy. How was it possible?

"The year 1928 was terrible: the infernal columns had received the order to deport the rural population to 'concentration camps' where famine and epidemics decimated them. At the least show of resistance, the Federates would massacre them. Harvests and flocks were seized, grazing land burned, and villages destroyed by the thousands. Despite this scorched earth policy, the Cristeros stood fast like latter-day Macabees.

"In 1929, the government renounced its policy of governing the countryside. Three-fourths of inhabitable Mexico was in the hands of the troops of Christ the King, victory was in reach especially as the riffraff in Mexico were fighting each other, and in the United States Hoover, who was not a Mason, was elected!

BETRAYED BY THE VATICAN

"Then they learned that the secret negotiations between the Mexican government and the Vatican had resulted in an accord. On June 21, the Mexican episcopate signed a 'resolution' of the conflict with the ruling power on the basis 'negotiated' by a US Jesuit, a Fr. Walsh. The accord provided for: (1) immediate, unconditional cease fire; (2) the resumption of public worship beginning the next day (June 22.)

"That was all. It restored them to the same situation that prevailed in 1926 with all the anti-Catholic laws then in effect, including the registration of priests! In the text, the Cristeros are called fanatics directed by a few third-rate priests; their revolt was an error, an imprudence, even a sin: they must lay down their arms under pain of excommunication...

"Six thousand Cristeros obeyed, and were immediately massacred. In three years, they had only lost 5,000 men in combat! The Mexican episcopate decreed the excommunication of the Cristero priests, but those who had not been killed during the war (180) had already been martyred...All was lost.

"The new president, the Masonic lawyer Fortes Gil, rejoiced. At the summer solstice banquet, he acknowledged his astonishment at the unconditional capitulation of a victorious army, and his intention to continue the fight: 'The fight did not begin yesterday. The fight is eternal. The fight began 20 centuries ago.'

Indeed, but the novelty was that the Vatican was not on the right side..."

Yom Kippur War: Would the Illuminati Sacrifice Israel?

On Oct 6 1973, Egypt and Syria launched a coordinated surprise attack on Israel.

Israeli defenders on the Suez Canal and the Golan Heights were outnumbered and overwhelmed. Israel took heavy casualties and was considering the nuclear option. *Was Israel really in mortal danger?*

Israel is the Rothschilds' personal fiefdom—their personal family army, nuclear arsenal and intelligence service, all in one.

Jerusalem is destined to be the pagan religious and governmental center of their World Government.

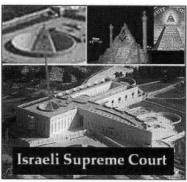

Masonic themed Israeli Supreme Court appears to envision a global function.

They designed and paid for the Israeli parliament (Knesset) and the new Masonic-themed Supreme Court Building, destined to arbitrate global disputes. Their mugs are plastered all over Israeli currency.

If Israel *really* had been in mortal danger, it would contradict our belief that the Rothschild bankers secretly control world events.

THE VINOGRADOV FILE

In 2012, Moscow-based, Israeli journalist Israel Shamir received a secret 20-page report written in Jan. 1975 by the Soviet ambassador to Cairo, Vladimir M. Vinogradov.

According to Vinogradov, a veteran diplomat who later became Russian Foreign Minister, the Yom Kippur War was a conspiracy organized by Henry Kissinger in cahoots with Anwar Sadat and Golda Meir. The respective motives were:

1. The US would replace Russia in the hearts of the Arabs by saving Egypt from another defeat. The price of oil would soar and the Arabs would show their appreciation by accepting US dollars for it.

2. Golda Meir (Israel) was willing to sacrifice 2500 Israelis dead and 7500 wounded to oblige its biggest benefactor. The US would also emerge as Israel's savior and therefore the ideal peace broker between a chastened Israel and an Egypt which has regained its pride. The Syrian army would be destroyed. Estimates suggest Arab dead and casualties were six times Israel's.

3. Anwar Sadat was isolated domestically and his prestige was at its nadir. He needed to placate the nation by avenging the 1967 defeat. Probably a CIA asset, he disliked the USSR and was opposed to socialism.

SIGNS THE FIX WAS IN

1. Like Stalin on the eve of Operation Barbarossa, Israel ignored the Egyptian troop build-up and warnings of imminent invasion.

2. After overwhelming Israeli positions on the east bank of the canal, the Egyptians did not advance into the Sinai, nor were there plans for this. They simply stopped. The Israelis were able to concentrate all their forces in the Golan and were able to defeat the Syrians. Hafez el Assad knew he had been betrayed by his ally!

3. When the Israelis began to move their forces south, Sadat vetoed an offer by the Jordanians to attack their flank.

4. Sadat ordered a 40 km gap be left between his Second and Third Armies. This allowed General Sharon to slip through, cross the Suez Canal and encircle the Egyptian armies.

5. The US saved Israel with an airlift of badly needed supplies; and it "saved" Egypt by ordering a stop to the Israeli advance to Cairo.

"Achieved by lies and treason, the Camp David Peace treaty still guards Israeli and American interests," Shamir concludes. "Sadat's name in the pantheon of Egyptian heroes was safe until now…[The war] sealed the fate of the Soviet presence and eminence in the Arab world… Thanks to the American takeover of Egypt, petrodollar schemes were formed, and the dollar that began its decline in 1971 by losing its gold standard—recovered and became again a full-fledged world reserve currency. The oil of the Saudis and of sheikdoms being sold for dollars became the new lifeline for the American empire."

CONCLUSION

Like the Yom Kippur War, most wars are choreographed. The outcome is determined in advance. Of course, the participants are not privy to these plans.

If there is a war with Iran, or a larger conflagration, the fix will be in. I don't think Israel will be destroyed, certainly not Jerusalem.

This doesn't mean Israelis won't be scared out of their wits. Zionism thrives on convincing Jews their very existence is under constant threat, like it was on Yom Kippur 1973.

CIA's Domestic Assassination Program: JFK & Mary Pinchot Meyer

Mary's Mosaic, a book by Peter Janney is a memorial to Mary Pinchot Meyer (1920-1964), JFK's confidante, adviser and lover.

Janney was a boyhood friend of Meyer's second son, Michael, who was hit by a car in Dec. 1956 and died. Janney recalls how Mary, despite her own grief, comforted him and the motorist who was hysterical. In Janney's memory, his friend's mother represented the ideal of womanhood.

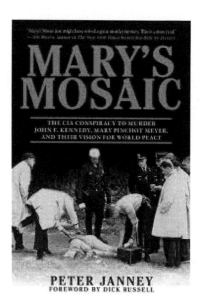

Janney's mother and Meyer were classmates at Vassar College. His father, Wistar Janney and Mary's husband Cord Meyer, whom she divorced in 1957, were both top officials at the CIA.

The book is an act of penance because although CIA Chief of Counterintelligence James Angleton ordered Meyer's murder (because she threatened to expose the CIA) Janney's own father and her ex-husband were both privy to the decision.

MURDER INCORPORATED

Despite the injunction against CIA involvement in domestic politics, the book reveals that JFK's assassination was only the most prominent of hundreds of US political assassinations. Consider names like RFK, MLK, JFK Jr., Vincent Foster and Senator Paul Wellstone. J. Edgar Hoover was probably murdered.

Two earlier Mary Meyer murder researchers, Leo Damore and John Davis, also died under suspicious circumstances. The CIA has many discreet ways to make murder look natural. Janney quotes William Corson, a CIA insider, "Murders are easy, suicides more difficult."

Another Janey source is Toni Shimon, daughter of "police inspector" Joseph Shimon, liaison between CIA, FBI, DC police and the Executive Branch from the 1940s-1980s. He told her political assassinations are part of doing business in Washington. He carried out a few himself.

Janney also suspects that Philip Graham was murdered by the CIA who then controlled the *Washington Post* through his wife Publisher Kathleen Graham and Managing Editor Ben Bradlee. This casts into doubt the *Post's* role in the Watergate Affair. Janney says the 18-minutes missing from the Nixon tapes included his threat to expose the CIA role in the JFK Assassination.

WHO WAS MARY PINCHOT MEYER?

Mary Pinchot Meyer is often described disparagingly as Kennedy´s "mistress." In fact, by 1963 she was part of his inner circle and perhaps his greatest influence.

An American blue blood, her father was a two-term governor of Pennsylvania. She was raised in NYC and travelled in the same social circles as JFK. A statuesque beauty, she was high-minded and had no time for the young Kennedy who was a philanderer like his father.

Coming of age during World War Two, she was preoccupied with world peace. She married Cord Meyer, an ex-Marine with a poetic temperament. She shared his commitment to the United Nations as a step toward "world federalism." These young idealists didn't understand the real agenda behind world government.

However Cord couldn't find a job in academia and Mary found herself the wife of a rising star in the CIA. She socialized with CIA families but was not afraid to voice her disapproval of CIA programs. After her divorce, she became an artist and experimented with LSD.

Like Aldous Huxley and Timothy Leary, who she visited, she believed that psychedelics were necessary for people to break the shell of socialization and experience divine consciousness. She started a group of Washington women dedicated to turning on the powerful men in their lives in order to prevent war.

In 1959, Meyer became reacquainted with Kennedy whose marriage was a sham. Mary turned JFK on to pot and LSD. Kennedy determined to make peace with Russia and Cuba and wind down the Vietnam War. His Nuclear Test Ban Treaty was passed in the Senate. His emissary was meeting with Castro on the day of his assassination.

Needless to say, LBJ reversed all of JFK's initiatives. As a direct result, about 1.5 million Vietnamese died. About 60,000 US soldiers died and $700 billion (in today's dollars) were wasted in a war which discredited, divided and demoralized the country.

Mary was privy to the power struggle JFK had waged with the CIA and military industrial complex. Recklessly she voiced her suspicions of Angleton. She had enough credibility and connections to cause him serious problems.

Her murder Oct. 12 1964, two days shy of her 44th birthday, while walking on a canal tow path, was as carefully orchestrated by the CIA as the President's murder. Mary struggled with her assailant and called out for help but was silenced by bullets to the head and heart. Such is the fate suffered by our truest and our best.

Leo Damore was actually able to interview the CIA hitman, now retired, who confessed. This journalistic coup may have cost Damore his own life but he managed to pass the information to a colleague who gave it to Janney.

THE ILLUMINATI

Janney's 550-page book is 25-year labor of love, meticulously researched and measured. Often the author is quite lyrical, giving it a novelistic page-turner quality.

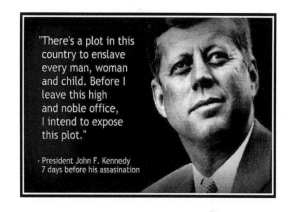

"There's a plot in this country to enslave every man, woman and child. Before I leave this high and noble office, I intend to expose this plot."

- President John F. Kennedy 7 days before his assasination

However, Janney does not understand that the CIA ultimately answers to the Masonic Jewish world banking cartel. He refers to an "invisible government" but this is the Illuminati world government. He says James Angleton was a mole but whose mole? The Mossad controlled him for the Illuminati bankers. They weren't going to let an idealistic President impede their agenda which depends on constant war and ever-increasing debt.

The mass media's complicity in the JFK coverup made possible the CIA-Mossad's next outrage, 9-11. It makes possible new false flags almost monthly, hoaxes like Sandy Hook and Boston Marathon. To be successful today, you have to collaborate with the satanic forces destroying America, or at least not challenge them. However, I doubt if ultimately the ruling class will enjoy the spoils of their treason.

Nevertheless, we may find hope in Peter Janney's courageous achievement. *Mary's Mosaic* is an impassioned defense of freedom based on knowing the truth: "The shining beacon of America—a promise unlike any other for humanity—was being extinguished... [due to] ignorance...I would do whatever it took, pay whatever price was required, to allow this story, this small but essential piece of history—to see the light of day." (391)

No matter how depressing, the Truth always is inspiring and so are people like Janney who risk their lives to tell it.

Excerpts from Oleg Platonov's *Russia's Crown of Thorns- Secret History of Freemasonry 1731-1996, (1996)*

By "Sonja" in Moscow

"One of the major tasks of the world's elite is to destroy national governments and establish in their place Judo-Masonic ruling regimes. For the past 150 years all western European countries have lost their national governments and are now ruled by cosmopolitan Masonic elites, whose interests are far from the majority of ordinary Germans, French, British and other western Europeans. The election show of two or three parties (the same in their essence) is a cover-up for the cruelest dictatorship of the secret world government and international Jewish capital.

Freemasonry today is completely different from what is traditionally believed. Ritual is no longer a priority; the Masonic job is done outside the Lodges. Top politicians of many countries openly acknowledge their involvement with Freemasonry. It is a sort of political trade union unifying unscrupulous politicians, financial swindlers and rogues of all kinds who seek personal profit and absolute power.

All major political decisions are made behind closed doors of Masonic organizations. Democratic elections are presented by a few candidates supported by the world's elite. This system of political power was introduced in Russia in the late 80s.

Masonic organizations are not united. They consist of "Mafia families" hostile to each other. We can witness a vivid example of Mafia fight in Russia now (1996). The ultimate goal of this fight is a split-up of the country and the holocaust of Russian people.

Today there are around 500 various Masonic Lodges in Russia (not including occult organizations and satanists Churches) with around 200,000 members. A large number of members (not less than 10,000) represent so-called "white masonry." The leading part belongs to the club-chain "Rotary." Other organizations of "White Masonry" are Order of Eagle, Magisterium, Reform, International Russian Club, Soros Fund.

"White Freemasons" consider themselves superior and elite, and possessing a special right to dominate and exploit other people. Their anti-Russian activities are of secret character.

FREEMASONRY A CRIMINAL COMMUNITY

Freemasonry in every aspect is a secret criminal community. Its goal is to achieve an international dictatorship based on Judaist doctrine of "Chosen People."

Russian Orthodox Church always condemned Freemasonry as a form of Satanism.

Freemasons have always been the evil enemy of humanity, still more dangerous as they tried to cover-up their criminal activities with a veil of deceitful arguments about spiritual growth and charity. Yet awful crimes committed by Freemasons put them outside of law. From 1725-1825, Masonic Lodges were prohibited in France, Sweden, Spain, Turkey, Malta, Austria and Portugal.

Notwithstanding these prohibitions Masonic ideology increased. Masonic influence was behind all wars, revolutions and cataclysms of 18th-20th centuries.

By the end of 19th century Freemasons directly influenced the policy of western European countries, playing a key role in governments and parliaments.

The stronghold of modern Freemasonry is the United States of America. The US is believed to be "the great Masonic super-power." Its government and top officials are members of Masonic Lodges.

Here is the list of military operations performed by US and based on Masonic aims and objectives:

1945	A-bomb blasts in Hiroshima and Nagasaki
1948-1953	Punitive operations against the Philippines people
1950-1953	Military invasion in Korea. Hundreds of thousands of Koreans perished.
1964-1973	Punitive operations in Laos. Thousands of victims.
1964	Bloody suppression of Panama national forces who were demanding the return of their rights.
1965-1973	Military aggression in Vietnam. Over 500 thousand Vietnamese perished. In Hitler-style peaceful villages were destroyed and burned to the ground. Mass murder of women and children.
1970	Aggression against Cambodia. Multiple victims of peaceful citizens.
1982-1983	Act of terrorism against Lebanon.
1983	Military invasion in Grenada. Hundreds of victims.
1986	Treacherous invasion in Libya.
1989	Military invasion in Panama.
1991	Large scale military operation against Iraq. Not less than 150 hundred thousand citizens perished.
1992-1993	Military operation in Somali. Murder of peaceful citizens.
1999	Aggression against Yugoslavia, thousands of victims, hundreds of thousands of refugees.

These are open military actions. Also, the US was largely involved in silent wars against Salvador, Cuba, Afghanistan, Iran, where they invested huge sums of money to support pro-American puppet regimes.

Total of victims perished as a result of Masonic US Presidents decrees during 1948-1999 amounts to more than a million people (not including the injured and destitute.)

The actions of US Presidents must be brought to international military tribunal and Masonic Lodges of all types must be strictly prohibited.

In Russia, Masonic Lodges were prohibited three times by special Tsarist decrees. The last prohibition had existed till 1917.

Despite the prohibition, Masonic Lodges functioned secretly. Signs of their activity can be traced in the 19th and 20th centuries (even during the Soviet rule.) Gorbachev's and Eltsin's decrees legalized Freemasonry in Russia. Masonic organizations seriously threaten the future of Russia.

The Korean War:
Another Illuminati Fraud

By Jim Perloff

In June 1950, Kim Il-sung, North Korea's communist dictator, invaded South Korea. American forces, under UN authority, came to South Korea's defence resulting in a three-year war that ended in stalemate. The artificially contrived war served at least two major Illuminati purposes—empower world government, and disenfranchise the U.S. Congress by declaring war without its authority.

• If President Franklin D. Roosevelt had not asked Joseph Stalin to enter the Pacific war, there never would have been a communist regime in North Korea.

• As a condition for entering the Pacific War, Stalin demanded—and received—some 600 shiploads of equipment and munitions for his Far Eastern army.

• Stalin waited until the United States had beaten Japan to join the Pacific War. His troops entered China just five days before the war ended. The atomic bomb had already obliterated Hiroshima.

• Korea had been a Japanese protectorate. In 1944, *Foreign Affairs*—the journal of the Council on Foreign Relations (CFR)—published an article suggesting Korea become a trusteeship ruled by the Allies including Russia. The Soviets occupied North Korea, while the U.S. occupied the south. No one asked for the Koreans' opinion.

• Stalin established a communist regime under Kim Il-sung in North Korea, building a 150,000-man army with hundreds of tanks and hundreds of warplanes. When the United States departed South Korea, it left only a constabulary force of South Koreans with small arms. They did not have a single tank or even one anti-tank gun.

• This arms imbalance made invasion of South Korea a certainty. In 1949, Mao Tse-tung consolidated communist control of China, securing Kim's rear. In January 1950, Kim proclaimed this would be Korea's "year of unification," calling for "complete preparedness for war."

• Sweetening the pot for Kim, America's ever-intriguing Secretary of State Dean Acheson (CFR, Scroll & Key, Committee of 300) gave a speech placing South Korea beyond America's "defensive perimeter." Victims outside the perimeter, he said, would have to rely "upon the commitments of the entire civilized world under the Charter of the United Nations"—intimating the role Korea would play in the Illuminati agenda.

• The Illuminati seek world domination. To govern the world requires a world government. *Protocol 5:11* said they intended "gradually to absorb all the state forces of the world and to form a super-government."

• World War I produced the first attempted world government—the League of Nations. The CFR was founded in 1921 in direct response to America's refusal to join the League. Council members drew up the plans for the League's successor, the United Nations. At the UN's 1945 founding conference in San Francisco, 47 of the American delegates were CFR members. David Rockefeller was long CFR chairman; his brother, John D., Jr., donated $8.5 million to purchase the land where the UN was built.

• Once the UN was established, the next step was to empower it by validating its peace-keeping credentials. (The UN Charter's first purpose is "To maintain international peace and security.") Hence the Korean War came into play.

• Nearly two years into the Korean War, the lead article for the April 1952 *Foreign Affairs* was entitled "Korea in Perspective." It summed up: "We have made historic progress toward the establishment of a viable system of collective security."

CONGRESSIONAL AUTHORITY

The Korean War fulfilled another Illuminati objective: usurping Congress's authority to declare war.

• The Protocols,(10) predicted: "In the near future we shall establish the responsibility of presidents.... We shall invest the president with the right of declaring a state of war." (A president is easier to control than a legislature.)

• Congress's authority to declare war has not been invoked since it ratified the UN Charter. President Truman sent troops to Korea without even consulting Congress. He explained: "We are not at war; this is a police action." The United States suffered over 100,000 casualties in Korea—but not to worry, this was just "a police action."

• Congress did not protest Truman's action very vigorously because the Illuminati were playing a trump card. The UN's strongest opponents in Congress were also anti-communists. They had condemned the Truman State Department for manipulating China's fall to communism. With Korea, Truman appeared to be atoning for that by sending troops to halt communist aggression. If Congress tried asserting its prerogatives, Korea could meanwhile fall to Kim Il-sung's advancing forces.

But the backstage Illuminists had no intention of "fighting communism." General Douglas MacArthur, commander of UN forces, learned this the hard way.

MacArthur not only repelled the invasion, but—following his soldier's instincts—pursued victory, liberating North Korea from Communism nearly to the Yalu River, which marks China's border. At this point, Red China poured its troops into the conflict. MacArthur ordered the Yalu's bridges bombed to keep them out, but within hours his order was countermanded by Washington—which would cost thousands of GIs their lives.

General MacArthur said of this: "I realized for the first time that I had actually been denied the use of my full military power to safeguard the lives of my soldiers and the safety of my army. To me, it clearly foreshadowed a future tragic situation in Korea, and left me with a sense of inexpressible shock."

This with the new concept of "limited war." Victory had become an anachronism, replaced by "containment," the idea originated in the famous 1947 "Mr. X" article in *Foreign Affairs*. MacArthur was soon dismissed from command in Korea—like Patton, expendable after serving his purpose.

Perhaps the greatest irony: the Soviet Union could have prevented the UN action in Korea simply by vetoing it as a member of the Security Council. After all, Kim Il-sung was their puppet. However, on the day of the Korea vote, the Soviet delegation was absent. They were in the middle of a walkout staged over the UN's failure to seat Red China. Secretary General Trygve Lie invited Jacob Malik, Soviet Ambassador to the UN, to attend the Korea vote, but he declined. Establishment historians call this a "Soviet blunder." But had Malik really goofed, Stalin would have had him nailed to a board.

The Korean War was not about victory on either side, but about validating the UN as "peacekeeper." Including civilians, some three million died on this altar to world government. When the war ended, Korea's North-South borders were restored to approximately where they had been at the outset.

General Mark Clark commented: "In carrying out the instructions of my government, I gained the unenviable distinction of being the first United States Army commander in history to sign an armistice without victory."

For the Illuminati, war is "revolutionary" because it consolidates Illuminati power and advances world government. Peace is "counter revolutionary." The Korean War, and indeed the North Korean prison state, were unnecessary and completely contrived.

James Perloff is author of several books; his latest is *Truth Is a Lonely Warrior*. His website is jamesperloff.com.

Book Six

The Illuminati at Work and Play

News Media Collaborated in 9-11 False Flag

Edward Hendrie is a lawyer. His book, *9-11—Enemies Foreign and Domestic* builds a powerful case that 9-11 was an egregious fraud and act of treason perpetrated against the American people. Clearly, a large segment of the US political, military and media class is complicit in the mass murder and/or cover-up, from the President on down.

Hendrie dissects and discredits the official story, and places the blame on the Israeli Mossad. He presents the attack in the context of numerous other Zionist false flags against the US (Beirut Marine barracks, USS Liberty) designed to change US policy. Hendrie effectively explains the broad religious context, i.e. the Cabalist and Talmudic Jewish vendetta against mankind. I haven't read anything for a while that so vividly exposes the control Illuminati bankers have over our lives.

Their ownership of the mass media is a large part of this control. Hendrie shows how the media was an active collaborator in the 9-11 fraud. As I suspected, no planes hit the Twin Towers or the Pentagon. The plane images were computer generated and synchronized with explosions in the buildings.

Hendrie shows that many of the "eye witnesses" were media employees and that many real eye witness reports of explosions but no planes were ignored.

Furthermore, the BBC reported the collapse of WTC-7, a 47-floor building, 20 minutes before it occurred. AP and CNN prepared obituary pictures for the 9-11 passengers three days before the attack occurred.

It makes sense to me that since no plane crashed at Shanksville or at the Pentagon, no planes were involved at the WTC either. These people have a consistent MO.

SUPPRESSING THE TRUTH

Hendrie shows that the "news" suppresses the truth and literally creates reality according to the Illuminati script.

The Twin Towers were designed to withstand hits by large passenger planes and that supposed fires ignited by jet fuels could not reach temperatures necessary to melt steel girders.

Hendrie attributes the fact that the two buildings and their contents became dust to a "direct energy weapon" related to HAARP. This weapon reduced almost everything to their molecular level. 1400 cars as far as seven blocks away melted or were deformed but trees and paper were unaffected, let alone burned.

Hendrie reveals that Category Three hurricane "Erin", packing 120 mph winds was about 200 miles from NYC at the time of the attack. He cites physicist Dr. Judy Wood who theorizes that the hurricane "acted as a massive Tesla coil creating field effects used by directed energy weapons on 9-11."

The purpose of 9-11 was to create a Zionist police state and to justify wars against Iraq, Afghanistan and Iran. Hendrie believes the Iraq war was prompted by Sadaam Hussein's decision to stop trading oil in dollars. Apparently, the bankers need petrodollars to support the burgeoning US debt and keep the $US from collapsing.

Hendrie speculates that the passengers of UA-93 were unloaded in Cleveland and murdered at a NASA facility at the airport. The damage at the Pentagon, which killed 125 people, was caused by explosions. The attack targeted offices where accountants were investigating the disappearance of $1.2 trillion.

Osama bin Laden died in late 2001 of Marfan syndrome. The "assassination" by Navy Seals was designed to rescue Obama, who was embattled by "birther" and other issues.

CONCLUSION

This 300-page book is carefully documented and throws our common dilemma into stark relief. We live in a theatre of the absurd where psychopaths and their enablers have taken control.

Hendrie makes clear that Cabalist Jewish bankers are at the heart of the conspiracy and Zionism is its most powerful instrument. He makes a convincing case that Mossad organized and executed the 9-11 attack. Senior members of the Bush administration were active collaborators. He cites admissions from insiders that this was an "inside job."

The 9-11 official story demonstrates how the Cabalists think they can turn their lies into reality using their ownership and control of the mass media. Our situation is analogous the movie *The Invasion of the Body Snatchers* where an alien force has invaded the peoples' minds and souls.

Related Video: "9-11 MISSING LINKS"
http://video.google.com/videoplay?docid=7877765982288566190

No Planes Hit WTC
http://www.youtube.com/watch?v=CUoqwUVOxHE&feature=share

Dan Senor: Portrait of an Illuminati Facilitator

According to his speech agent, Dan Senor "was the civilian face of the Coalition Authority to Americans, Europeans, Iraqis and the world."

Dan Senor shows General Mark Kimmitt the way to Baghdad.

He was only 32-years-old when he became spokesman for Ambassador Paul Bremer, and the Coalition Provisional Authority after the 2003 Iraq invasion.

The optics weren't good: ambitious young Canadian Jew, graduate of Hebrew University in Jerusalem, the face for the "US" invasion of Iraq?

By now it's clear Zionism is an expansionist ideology; apparently they didn't care who knew, even in 2003.

Flash forward to October 2012. Senor, now 41, is "foreign policy adviser," aka Zionist handler, for Presidential candidate Mitt Romney.

In Jerusalem, he committed his boss to "respecting" any Israeli attack on Iran. Later, Romney backed off only slightly, saying "no option was off the table." Romney was on his way to a $50,000 a plate fundraiser in the Israeli capital. Such is "American" democracy.

Dan Senor's career is a textbook example of how to succeed by serving the Illuminati bankers' Zionist Division which includes Israel, the US and Western Europe.

Some highlights:

Dan Senor graduated in history from the University of Western Ontario in London Ont., and took graduate degrees at Hebrew University and Harvard Business School.

Interned at AIPAC (Israel's Washington Lobby) and on Capitol Hill with Michigan Senator Spencer Abraham. Caught the eye of Neo Con boss William Kristol who famously said the Iraq war was conceived by 25 Jewish intellectuals in Washington.

Worked for the Carlyle Group , the tenth biggest defense contractor in the world which specializes in starting the wars that require its products. It hires retired politicians like GHW Bush who are able to get funding for weapons even if the Pentagon doesn't want them.

Senor then started his own "private equity" and hedge fund firm with John Kerry's millionaire stepson Chris Heinz (yes, that Heinz.) He also joined the Council on Foreign Relations and many other "think tanks." He co-authored a flattering book about entrepreneurship in Israel with his brother-in-law, and was a talking head on Fox-TV.

MARRIAGE

What caught my eye is that this uber Jew, a man who keeps kosher, married a shiksa, Campbell Brown, formerly of CNN. This illustrates that the Illuminati are not strictly-speaking Jewish. Although they run organized Jewry, they intermarry with Freemasons of all ethnic origin. The Illuminati are Cabalists, a satanic secret society within Judaism and many other religions and groups.

For real Jews, marrying a shiksa is a serious breach. It essentially means the children, in this case two sons, are not Jewish.

Senor met Brown in Baghdad in 2003 and they married in 2006 in a civil ceremony in Colorado. *The New York Times* Society Page reported that, "the couple vowed before 150 guests not only to stay together forever but 'to repair one small piece of the broken world.'

This is a popular conceit among Cabalists who believe they are "healing the world" by destroying it. Pure Satanism.

Campbell's father, Jim Brown ran unsuccessfully for Louisiana governor in 1987. He was elected insurance commissioner in 1991 and served until his resignation in October 2000 when he served a six-month prison sentence for lying to the FBI about the status of an insurance company. Brown was barred from practicing law until 2008.

I can't confirm Jim Brown is a Mason but he was surrounded by them and apparently he was corrupt.

CONCLUSION

Dan Senor is an example to all ambitious young Jews (and non-Jews) on how to succeed today.

Lend your talent to the Illuminati bankers. Go to elite schools and work for Illuminati fronts. Help them start gratuitous wars and squeeze the wealth out of the countries they conquer, even if millions are maimed, starve or die.

Help the bankers extinguish the human spirit and reduce everyone to animals. Ensure the devil wins his wager with God and humanity is a failed experiment.

If you have any moral qualms, tell yourself and anyone who will listen, you're "healing the world."

The Rothschild They Murdered

People used the word "gentle" to describe Amschel Mayor James Rothschild.

He was the only son of Victor Rothschild's second marriage to Theresa Mayor, and heir to the Rothschild dynasty after his older half-brother Jacob.

Amschel's obituary stated: "Where his father was of large and pugnacious build, Amschel Rothschild was tall, thin and strikingly graceful [after his mother]. His bushy head of hair ... emphasized large, sad brown eyes. He was precise, almost obsessively tidy, enjoyed making difficult cocktails and revisiting old jokes. He loved his farm, his children, restoring old outhouses, extending his lawns, going to bed early."

Amschel Mayor James Rothschild, 1955-1996, pictured here in 1977 at age 22

As a teenager, he raced motorcycles and later vintage cars and bi-planes.

"He started racing classic cars in 1974, owning successively a Lotus 10, an AC Cobra, a famous 1954 250F Maserati, a 1964 Willment Daytona Coupe in which he won two Historic Sports Car Championships..."

He married brewing heiress Anita Guinness in 1981 and had three children, Kate (b.1982); Alice (b.1983) and James (b.1985.) He farmed during his twenties and didn't join the family business until 1987 at age 32. He served an apprenticeship before being appointed Executive Chairman of Rothschild Asset Management in 1993. His obit continues:

"Amschel was regularly billed as the heir presumptive to Sir Evelyn de Rothschild for the chairmanship (Sir Evelyn's children being still too young to be candidates), though newspaper reports would be sniffy about his prospects; they implied his profile was too low, that with his gentle manner, he was too "nice," that he lacked the killer instinct."

On July 8 1996 he was found dead in the bathroom of his suite at the Bristol Hotel in Paris. According to the official story, he had committed suicide by hanging himself with the belt of his bathrobe. Thanks to the now defunct *The Spotlight* we have the truth:

Rupert Murdoch Ordered Editors World Wide To "Spike" The Story

-----

Exclusive To The Spotlight
August 5, 1996
By Sasha Rakoczy

French police have determined that Amschel Rothschild, heir to the fabulous Rothschild banking fortune, was murdered, according to well-placed European sources.

But, French Prime Minister Jacques Chirac has ordered police to close their investigation. Media outlets worldwide have ignored these mysterious developments. Some have reported the death was a suicide, other outlets disregarded the death altogether.

As if obeying an invisible choir-master, the world's competing news organizations silenced their strident sensationalism this month to cover up the mysterious death.

In the United States, newspapers controlled by Rupert Murdoch, the foreign-born owner of the world's largest media empire, either studiously ignored reports that Rothschild had met a violent end, or relegated it to the back pages as a mere "heart attack."

A Spotlight inquiry has established that Rothschild, 41, a billionaire investment banker and a noted sportsman in excellent health, was discovered lifeless on the floor of the bathroom of his suite at the luxurious Bristol Hotel in Paris on July 8 at 7:32 pm.

Police found that he had been strangled with the heavy cord of his own bathrobe. One end of the cord was attached to a towel rack, as if to suggest that Rothschild's violent death was self-inflicted.

"The [French] crime scene investigators never called it 'suicide,'" reporter Theirry de Segonzac told The Spotlight in a telephone interview from Paris. "After photographing the body, one of the detectives gave the towel rack tied to the body a strong tug. It came right out of the wall."

Had Rothschild really attempted to hang himself from that rack, he would have ended up with nothing worse than a couple of holes in the wall, de Segonzac said.

There was no suicide note, no discernible cause or reason for a finding of suicide, knowledgeable sources say.

Rothschild, an athletic and imperious figure in early middle age, was a renowned race car driver and the husband of Anita Guinness, herself one of the world's wealthiest heiresses. The couple had three children who spent most of their time on the family's baronial estate in Suffolk, England.

Rothschild had arrived in Paris to take over one of the many family consortium's French assets—management operations which were to be merged with N.M. Rothschild's London-based investment banking center.

"Far from being 'troubled,' Amschel Rothschild's star was on the rise and he relished his success," says an executive at Keefe, Bruyetter and Co., a respected Wall Street monitor of the financial services industry. "I don't believe for a moment he suddenly went and killed himself. There's much more to this story."

But with frantic speed—within an hour after the body's discovery—authorities and news executives in both France and Britain launched an unusual joint offensive to preempt a public inquiry or a press investigation into the circumstances of Rothschild's death.

"Murdoch sent a hotline fax to his 600-odd editors and news managers around the world, ordering them to report Amschel's death as a heart attack, if at all," said British broadcast reporter Ian Gooding.

"No one around here has ever seen such pressure to kill a front-page story. But in the end, the cover-up was complete."

CONCLUSION

By the way this story was buried, it is obvious that Amschel was murdered.

Apparently the Illuminati are not immune to lethal attack, when they administer it themselves. If an enemy of the Rothschilds had done it, believe me you'd know.

The Rothschilds appear to have a secret compact. Each member of the dynasty will die if he refuses to advance the plan for the subversion and enslavement of the human race outlined in *The Protocols of Zion*.

Obviously Amschel Mayor James Rothschild did not have "the killer instinct." We don't know the details but he became an obstruction.

Amschel's story is a great tragedy. A sensitive, intelligent and good man is born into a megalomaniacal family of generational Satanists. He discovers he must be a ruthless predator. It's not in his character. He has a soul. He resists and is murdered.

Let's always remember this good man.

Bursting the Malachi Martin Bubble

Powerful forces have maintained the fiction that Malachi Martin left the Jesuit Order voluntarily or on principle. In fact, this prominent church critic was forced to leave the priesthood because he was a scoundrel and a philanderer.

By 1962, he had alienated the affections of at least four housewives and then dropped them.

When one spurned woman asked Martin's brother in Dublin where Malachi was, she was told:

"Dear girl. I don't know. I must tell you, you are the fourth woman who has come here asking me the same question about Malachi. All of them have essentially the same story to tell. That they were in love with Malachi and thought Malachi was in love with them."

Malachy Martin

"Four woman?" she demanded. "The same story?"

He nodded, and said, "And one rather attractive young man."

This account can be found in Robert Kaiser's book, *Clerical Error* (2002.) The woman was his wife. (pp.284-285)

Kaiser was the TIME magazine correspondent in Rome in the early 1960s. Martin was a source who became a close family friend. Martin didn't just break up Kaiser's family. (Kaiser and his wife Mary had two young children.) It was much darker. To allay suspicions, Martin mobilized a network of influential contacts to smear Kaiser and have him committed as a paranoid schizophrenic.

ZIONIST AGENT AND LIAR

Martin's books exposed satanic practices in the Catholic church, and the Pope's role in the New World Order. While pretending to be against world government and the decline of traditional faith and practice, Martin went a long way to discredit the church. His many books were published by Illuminati Jewish mind-controller Simon and Schuster, which was a sign that something was fishy.

Kaiser's book, on the other hand, is published by *Continuum* which bills itself as "unconstrained by the interests of any global media group or academic institution, and based in London and New York."

In it, Kaiser recalls that Martin started hanging out with two officials of the New York-based American Jewish Committee and flashing $100 bills. The Jews were particularly concerned that the 1962 Second Vatican Council pass "the Jewish Schema" which absolved Jews of blame for Christ's Crucifixion and by implication accept guilt for 2000 years of anti Semitism.

This is a typical example of how Illuminati mind-controllers invert good and evil. The Crucifixion of Christ was part of an ancient conspiracy against God and man now reaching fruition with the New World Order.

"Martin was their lobbyist." Kaiser wrote. "These Jews were using him and paying him well for his help. (190)

Martin was the secretary to Cardinal Augustin Bea, a Marrano who spearheaded the Schema and a general liberalization of church dogma and practice. According to an article in *Wikipedia*, Martin passed confidential documents to the American Jewish Committee, which is a front for Illuminati bankers. He also wrote under pseudonyms many inflammatory articles for Illuminati magazines like *Harper's* describing the foot dragging of Vatican conservatives.

Martin had a reputation as a liar. Mark Owen cites psychiatrist M. Scott Peck's book *Glimpses of the Devil* about possession and exorcism. According to Peck, Martin, although a formidable scholar and polyglot (17 languages), could by turns be a "pathological liar" and a "leprechaun."

In an email, Owen told me that Peck said that in his book *Hostages to the Devil* Martin took credit for exorcisms that were actually performed by Peck.

MATURITY

Bob Kaiser's book, *Clerical Error* is also about attaining maturity. Kaiser spent 10 years as a Jesuit himself. He makes the point that immaturity is really a function of having "idols and "taking guidance from "authorities" like the Jesuits or "experts."

Kaiser was fooled by Martin's collar and couldn't see what was happening in his own home. Then instead of taking action, he sought help from the Jesuit Order, who prevaricated. His so-called friends didn't alert him.

Kaiser learned that maturity is not so much gaining wisdom as gaining confidence in one's own judgment, *trusting oneself* no matter one's limitations.

"Thou shalt have no other gods before me" is really an order from God to all of us: to take charge of ourselves, think our own thoughts, and feel our own feelings. In other words, to grow up." (262)

For a lot of us, maturity has been realizing that no one knows very much, and there are a lot of unscrupulous, stupid and evil people in the world ready to exploit us.

How the Illuminati Recruit & Network

What do Facebook's Mark Zuckerberg, NHL Commissioner Gary Bettman and CNN's Wolf Blitzer have in common? How about *Chicago Tribune* owner Sam Zell, and pop singers Simon and Garfunkle?

At university, they were all members of the Jewish college fraternity Alpha Epsilon Pi which has 10,000 members in 155 chapters in the US, Canada, the UK and Israel. Apparently some non-Jews who espouse its "purpose and values" are admitted.

Affiliated with the B'nai Brith, this fraternity is one way Jews get recruited by Freemasonry and get a shot at the inside track in the New World Order.

At some campuses, 50% of Jewish students join Jewish fraternities and make up that proportion of fraternities in general.

the Alpha Epsilon Pi fraternity's coat of arms consists of many occult references

Although most students join with the vague sense they are networking, they have no idea they are joining a Luciferian organization secretly dedicated to enslaving mankind according to the formula set out in *The Protocols of the Elders of Zion*. They are gulled by the empty talk of a campus "brotherhood" and serving the Jewish community.

But the coat of arms of the fraternity is a clue to its real occult (i.e. satanic) designs.

At my request, Texe Marrs kindly deciphered the emblem.

1) The skull on the book (no doubt a Holy book,) implies a faith in death and mortality, but it is counterbalanced at right by the diamond (lozenge shaped icon) which is the hope and promise of immortal life (esoterically, the diamond is the phallus, sign of the generative power.)

2) The *fleur de lis* at left is symbol of royalty—and has an esoteric sexual meaning as well. It is known as Satan's flower.

3) The six-pointed star on the Menorah symbolizes the completion of the Jewish mission, which is to consummate their hoped for Kingdom and sovereignty over all. We have in the star six triangles, six points, and six lines (in the internal hexagon at center.) Thus, 666.

(4) The "Aladdin's" lamp connotes light and knowledge—esoteric, divine wisdom. The rampant lion is also symbol of royalty and particularly of the Tribe of Judah. The triangles, with blue background, sign of the four corners of the world, or universe.

Pretty weird for an organization dedicated to Jewish brotherhood and service, wouldn't you say?

According to a B'nai Brith article,

"To join fraternities like AEPi, students must first go through initiation, which varies by chapter. This involves secretive rituals dating back to a fraternity's founding, which are celebrated at the start of every school semester. They are then required to pay an initiation fee of $425. Chapter fees vary each semester after that depending on the events held by each individual chapter and range between $275 and $750 a year."

"Once members become alumnae upon university graduation, they don't have to pay a cent and they'll still have their lifetime membership. Most importantly, they'll maintain friendships with people they regard as family."

People joining this or any fraternity should not expect to make a deal with the devil on the first day. This is a subtle process of indoctrination and sifting lasting many years. Most will have to join the B'nai Brith.

Over a long period of time, people willing to sacrifice any shred of decency will be identified and promoted. By this time, doing evil in the service of the Luciferian NWO will seem to be good.

CONCLUSION

Society was naive to think it could reject God without embracing Satan. They are like light and darkness. Remove the light and you will have darkness. (I define God in terms of spiritual absolutes like Truth, Love, Goodness & Beauty.)

Society was naive to think that those advocating "secularism" and "the separation of church and state" did not have a hidden agenda. They were Satanists and their dupes.

We become what we worship (obey.) Increasingly, society resembles a satanic cult and people are degenerating into demons. Freemasonry, with its recruitment centers at college fraternities and sororities, Jewish and non-Jewish, plays a key role in this process.

So, if you're a student, Jewish or not, and want to sell your soul and betray your community for personal gain, now you know how.

Henry Makow PhD   211

Bohemian Grove: Illuminati Meet This Week for Satanic Rituals

The satanist cult that has colonized mankind meets every year during the third week in July at Bohemian Grove 80 miles north of San Francisco.

Over 2000 members—the political, corporate, cultural and military elite of the world—gather for satanic rituals, possibly including human ritual sacrifice. They have been meeting here since the 1880s.

According to "Treee," a young Las Vegas woman who claims to have contacts inside the secretive club, a ritual sacrifice of Mary Magdalene takes place Tuesday July 21; and the ritual sacrifice of Jesus Christ takes place Wednesday, July 22. A human body or effigy is burned in front of an large owl symbolizing Moloch, the pagan Canaanite God. Alex Jones filmed a similar ceremony called "Cremation of Care" July 15, 2000. It can be viewed here: https://www.youtube.com/watch?v=r5dHhvpHIjM

SATANISTS AND THEIR PERVERSIONS

Alex Jones points out in his film that their "Cremation of Care" programme actually shows a baby's body being devoured by the flames. Another YouTube photo montage taken from the estate of a BG member leaves little doubt that serious satanist practices take place. One of the pictures shows a dead body, presumably a human sacrifice.

http://www.youtube.com/watch?v=URimMtIwDoY

As for perversion, let's start with the trivial. In 1978, the club actually argued in court that it shouldn't have to hire female staff because members at the Grove "urinate in the open without even the use of rudimentary toilet facilities" and that the presence of females would alter club members' behavior."

An all-male enclave, Richard Nixon was heard on the Watergate Tapes describing it as "the most faggy goddamn thing you could ever imagine, that San Francisco crowd that goes in there; it's just terrible! I mean I won't shake hands with anybody from San Francisco."

In the 1989 Franklin Coverup scandal, Paul A. Bonacci claimed that he had been kidnapped and flown to the Grove by Republican leader Lawrence King and was forced into sexual acts with other boys.

In Ch. 18 of *The Tranceformation of America*, Cathy O'Brien writes "I was programmed and equipped to function in all rooms at Bohemian Grove in order to compromise specific government targets according to their personal perversions.

'Anything, anytime, anywhere with anyone' was my mode of operation at the Grove. I do not purport to understand the full function of this political cesspool playground as my perception was limited to my own realm of experience. My perception is that Bohemian Grove serves those ushering in the New World Order through mind control, and consists primarily of the highest Mafia and U.S. Government officials.

"I do not use the term "highest" loosely, as copious quantities of drugs were consumed there. Project Monarch Mind-Control slaves were routinely abused there to fulfill the primary purpose of the club: purveying perversion. Bohemian Grove is reportedly intended to be used recreationally, providing a supposedly secure environment for politically affluent individuals to "party" without restraint. The only business conducted there pertained to implementing the New World Order, through the proliferation of mind-control atrocities, giving the place an air of "Masonic Secrecy." The only room where business discussions were permitted was the small, dark lounge affectionately and appropriately referred to as the Underground.

"My purpose at the Grove was sexual in nature, and therefore my perceptions were limited to a sex slave's viewpoint. As an effective means of control to ensure undetected proliferation of their perverse indulgences, slaves such as myself were subjected to ritualistic trauma. I knew each breath I took could be my last, as the threat of death lurked in every shadow. Slaves of advancing age or with failing programming were sacrificially murdered "at random" in the wooded grounds of Bohemian Grove, and I felt it was "simply a matter of time until it would be me." Rituals were held at a giant, concrete owl monument on the banks of, ironically enough, the Russian (rushin') River. These occultist sex rituals stemmed from the scientific belief that mind-controlled slaves required severe trauma to ensure compartmentalization of the memory, and not from any spiritual motivation.

"My own threat of death was instilled when I witnessed the sacrificial death of a young, dark-haired victim at which time I was instructed to perform sexually as though my life depended upon it. I was told, the next sacrifice victim could be you. Anytime when you least expect it, the owl will consume you. Prepare yourself, and stay prepared." Being "prepared" equated to being totally suggestible, i.e., "on my toes" awaiting their command."

IMPLICATIONS

Supreme Court Judge Sonia Sotomayor is a member of the all-female "Belizean Club" which is the female equivalent of Bohemian Grove. The emerging picture is that the world elite is chosen by virtue of being sexually and morally compromised so they will obey the dictates of Cabalist central bankers who are establishing the New World Order.

Bohemian Grove is more evidence that our natural leadership has been replaced by Satanists and perverts. We cannot take ourselves seriously as a society as long as we allow these impostors to control us.

We must nationalize the central banks, and take control of our own credit. We must ensure that all political campaigns are publicly funded. The media and movie cartels need to be broken up and redistributed. The central bankers and their lackeys must be banished or the human race is doomed to further degradation and possible destruction.

Jewish Jokes About Goyim & God

Jews love Jewish jokes as much as anyone. Many focus on how money-minded Jews are supposed to be. I love this Woody Allen one-liner: "See this pocket watch? My grandfather sold it to me on his deathbed."

Recently, I read some jokes meant for Jewish eyes only. They came from a Chapter "Jacob and Esau" in *Jewish Wit and Wisdom* published in 1952. Many reflected the traditional Jewish-Gentile relationship down through the centuries. The first one emphasized the view that Jews are smarter than others.

Q: Why were Gentiles invented?
A: Somebody has to pay retail

A rich man left his fortune to his three friends, an Irishman, a German and a Jew. The only stipulation was that each had to put a $100 bill in his coffin just before it was lowered into the ground. At the funeral, the Irishman and the German both gladly fulfilled their obligation. Then it was the Jew's turn. He picked up the two hundred dollar bills and left a cheque for $300 in the coffin!

This is fairly benign compared to what came next.

Two Jews, one from London and one from a small shtetl (village) in Poland met at a spa in Germany. The Londoner asked his Polish friend how many Jews were in his village. 700. And how many goyim? 45. And what do the Jews do? They are artisans and shopkeepers and traders. And the goyim? "They make themselves useful to the Jews. They sweep out the stores and on Sabbath make the fires and remove the candlesticks."

Then, it was the Pole's turn. On learning there were 200,000 Jews in London, and seven million goyim, he quite rightly inquired, "What do you need so many goyim for?"

This story nicely illustrates the parochial quality of many Jews. Is it good or bad for the Jews? is a common reflex. Call it a "self-referential" quality, where the world revolves around them, and they create reality according to their prejudices and self-interest. (Is it a coincidence that the mass media and Hollywood are dominated by these "reality-creators?" And they have used this power to divert gentiles from the diabolical Judeo Masonic conspiracy?) This Jewish "solipsism" now passes as "Modernism."

In his book, *Sex and Character* (1903), the Jewish philosopher Otto Weininger labeled it "subjectivity" and compared Jews with women, saying neither are able to see situations objectively, or in moral terms. Everything is a reflection of their emotion, vanity and self-interest. Have you noticed that people in general are becoming more selfish and self-centered as Christian influence fades?

The joke also reminds me that while Jews have convinced themselves and the world they are the victims of irrational "hate," the Talmud tells us the hate actually originates within Jewish ranks. The rest of us cannot conceive that certain people would set themselves up in opposition to the human race and actually succeed.

The notion that the goyim will serve "the Jews" motivates the Illuminati in general. (The Illuminati include Freemasonry.) This explains why the human race is kept in a state of arrested development, in a perpetual adolescence. This is why there is no common effort to lift humanity to a higher spiritual and mental plane. On the contrary, the general effort is directed at degrading, re-engineering and indoctrinating it for permanent servitude.

GOD

The following joke (from Wikipedia) illustrates that Judaism may be deficient as a religion. You cannot have religion without God.

Two Rabbis argued late into the night about the existence of God, and, using strong arguments from the scriptures, ended up indisputably disproving His existence. The next day, one Rabbi was surprised to see the other walking into the Shul for morning services. "I thought we had agreed there was no God," he said. "Yes, what does that have to do with it?" replied the other.

Many observers have noted that Judaism is about empty observance and conformity rather than a living relationship with God. Arthur Koestler famously said "Judaism teaches Jews how to cheat God." The following stories suggest some Jews think God is a wily businessman they cannot outfox. This is also from Wikipedia.

A poor man walking in the forest feels close enough to God to ask, "God, what is a million years to you?

God replies, "My son, a million years to you is like a second to me."

The man asks, "God, what is a million dollars to you?"

God replies, "My son, a million dollars to you is less than a penny to me. It means almost nothing to me.

"The man asks, "So God, can I have a million dollars?"

And God replies, "In a second."

I found this last one (from the book, p.361) quite shocking:

A Jew buys a lottery ticket and goes to the synagogue where he promises God that he will donate a new scroll if he wins. When he fails to win, he exclaims "the Jewish God is no businessman," and goes to the Christian church where he promises to pay for a new roof.

He wins a large prize but welches on his promise. Instead he returns to the synagogue where he praises the Jewish God in these terms: "You knew all along that I wont keep my promise so you ignored me. But the Christian God naively believed me. After all, there is no God like the Jewish God."

These stories suggest that some Jews see God as a wily businessman. They have created God in their own image. They are their own God. Unfortunately, their God has become ours.

"We Day:"
Illuminati Target Our Children

*Work for peace—only in a peaceful world can great change be achieved,
former Soviet president Mikhail Gorbachev implored 18,000 Manitoba
children this morning.*

*"Be united, and don't allow anyone to divide you. Never fear those who are
trying to intimidate you," said the Nobel peace laureate at the second We
Day Manitoba.*

"We need to move to a world without nuclear weapons," Gorbachev said.

"I like you guys—I love you!" the 81-year-old said to thunderous applause.
—Winnipeg Free Press, Oct. 30, 2012

Why would Illuminati heavyweights like Mikhail
Gorbachev (Al Gore and Paul Martin at other
venues) take time to address 18,000 school children?

The local business elite, Trilateral Commission
Member Hartley Richardson, *Free Press* owner Bob Silver and Jets owner Mark Chip-
man sponsored this Winnipeg event. This is proof society has been totally subverted,
and not just by Jews.

They keep talking about "changing the world." They are referring to satanic Illuminati
rule. This is why "the change" is always for the worse.

Our correspondent SPH writes:

I had never heard of "We Day" until my 12-year-old-son asked me if I had any pennies
that I didn't want. This highly publicized event was held in Winnipeg Oct 30, 2012 and
various dates throughout the year in other Canadian cities.

"We Day" is self described as "an educational event and the movement of our time—a
movement of young people leading local and global change."

The basic angle is that awareness of the world's great injustices and inequalities is raised, and then the question that is directed at our children is, 'what can WE do about it?"

Tickets cannot be purchased for this event. Kids are welcomed for free, but there is a catch. Each child is expected to commit him/herself to at least one act of local and one act of global charity through *Free The Children's* year-long engagement programs. *Free the Children* is a charity founded by Craig Kielburger ("We Day" front-man since he was 11.)

While "We Day" is not specifically a charity, it works closely with charitable partners, and their goal is to inspire our children to become Illuminati widgets of tomorrow. Children are encouraged to attend workshops and even summer camps geared toward activism, public speaking and fund raising. This is very typical of Illuminati Communist recruitment.

All major charitable organizations are fronts for generating as well as laundering money, while creating an air of good will.

Organizations like the Red Cross are just more tentacles of the illuminati's international power structure.

HIDDEN AGENDA

Although the causes represented here will seem noble to the average person, the true goals of this organization are beyond most people's comprehension. Most people believe that global warming is a real thing, and not a contrived crisis and pretext to advance the Illuminati agenda.

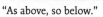

"As above, so below."

They are preying on our collective guilt as the lucky ones who live in a developed county. Like the Hitler Youth were indoctrinated in anti Semitism, our children are being similarly inculcated in the Globalist mindset.

"We Day" is "awakening the spirit of volunteerism," and "educating, engaging and empowering socially conscious youth to become agents of change."

The grooming of our children takes place early. Under the guise of charity, human rights and equality, they are selecting the most creative and energetic of our youth and twisting their sincere efforts in favour of their satanic agenda.

Proof that all is not quite right can be easily gleaned from their website. Immediately my attention is drawn to their logo/hand sign. It is identical to one of the hand signs of power as illustrated in H.P. Lovecraft's *Necronomicon*. Although considered by the mainstream to be a work of fiction, Lovecraft's is tied to Freemasonry and the occult.

Also, the """We Day""" dance, among other moves, makes very obvious gestures that go from pointing straight up to pointing down. Very similar to the gesture for the Hermetic maxim, *"As above, so below."*

The """We Day""" website includes numerous informational videos on a variety of subjects. Professor Jonathan White hosts a series titled 'Ask the Professor' and is seen giving the Hebrew 'shin' hand sign.

One such video on globalism highlights the economic disparity between the developed and developing nations. Surprisingly it also goes so far as to point out the crooked dealings of international banks that result in a never ending cycle of indebtedness for third world countries. But as frank as this presentation is, it does not name any specific institutions (IMF, BIS, World Bank.) There are no solutions suggested. We are meant to believe that real change comes from collecting pennies.

When the professor asks the viewer "what can we do?" it is followed with some fun facts under the heading "How do our choices as consumers affect the world of wealth and poverty?"

We are given figures about the developed world's discretionary spending and the costs of reducing world poverty. For less than the cost of what we spend on things like cosmetics ($18B) or ice cream ($11B), we could provide basic health and nutrition ($15B) or provide clean water and sanitation ($9.5B) to everyone on the planet. It also mentions the world's annual military budget at 1.5 trillion, but clearly it is the middle class that is at fault for the state of the world.

He also mentions that $12 Billion would provide "reproductive rights for women all over the world," whatever that means.

Other reasonably radical suggestions are made, such as a 1% tax on the entire world's population could fix everything.

If anything, these statistics make it clear how easily the worlds ruling elite could instantly rectify all of the injustices on our planet, if only that suited their plan. Ultimately the children are left with a nameless sense of grievance.

CONCLUSION

"We Day" is brainwashing pure and simple. With catchy tunes, a fun dance and uplifting ideals, our kids are drafted into a cadre, an insipid Western version of the Red Guards. They can be channelled into any number of Illuminati causes.

FIRST COMMENT FROM DAN:

I recognize the occultist signatures behind this "We" operation.

David Spangler defined their concept of "holarchy" this way: "In a hierarchy, participants can be compared and evaluated on the basis of position, rank, relative power, seniority and the like. But in a holarchy each person's value comes from his or her uniqueness and the capacity to engage and interact with others to make the fruits of that uniqueness available."

The way I've seen this actually play out when applied to a group of children or adults is everyone loses individuality in hypnotic group activities under direction of leaders.

When I was in OTO, the priest and priestess poses were part of the rituals—(LVX means light.) These people believe physical motions and poses help bend and shape 'force' according to will.

The Sign of "Osiris Slain"   "L"   "V"   "X"

This is done individually or by the group at "Resh," facing the rising or setting sun.

The photo of the girl doing the "We" song, she is signing NOX (darkness.)

The OTO priest and priestess would demonstrate the poses for us to imitate, without telling us what they thought we were doing.

I had 19th century occultist Pascal Beverly Randolph's opus *"Sex Magick"* in which he explained that by putting a person into certain positions you can gain control over them. (This gets very near to S&M thinking.)

Does Decline of Grammar Signify Decadence?

A disturbing sign of cultural decline is that more and more people cannot write a proper sentence.

A sentence is the basic unit of written communication. If we learn only one thing in school, it should be to write a sentence.

Increasingly I am posting submissions and material from other sources. I also post email response. About one in three contributor cannot write a sentence.

A sentence begins with a capital letter and ends with a period. It must contain a noun and a verb, a subject and a predicate.

"The dog (noun) chases (verb) the cat." "The dog" is the subject. "Chases the cat" is the predicate.

Yet I have an acquaintance who somehow attained a Master's Degree in Social Work and cannot write a sentence.

He is engaged in a custody battle and is writing his own affidavits.

"Your inability to write a sentence discredits you," I tell him.

He just laughs and acts like I am an old pedant defending his turf.

"You sound like one of my old professors," he says.

"I would have flunked you," I say.

He wouldn't appear in court wearing pajamas but thinks nothing of submitting documents that discredit him.

His children's welfare is at stake. He cannot defend them effectively. Everyone who cannot write is similarly handicapped.

GRAMMAR BECOMING AN ANACHRONISM?

Just as our grip on culture in general is becoming more tenuous, increasingly, English grammar is treated like an anachronism.

The popularity of texting may be a factor. People think they can write like they talk, in a stream of consciousness.

But this doesn't explain why schools don't require English proficiency as a condition of graduation. What else is an education for?

Writing a sentence is the equivalent of knowing how to add two plus two. I suspect that a subversive force is behind this cultural disintegration. Flouting the rules of grammar is treated like another form of liberation and revolt.

At the same time, the rules for plagiarism are being relaxed and the objectivity of Math is being challenged and fudged.

Ours is a satanic era where the laws of God and nature are distorted and reversed. Why would the rules of grammar be exempt?

ANOTHER EXAMPLE

Recently, I posted a powerful article by "Duran" about how young men are being psychologically destroyed in school.

In that article, Duran's periods were originally all commas and there was little to no capitalization. This talented young man transferred to an all-male private school and graduated with flying colors.

Yet, he still cannot write a sentence, and like my social work friend, doesn't think he needs to. The same applies to some other valued contributors.

I was lucky to attend public high school in Ontario in the 1960s when the rules of writing were drummed into our heads, and we were expected to master a wide range of knowledge: history, geography, sciences, languages, math. My teachers were young, smart and dedicated.

But clearly the education system today is more concerned with grooming youth for gay sex than equipping them with the skills and knowledge necessary to succeed.

We are witnessing a return to mass illiteracy. The culture is moving away from text and becoming verbal and visual. The hidden agenda is to dumb down the new generation, and to make them ineffectual and easier to control.

Sheep don't need to write. They just need to bleat.

FIRST COMMENT FROM HB:

This is a topic that really resonates with me. I worked at a prominent law firm a few years back, and often had to rewrite memorandums and briefs composed by young associates. When graduates from highly respected law schools are unable to write a 2 or 3 page memorandum without multiple spelling and grammatical errors, you know something is amiss.

The worst offenders were African-Americans brought in to satisfy the diversity committee, some of whom were honest-to-God functionally illiterate, but the general decline in standards was evident across the board. Looking beyond the office environment, I see that neither my nephew or niece (aged 16 and 17 respectively) can read or write beyond a sixth grade level.

The eldest will be heading for college next year and I predict that in spite of her deficient language skills, she will graduate with an above-average GPA simply because most colleges are more concerned with boosting enrollment and looking good themselves than imparting actual skills to their hapless students.

Book Seven

Last But Not Least

Cohabiting With a Monkey

I have a confession to make. I've been living with a monkey for most of my life.

I call him "Curious George." (He is very curious to me.) We're an odd couple. He is always posturing and foraging. I try to keep him in check.

His vulgarity is a constant embarrassment. It seems that at a young age, his mind was corrupted (programmed.)

Curious George

When he sees a fertile female, he doesn't see a human being. He sees a hypothetical sexual partner. He's thinking, "Wow, she's cute." This is "Sex-obsessed George."

When his best friends suffer some misfortune, he does feel compassion. But there is a tinge of satisfaction. This is "Schadenfreude George." Or should I say, "Insecure George?"

Paradoxically, George is not a jealous monkey. He accepts that there are smarter, more talented, more hard-working monkeys, who are more deserving than him.

Sometimes I think of George as an airplane and I am his pilot. I have to fuel him up at least three times a day, clean his cabin and empty his toilets. I change his oil about once a week. Sometimes his batteries wear down so I give him a nap.

I sit in the cockpit in front of a computer screen. George wants a drink. George needs stimulation. George is always "wanting" something.

This is "Bean-counter George." He tries to increase his store of coupons (called "money," very useful for acquiring food.) He also thrives on getting recognition from other monkeys and gets quite angry if they act like, well ...monkeys!

EDUCATING GEORGE

George lives on a planet that has been overrun by his kind. It is a large zoo without cages. He is surrounded by bad examples. It's "cohabiting with six billion monkeys."

The planet is ruled by a clique of evil monkeys who "corrupt in order to control." They don't want simians like George challenging their supremacy.

Everywhere George looks, he is encouraged to be his worst.

Porn, violence, greed etc. are pushed in his face. George rarely gets accurate information or sees positive role models.

I try to shield him from all the filth and instead, expose him to truth and uplifting experiences.

I wish I had home-schooled him. He wasted most of his life listening to other monkeys.

WHO IS GEORGE?

As you have probably guessed, George is an animal that has served as the vehicle for my consciousness for some 64 years. I figure he's got about 18-25 years left before he expires and I must hitch another ride.

(Apparently, the Creator has chosen this method of self-expression: Inject Himself into a higher Primate and hope the seed will grow. Unfortunately this plant primate is in some danger.)

George is definitely not the virile young ape he once was. There are many signs of wear and decline.

George is so demanding that I often forget I am not him. That distinction is what distinguishes me from an ape. It's what makes me "human."

The whole cosmic drama takes the form of domesticating our ape vehicles. I must regularly unplug the "George" computer. I want soul to experience itself instead of George.

I must increase consciousness through meditation, prayer and reading the New Testament. *"The Lord is thy shepherd. Thou shalt not want."* Hear that, George!?

Our would-be masters want to erase the idea of God consciousness. If we are just animals, they (not God) will shape and control us.

I wish George were like a horse instead of a monkey. Horses are vehicles by nature. They are graceful, peaceful and take direction.

I think God would like us to be more horse-like. It's a step toward becoming more like Him!

Is "Temptation" an Outmoded Concept?

Rule your mind or it will rule you. —Horace

I can resist anything except temptation. —Oscar Wilde

A man may conquer a million men in battle but one who conquers himself is, indeed, the greatest of conquerors. —Buddha

And lead us not into temptation, but deliver us from evil. —The Lord's Prayer (Matthew 6:9-13)

Most people act like the concept of "temptation" is a relic of a bygone era.

Yet in their hearts, I think they know the concept has never been more timely and urgent than it is today.

A woman asked a newspaper advice column recently: "I've been in a relationship for many years with the same guy. I love him, but I've recently discovered I might be more attracted to members of the same sex. Should I tell him? Should I end it? Is there something psychologically wrong with me?"

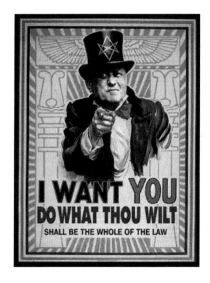

The psychologist Dr. Joti Samra replied: "First and foremost, there is absolutely nothing that is psychologically wrong with you for having questions about your sexual orientation.... One's true sense of sexual orientation is not a choice ... If you feel that your partner is someone you could talk to openly, and without judgment, you could certainly gently raise the issue with him."

This lady has a passing fancy for other ladies. No wonder, the media is promoting it full time. It's chic. So she raises it with her boyfriend. If he isn't also brain-dead, he won't be happy to learn that his future wife, and the mother of his children, his rock and solace, is a closet lesbian.

Wouldn't it be smarter to shut up and let it pass?

Do we have to indulge every attraction we feel, even if it's destructive to us and the people we supposedly love?

Say she were attracted to other men. Should she discuss it with him? Act on it? Most heterosexuals are sexually attracted to many members of the opposite sex. But if they are already committed to someone they care about, they control it. They recognize it as temptation.

Suppose this woman was sexually attracted to children? Would the psychologist be OK with that as well?

"One's true sense of sexual orientation is not a choice..." Believe me, this kind of logic leads to pedophilia and bestiality.

People will resist eating fats and sugars because they're unhealthy. But they think nothing of indulging toxic and self-destructive desires like porn or gambling.

True religions see man as the interface between spirit (God) and matter (animal.) Man is like a little boy (spirit) riding an elephant (body.) He must restrain his animal instincts. He must be able to recognize temptation and resist it.

There are two possible strategies. One is to indulge the desire and show the elephant that the thing it wants is not that great. In fact, it's drab and boring. It's best if the temptation can be discredited and the desire just disappears.

If that doesn't work, and indulging the temptation makes it grow more powerful and destructive, one must quit cold turkey.

DEVELOPING RESTRAINT MUSCLES

Have you noticed that *nine* of the Ten Commandments are proscriptions?

They tell us what we shalt NOT do. Surely this is an important clue. We worship God by *disciplining and controlling* our lower nature.

The only affirmative Commandment is to *"honor your father and mother."* The other nine are concerned with obeying, i.e. self-discipline:

You shall have no other Gods; not make idols; not take His name in vain; not work on the Sabbath; not commit murder; not commit adultery; not steal; not bear false witness (lie) and finally, not covet your neighbor's wife or possessions.

In contrast our secular-Satanist society finds salvation in self-indulgence, not self-restraint. "Do what thou wilt," is the satanist motto.

We are like Eve in the garden, subjected to temptation 24/7. Money. Sex. Food. Material things. Power. Fame. TV is full of gorgeous bodies.

They have abolished the very concept of temptation. We have been disarmed, and made vulnerable to all these appeals.

We see it. We want it. We are no longer able to discern what is good and what is self-destructive. We need to rediscover self-restraint. An alarm must go off in our mind every time we are tempted.

Quickly we'll discover that the rewards of self-restraint far exceed self-indulgence. We will feel as much self confidence and pride from exercising our spiritual muscles as we do from an intense physical workout.

Spiritual discipline gives life challenge and definition. We become Self-centered in terms of our higher self, obeying a new Master. As we purify and exert ourselves, we begin to enter into the fourth dimension, the moral dimension. We begin to experience the person we were meant to be.

The End of Women

I have been attending a small vegetarian cooking class. The teacher is a woman aged 70 who could pass for 55. There is another female classmate, a French Canadian retired teacher in her 60s who is also quite vivacious.

Normally I don't notice women my age (64) but there is something uncannily different about these ladies. I felt so relaxed in their presence that I almost fell asleep. Then I realized what it was: these women are feminine. I had stumbled upon a species that is almost extinct: "woman."

Like myself, these women came of age in the 1960s, a time of transition. But, in high school, girls still took Home Economics and boys took Shop. Boys asked girls out on "dates"—to dances or the movies. Premarital sex was still frowned upon and illegitimate children were called "bastards." A popular song had the chorus: "Love and marriage, love and marriage, go together like a horse and carriage." We were taught to question authority, not our gender.

What is it about these two cooking class women that define "feminine?" If I had to choose one word, it would be "vulnerability." These women do not kill their own snakes. They rely on a man, their husband, to protect them and for direction. *They do not compete with men.*

Another key word is "sacrifice." They are dedicated to their families and are cherished in return. They are loved not for their looks, careers or repartee but for their contribution to their families.

Another key word is "surrender." You feel that a loyal man with vision and determination could earn the life-long devotion of women like these. This is how two people become one.

Surrender and sacrifice, based on trust, is how a real woman loves. Of course, a man must earn and keep this trust. A wife's sacrifice inspires a man to sacrifice, i.e., to provide for his family.

Both men and women have been grievously injured by the Illuminati social engineers who have undermined gender and marriage with the complicity of our government, media and education system. Women have been "empowered" and men emasculated. The purpose is to neuter and re-engineer humanity as a slave race.

Women were designed by nature to sacrifice and surrender for family. But feminism taught young women to be "strong and independent" and regard men, marriage and family with suspicion. As result, women have been deprived of fulfillment they crave and can only achieve through selfless dedication to a loving husband and children. This also extends to their sexual fulfillment.

Women used to be essentially different from men. Their focus was the home. Their spirit made them a refuge and harbor for a man. Their energy balanced his energy.

Young women today are so busy pursuing careers, they are barely distinguishable from males. Feminism has fitted many with a psychological penis.

Many young women suffer from "personality deficit disorder." They may have looks but little personality, style or charm. They can't be men, and don't know how to be women. They are mutants.

Men think they have a shiny red sports car. But when they look under the hood, there is no engine (i.e. character.)

In contrast, there is a lightness and charm about feminine women of my generation. They don't take themselves so seriously. They are still girlish and attractive in their 60s and after.

Under the guise of gay and women's "rights," the Illuminati has waged war on gender and has crippled heterosexuals psychologically. Men today are always portrayed as boyish, feminine and pussy-whipped. Women cannot love these men.

The essence of masculinity is power. My advice to young men is to find a rewarding career that you enjoy. Define a vision for your life and a place for a woman in it. Then help a young woman rediscover her fundamental feminine nature by accepting you as her leader. You must be the boss or she won't respect you. You'll be her brother or son.

Men - Design Your Perfect "10"

Lately, I have been thinking about a great woman I knew when I was 24. I ignored Liz because I wasn't attracted to her sexually. She was average looking but there was no chemistry.

She had many of the qualities in the left-hand column below, and she liked me. But my tastes and even my ideas had been formed by PLAYBOY.

I had been brainwashed by my cult-ure to believe that "sexual attraction" is 75%-90% of what male-female relationships are about.

I thought marriages were based on sexual attraction. You had to live together before marriage to make sure you were "sexually compatible." Sex was the Holy Grail.

A Victoria's Secret model, the perfect 10?

I was thinking about Liz lately, wondering what her life has been like.

I was thinking about her because I am 64 and now realize that sex is a relatively small part of a good marriage, say 20%.

What if I knew this back then? I wouldn't have had three failed marriages by the age of 50, two largely based on sexual attraction.

I am happily married now but how different my life might have been. I might have had a family.

MEN, DESIGN YOUR PERFECT "10"

You can choose 10 of the 20 qualities listed below. If you choose only from the right-hand column, you will get the woman in the picture above, but she will have none of the qualities in the left-hand column. Put another way, what are you willing to give up for sex appeal?

Character (Honest, Fair)	Sex Appeal
Personality (Cheerful & fun)	Sex Appeal
Great Sense of Humor	Sex Appeal
Intelligent and reasonable	Sex Appeal
Skills & Talents	Sex Appeal
Warm and loving	Sex Appeal

Devoted & Loyal	Sex Appeal
Common Beliefs & Interests Great conversation.	Sex Appeal
Incredible Cook & Homemaker Good mother to your children.	Sex Appeal
Unselfish, Interested in Others	Sex Appeal

What Being Jewish Means to Me

This Epilogue was inspired by an email from David Massada, my French translator:

> You know Henry, when I did the first translation, it was all about putting you in the map in France, and I don't want to sound too pretentious, but I believe we achieved just that!
>
> You're now at the core of the few authors dealing with the subject and with the regular updates from the blog, I know that we get a constant flow of new people gaining awareness of your work...
>
> Now, I sometime have the hardest time to make French people understand that as a Jew, you can support a national viewpoint. Because everyone tends to believe that a Jew is international per se, and that he's supposed to hate the country where he settled (I think it might be true historically, and I don't know if you would agree with that...) So I end up fighting tooth and nail to present you as a Canadian citizen, and not a member of a worldwide tribe... (I know it's crazy but it's the prejudice against Jews in general...)
>
> I also often get the smart remark that you can only be a shill because otherwise the Jewry would have shut you down with all the nailing you've been doing... (I personally believe that you must stand a lot of pressure as those articles are ripping the cover off of freemasonry and all Jew's many proxy in general...)
>
> It's frustrating, I wish I could do a video interview of you with a good set of questions that would cover all this things, so you could clarify for the French audience...

REPLY:

I am an assimilated Jew. My Polish Jewish parents survived the Second World War by passing as Catholics.

After the war, they wanted nothing to do with the identity that almost cost them their lives. They gave their children common English names. Jewish observance was limited to lighting candles on the Sabbath.

I have always identified with the human race first, my country second, and being a Jew third.

Until the age of 50, I was a typical brainwashed, dysfunctional, liberal, socialist, zionist, feminist Jew. My return to health began when I started to question these memes and obey my own instincts and perceptions instead. I discovered the Illuminati conspiracy which has become my work.

In contrast to the Cabalist Jews, I believe I express the authentic Mosaic Jewish spirit, a commitment to universal truth and morality. (This spirit is not exclusively Jewish.) I have always sensed there is an immanent moral order, an intuition that inspired my game *Scruples*.

WHY DO I REMAIN JEWISH?

When I was young, a friend's father used to say, " *Henry. You can't jump out of your skin.* "

My interest in learning, writing and teaching, my idealism and my sense of humour are all Jewish qualities. (So are many of my bad traits.) I cannot deny who I am.

I support any religion that upholds a moral order and family values. As you know, I believe God is synonymous with absolute spiritual ideals like truth, justice, love, order and beauty. I do not join a religion because I want a direct relationship to God. But I support everyone who finds sustenance in religion.

In general, I have had little to no reaction from Jews, either positive or negative. The same applies to Freemasons. I am ignored, a tiny ghat on the tail of an elephant.

In 2007, the Canadian Jewish Congress tried to force me to remove all references to Jews from my web site. However, nothing came of it. The "hate laws" in Canada were changed because Muslims started to use them to their advantage.

Obviously, I do not expect to influence the course of world events. I write to empower my readers. Ignorance is not bliss; it causes suffering.

"JEWISH SHILL"

I would serve the Illuminati Jewish purpose if I actually promoted anti Semitism.

On the contrary, I show that Jews are not all brainwashed. A few like me are capable of being objective, truthful and fair. As result, I have won more friends for "the Jews" than anyone. I combat racial prejudice and anti Semitism.

For this reason, I don't expect the B'nai Brith to hold a Gala Dinner in my honor, since it thrives on anti Semitism which forces Jews to contribute money and conform.

Of course, I am critical of the majority of Jews for being used, but this applies to most groups today.

Far from "hating" my homeland, I have always been a Canadian nationalist. My Ph.D. is in Canadian literature. Our political leaders like Harper, Obama, Cameron and Hollande are the real "Jewish shills," Freemasons and national traitors.

We should not be prejudiced. I am proof that each individual has a unique character and learning curve.

At the same time, I find the physical and cultural traits of other races and nations attractive. I want to see these differences preserved in order to resist the Illuminati agenda. We are one big family, each bringing something unique and beautiful to the table.

Human beings all want the same thing—to enjoy the precious gift of life.

We are the Family of Man, children of God who looks out through our eyes, the windows of the soul.

We should dedicate our lives to serving and praising Him. We should not allow the Illuminati to usurp our Birthright.

14829275R00134

Printed in Great Britain
by Amazon.co.uk, Ltd.,
Marston Gate.